A B C
of
FRENCH
FOOD

A B C

of

FRENCH

F O O D

Foreword by Egon Ronay

Introduction by Jacques Pépin

Len Deighton

BANTAM BOOKS

NEW YORK · TORONTO · LONDON · SYDNEY · AUCKLAND

*This edition contains the complete text
of the original hardcover edition.*
NOT ONE WORD HAS BEEN OMITTED.

ABC OF FRENCH FOOD

*A Bantam Book / published by arrangement with
Century Hutchinson Limited*

PRINTING HISTORY

*Century Hutchinson edition published May 1989
Bantam edition / April 1990*

Library of Congress Cataloging-in-Publication Data

Deighton, Len, 1929–
   ABC of French food / Len Deighton ; foreword by Egon Ronay ;
   introduction by Jacques Pépin.—Bantam ed.
      p.   cm.
   ISBN 0-553-05759-6
   1. Food—Dictionaries. 2. Cookery, French—Dictionaries.
I. Title.
TX349.D48 1990
641.5944'03—dc20   89-18157
                                                       CIP

Published simultaneously in the United States and Canada

PRINTED IN THE UNITED STATES OF AMERICA

DH   0   9   8   7   6   5   4   3   2   1

Dedication

To M. Aschieri the mayor, M. Guglielmero the headmaster, M. Boselli the wood carver, M. Plantey the rose cultivator, M. Selvini the garagiste, M. Durbise the RAF veteran who teaches chess and skating, M. Grosdenier the patissier, M. Capizzi the policeman and Patrick the judo instructor. To Mme. Viande at Pressing Napoleon, Mme. Danielle Pappatico the cleaning lady, Mme. Gazia the mushroom dealer, M. Lavalade the fishmonger, M. Tomi and M. Bolignano the taxi drivers, M. Gomes the butcher, M. Molinengo, M. Vitali the tiler, M. Galland the *traiteur*, M. Auzou the grocer and M. Connan the insurance consultant, and to all their families I dedicate this book.

Preface

Before you buy this book, borrow it or even steal it, perhaps I should explain that it is not a lexicon nor an encyclopedia. It is not intended to provide a complete dictionary or even a glossary of culinary French.

So what is it? It is an edited version of my loose-leaf notebook. In 1952 I got a scholarship to the Royal College of Art largely because the examiners were surprised that I could produce a sketchbook. Nowadays I still like to make notes and drawings about people, places, food and anything else I need to research. Thousands of loose-leaf pages are filled with my scribbles; the result of countless conversations about food. Many, if not most, of them were culled from the brains of professionals: chefs, waiters and restaurateurs, greengrocers, gardeners, chemists, fishery officers, fellow amateur cooks and customers. More pickings came from conversations and culinary experiments by my wife and my children: all better equipped to cope with the French—their temperament, their language and their food and cooking—than I will ever be.

Because of the limitations of space there are some aspects of French food that I have not dealt with, such as French cooking outside France. During the time I lived in Munich I was able to see and sample the highly regarded French cooking of that always food-conscious city. German chefs, many of them working in top restaurants in France (and notably Anton Edelmann from Bavaria at the *Savoy*), are having a great influence upon

French cooking. Regular visits to southern California gave me a chance to see the staggering—and quite different—changes that French cooking has undergone there, some of which have come from French chefs working with California's superb produce.

London, of course, has been under the direct influence of French cooking ever since Escoffier, and I have always liked the way that certain English restaurants, mostly in grand hotels, have developed menus on which fine British and classic French dishes find happy accord. As a longtime devotee of my mother's bread and butter pudding—made with eggs and cream—I was delighted to see the way that Anton Mosimann (from Switzerland) produced a version of it, when at *The Dorchester*, that is now seen on menus all over the world, including France.

Apart from brief mentions in other contexts nor have I dealt with French chefs working abroad. This means that I have not included here the remarkable story of the Roux brothers, who came to England and, as well as running the finest retail luxury food shop in Britain—*Boucherie Lamartine*, London—and all sorts of other food-connected activities, including the best British TV cooking series and superb cookbooks, run a three-star restaurant each!

Whatever is the way forward, we are fortunate to be living in an age when so many hard-working, passionate and dedicated men and women feel so strongly about food that they will argue about it. It is to further that argument, and provoke more, that I wrote this book.

Len Deighton

"God sends meat, and the devil sends cooks."

CAPTAIN FREDERICK MARRYAT

(Seafarer, novelist and gourmet)

"Reality must take precedence over public relations,
for nature cannot be fooled."

PROFESSOR FEYNMAN

*(Minority Report of the Presidential Commission
on the space shuttle Challenger accident)*

Foreword

by Egon Ronay

The most fascinating books about gastronomy are not those written by chefs, however legendary, nor by professional food writers, however famous. But when the pen of Alexandre Dumas *père* or the irreverence and orginality of Voltaire or the analytical approach of Brillat-Savarin is brought to bear on the subject, the result would be wasted on the bookshelf or in the kitchen, or even on the coffee table. The place for that rarity, a great writer's musing on gastronomy, is the bedside table—at any rate mine is.

And that's where Len Deighton's should be kept, for the stuff that he conjures up so enticingly is what food enthusiasts' dreams are made of. However deprecating he may be about his own book in the acknowledgments ("uneven, incomplete, opinionated"), it is precisely his unorthodox approach, his outspokenness against the tide and his highly individual opinions that make it so readable. Yet its bedrock is knowledge: his beginnings in professional kitchens in France are only too clear; so is his reverence for solid traditions. Tamper with the ancient and well-tried roots of cooking, and you find yourself in a blind alley lit by nothing but gimmickry. As for *nouvelle cuisine* and *menu dégustation* ("like a cocktail party without the wooden sticks")—you can keep them. "Not opposed to experiment," he says, "I do not wish to be experimented upon." Food-fools are not suffered easily and fashion-blinded chefs are given short shrift.

When it comes to food, this writer of highly respected, tense prose can turn endearingly lyrical: "Tripe eaters are poets deep down," he remarks. At times he sorely tempts: "Wonderful; I can almost smell it," he adds to his way with *poularde à l'estragon*; I simply *had* to try it the next night.

Len Deighton wrote his thrillers with his head. This book he wrote with his heart. It is an enthralling, instructive, highly individual and hugely enjoyable *tour de force*.

Introduction

by Jacques Pépin

More than 500 cookbooks and books about food have been published each year during the last ten years in the United States. It is a full-time job to sort out a few good ones from the plethora of boring, pretentious and unreliable offerings that appear yearly along with the crop of plagiarisms of the previous year's successes. Yet, there are good food books published that provide worthwhile, educational reading, and the *ABC of French Food* is one of them.

In this *abécédaire* portrait of French food, the most common names, expressions and culinary terms are reviewed through the criterion of *bon-sens* (good sense). This "cuisine through the alphabet" situates itself between a dictionary and a glossary of culinary terms without having the dryness of a dictionary or the technical narrow-mindedness of a glossary. It is easy to look at, easy to find expressions in, and easy to pick up and find information in as the need arises.

With the confusion created by *nouvelle* cuisine in the last twenty years, common names used in the kitchen or in relation to food have lost their specific meanings and are open to any interpretation. This book starts the much-needed process of clarification and a structured, organized body of information is certainly a distinctive and inherent aspect of French cuisine and French culture.

The *ABC* approach to French food is more humanist than the technical approach of the chef. Along with the food, it incorporates the whole dining experience as it relates to a specific country and civilization. It is versatile, personal, entertaining and informative without being monotonous. The author brings in his family, discusses his ideas about food, new equipment, the chefs—known and unknown—that he admires, restaurants, cookbooks, wines and areas of France, as well as the food of those areas. The explanations are sometimes lengthy, sometimes brief, as the mood strikes the author.

There is no affectation in the *ABC of French Food*, only an honest effort to explain and interpret, in a personal and subjective way, cooking expressions, customs, recipes, and names associated with French food. The book's intentionally limited scope makes it relaxing to read, and the author is never far away behind his explanations and always ready to let the reader know his likes and dislikes. Attentive to the goodness of a simple meal as well as aware of the pretension of some "great" restaurants or "great" chefs, he understands the dichotomy of the cook, who sometimes creates sublime concoctions and other times destroys good, basic ingredients in the name of *haute* or *nouvelle* cuisine. This ambivalence is reflected in the motto stated at the beginning of the book: "God sends meat, and the devil sends cooks."

Len Deighton is rational in his definitions of dishes but is always ready to question and discuss the conventional meanings. In the case of *bouillabaisse*, for example, he gives a good description of this particular fish stew from the south of France, then lets the reader decide whether it can be done well in every part of the world or whether, as people in the south of France insist, it can be done well only along the Mediterranean coast, specifically in Marseille.

The author blatantly criticizes the *charollais*, considered by many Frenchmen to be the best beef in France, calling it "chewy" and "far short of Aberdeen Angus or almost any American beef cattle." In almost the same breath, however, he tells you that French butchers are the "world's best." These clear, opinionated comments on the French and French food are in tune with the French spirit, which thrives on controversy.

The *ABC of French Food* is a fascinating companion of shared experience, an index as well as a memoir, a biographical diary, and a record of family outings. It is easy to read, to the point, informative and fun, an ideal gift for anyone interested in cooking generally and French cooking in particular. This book is a must for anyone wanting to increase his knowledge beyond the mere surface of the recipe and to truly understand French cuisine.

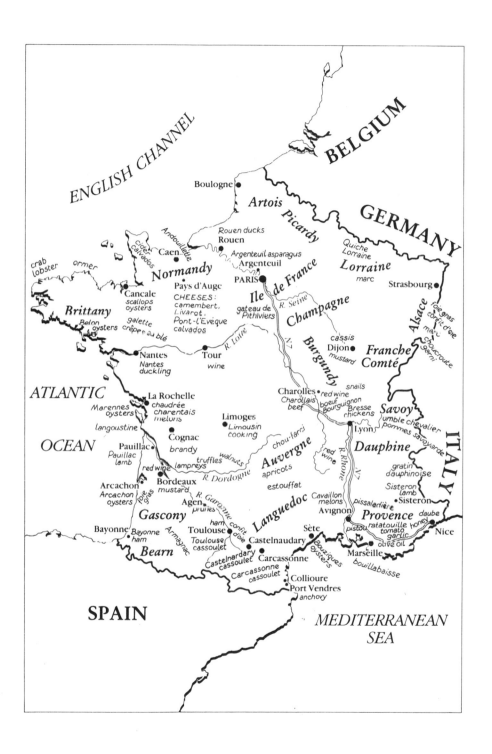

Abricot: apricot. A rather tough-skinned but delicately flavored Chinese fruit that has been eaten for about 4,000 years. It reached Europe around the time of Christ, but disappeared to be rediscovered in the fifteenth century. Like me, it thrives in a warm, frost-free temperate climate, which is not easy to find. Delicious "musk-apricots" are grown in the south of France and jam apricots in the Auvergne. In the Middle East it is revered, and in Egypt the tourist soon learns to say *"Bokra fee mish-mish"*—tomorrow there will be apricots. Nowadays the best crop is found in sunny California, but when Thomas Jefferson—horticulturist, Francophile and U.S. President—visited France, he said that only its pears and apricots were superior to those grown in his U.S. orchards.

Many gourmets are passionately devoted to these lovely aromatic fruits. Egon Ronay tells me that despite the severe winter frosts, Hungarian apricots—from the region around the town of Kecskemet— are without doubt the finest in the world.

I include apricots in this book because the French have a great passion for them, especially for apricot jam, **confiture d'abricots**, which, in my experience, they prefer to make from dried apricots rather than fresh ones. Jam made from fresh apricots, with kernels included, is even better.

Abricoter means to glaze. The liking the French have for apricot jam, its golden color and delicate flavor, makes it the favored coating with which to glaze confectionery, an apple tart, for example. So the word abricoter is used to describe this glazing process even when redcurrant jelly or some other glaze is being used.

Agneau is lamb, specifically an animal between four and nine months old. The choicest weigh about 22 pounds. The meat is tender and flavorful, and breeders keep supplying lambs of this size to the shops right through the summer.

Mouton (mutton) on sale in the butcher's shop is mostly the meat of breeding ewes between three and four years old. Such meat is tough, and suited only to boiling or pot-roasting, but it is very flavorful. Ever since Edwardian days many people have considered lamb bland and insipid compared with the stronger-flavored mutton. On the other hand some people find the distinctive flavor of mutton disagreeable. I like it, and so do many others, for a specialized market for mutton exists supplied by breeders with animals that might be anything over two years. This sort of mutton is expensive and difficult to find. The meat needs hanging for at least a week if it's to be roasted.

Agneau de lait is suckling lamb, a milk-fed animal which has been weaned but not started grazing. It's likely to be only a month old. For anyone who likes to eat lamb this is the most delicate and delicious meat of all. Such animals are small, no more than about 11 pounds. When I bought a leg recently it weighed only 2 pounds 14 ounces. It was the size of such cuts that persuaded an unknown chef to wrap one in pastry and produce the famous **gigot en croûte.** At *Baumanière*—a three-star restaurant in Provence—it's a specialty. Their recipe[1] calls for the lamb to be cooked in a hot oven for 15 minutes and then cooled before being wrapped in pastry and cooked again so the original concept is lost. The only way to make the real thing is by putting raw lamb into raw pastry and cooking it only once.

The season for baby lamb is short. Eat it at Easter; by late May or early June it will all be gone. But Anton Mosimann in his private dining room at the *Dorchester Hotel* in London served me baby lamb on January 7! Where had it come from? "Eat up!" he said. Performing miracles is everyday work for a master chef. French sheep farmers produce a lot of baby lamb, which provides a surplus of ewes' milk, which is then sold for cheese making. In countries where ewes' milk cheese is unknown, baby lamb is more difficult to find.

Agneau de pré-salé. Lamb which has grazed on salt flats or coastal northern grasslands is said to taste of the grazing. Other regions also claim such special lamb. **Agneau de Pauillac** is found in coastal parts of the Médoc. **Agneau de Sisteron** is famous throughout France. In Provence the local lamb is said to taste of herbs, such as wild thyme. Such claims should not be taken too seriously but most French lamb is excellent.

Aiguillette: Specifically this means a long thin muscle that separates easily from a breast of poultry or game. In practice French chefs carelessly use the word when they mean whole breast sliced lengthwise into strips of the same dimension as the aiguillette. As a guide to how big these strips should be we can refer to the recipe prepared at *Les Frères Troisgros,* Roanne. Their **aiguillettes de col-vert aux mousserons des prés** consist of strips of roasted mallard duck breast with mushrooms, liberally accompanied by a rich sauce. The sauce is made from **crème fraîche double,** duck livers and duck stock prepared with brandy, red wine and **demi-glace.** They advise cutting the duck breast into five aiguillettes. A raw duck breast prepared for grilling, frying or cutting into aiguillettes is called a **magret.**

Aiguillette is also the name given to a cut of beef: the top of the rump. It is also called the **pointe de culotte** or **pièce de boeuf.**

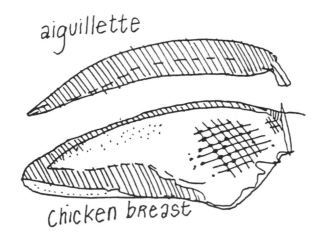

aiguillette

chicken breast

Ail: garlic. Because it is a relative of the lily this perennial is usually categorized as growing only in warm climates. Actually it's a tough little plant that has been found all over the globe since recorded history. It flourishes in many northerly gardens in Europe and America. Writers from Aristophanes to Shakespeare, gurus from Mohammed to Gandhi and scientists from Pliny to Pasteur have all mentioned this curious bulb with varying degrees of enthusiasm. All sorts of wild claims have been made for garlic as a medicine and as an antidote to bites of snakes and insects. It is given to our dogs as a cure for worms, and whenever I sneeze in Russia someone tells me that it is the only effective cure for the common cold.

In France garlic is used in country dishes rather than in haute cuisine, and is more prevalent in the cooking of southern France than in that of the northern regions. Garlic soup and garlic stuffings for chicken are favorites. The chef has to distinguish between the powerful effect of raw garlic and the quite different flavor of it when cooked. Like onions and leeks, to which it is related, garlic loses much of its irritant power when heated. So garlic served in large amounts (for example, the garlic purée which is well known as an ingredient of sauces and other mixtures but lately is being served as a vegetable) must be well cooked.

Purée d'ail: garlic purée. For this the chef uses several heads of garlic (cloves separated, chopped in half and skin removed) that have been blanched in boiling water for three minutes. They are then gently fried in butter—lid on so that the butter doesn't brown or even darken—before being mixed with **sauce béchamel.** Sieve it before serving.

The real garlic enthusiasts who want a purée don't bother with the sauce béchamel; they cook garlic by the potful and make it smooth in a food processor.

But the chef must be aware of the fact that some people just can't digest garlic. And for many others just a rub of garlic round the salad bowl or cooking dish will be enough. If you want more, use a garlic crusher. There are excellent designs which are very easy to clean. Don't imitate those foolish TV cooks who crush garlic by thumping it with the side of the knife. The spattered particles and juice will stay in your clothes and turn rancid, producing a smell almost impossible to remove. Red-skinned garlic **(ail rose)** is said to be the best, but it's not easy to distinguish the difference in flavor. Garlic can be used to make garlic vinegar or garlic oil for use in salads or cooking (in either case sieve the garlic pieces out after 24 hours).

Ail vert. Looking rather like a white lumpy onion, this "green garlic" has been picked before the cloves have formed. There is a slight difference of flavor, but it is mostly used in salads by restaurateurs who like to have fashionable ingredients on their menus.

Aïoli: literally garlic oil. A powerful Provençal sauce of raw garlic and olive oil (a combination that even some garlic lovers find indigestible) beaten with egg yolk into a creamy emulsion. Used originally on Fridays to provide flavor and excitement for a meal of poached fish, nowadays it's served all week through and can be found alongside such dull dishes as cold cooked potato, beans, carrots and so on. A fierce, cayenne-flavored variant is called **rouille** (literally "rust") on account of its color, and served in the south of France with various fish soups and stews.

A la Mode: in the fashion. In France expect **boeuf à la mode** to be braised and served with vegetables. In similar style **tripes à la mode de Caen** is prepared in a special locally made **marmite** (a tall pot with narrow top to minimize evaporation) and is cooked for about 12 hours with calf's foot to make a rich, fatty stew which, purists insist, must remain fairly light in color. But à la mode means anything the menu writer wants it to mean: in the United States it means your pie will come with ice cream.

Albumin: water-soluble protein importantly found in many foods such as egg, milk, blood and fish. It is a delicate substance very vulnerable to heat. It provides problems for the cook because of the way it suddenly coagulates at 140°F and then hardens and separates at a temperature of 178°F. For this reason egg custards—and all fish—must be cooked very gently so they don't get hotter than this. If you see bubbles in your baked egg custard—or someone else's—it's a sure sign that the mixture became too hot. Very few egg custards are cooked properly.

Steaming is a good way to cook such foods because the heat of it is less than that of boiling water. "Coddled" eggs are put into boiling water without heat and left for seven or eight minutes according to the volume of the water. Try it: they taste much better than a "boiled" egg and the egg white will be delicate and flavorful. Uncooked lobster contains clear colorless liquid albumin which looks exactly like egg white when cooked. For this reason it's best not to pierce the shell of an uncooked lobster.

Frozen foods lack albumin, so a mousse made with frozen fish is more likely to separate. Fresh cod will give you a better mousse than frozen sole. (The word albumen is sometimes used as a synonym, but albumen more specifically refers to egg white.)

Alcool blanc. Distilled alcohol is a recent discovery, and when these "burned wines" (or brandies) became popular, country people began to brew their own alcohol from whatever was available. In Alsace cherries were used, in Ireland potatoes, and in Lorraine they discovered how to make a wine alcohol from marc, the crushed grape residue left over from wine-making. No one ever gave those homemade potions a name, so they are simply called **marc.** Nowadays there is a dazzling selection of fruit alcohols available, most of them clear or "white." The ones aged in wood darken and are not alcool blanc. **Framboise** and **poire** are my favorites, but the drinker should beware: not all such drinks are distillations of fruit. Some of the ones on sale at fancy prices are simply grain spirit plus flavorings.

Allumettes: matchsticks. Vegetables, such as carrots and potato, cut into small square-sectioned sticks are called **juliennes.** When potato juliennes are deep-fried golden and crisp, the result is called **pommes allumettes**, matchstick potatoes. The word allumettes is also sometimes applied to very small items of puff pastry served as savory **amuse-gueules** or sweet **petits fours.**

Alsace. The most easterly region of France stretches from the forested mountains of the Vosges to the very flat plain of the river Rhine, which marks the German border. The hillsides of Alsace are noted for their vineyards, which produce famous Riesling and fruity Gewürztraminer wines, and for the high grazing that produces distinctive local cheeses. No less notable are the beautiful villages which in the weeks of summer attract countless busloads of tourists to their narrow streets and alleys. But Alsace returns the compliment, for just as Brittany supplies to the navy the bulk of France's sailors, so Alsace—where learning foreign languages is second nature—supplies a large proportion of highly skilled waiters and restaurant managers to the dining-rooms of France and to the rest of the world.

Alsace has spent about half of the last century under German rule and this has made its cuisine unique and superb. The most famous restaurant of the region is *L'Auberge de l'Ill* at Illhaeusern, but this whole region abounds with unpretentious restaurants in which you'll find some of the finest and most genuine cooking in France. Perhaps it's the mountains, or the geography, or the communications, or the cold climate that have so far kept that blight of modern French cooking—nouvelle cuisine—from destroying this local cooking. Perhaps it is the fact that the German visitors, upon whom the economy of this region depends, are not attracted by French nouvelle cuisine when remarkably similar German nouvelle cuisine is available at home. Alsace's regional cooking is inimitable.

Many dishes show the German influence. The German *Sauerkraut* becomes **choucroute garnie**, with a selection of sausage and smoked pork, some boiled meat or poultry, plus such things as brains, pig's ears and dumplings too. Even the names sound different here. The local dish **beekenhofe** or **Bäckeoffe**—a baker's oven—is a slowly cooked stew, in which pork and mutton, potato and onion are cooked until the ingredients blend.

Those cruel winters that make so many local inhabitants find an urgent excuse for visiting distant relatives have given rise to a tradition of preserving and pickling. Geese—in particular the ones that have been raised for **foie gras**—are preserved in their own fat to make **confit d'oie**, a local delicacy.

Alsace is famous for its **alcools blancs**. These **eaux de vie** or schnapps are made from local fruit and local wine. I have always liked them and prefer a good one to anything but the finest brandy for an after-dinner drink. The local **marc de Gewürztraminer**, made from the residue of pressed grapes, is particularly good and a real one is difficult to find outside this region.

Amande: almond. The almond tree blossoms very early. Although the tree grows in England and in the northern part of the United States, it can only flourish in regions that enjoy a frost-free winter. Almost all American almonds grow in California. In Europe the best almonds are found not in France but in warmer parts: Italy, Spain and Portugal. Sweet almonds are preferred by the chef because these are so versatile. The alternative—bitter almonds—can be lethal in anything but very small amounts.

Originally almonds were used to thicken soups, stews and puddings, but nowadays the almond is not found extensively in French cooking. Even the best-known recipe—**truite aux amandes**—probably originated in Germany. Less well known is the wonderful **gâteau de Pithiviers**, a closed flaky pastry tart filled with almond paste and flavored with a trace of rum. Marzipan (**massepain**), a simple combination of ground almonds and sugar with sometimes a little lemon juice, is the world's most popular nut recipe. Just as delicious is **pralin aux amandes**. For this sugar and almonds, plus a dash of vanilla, are heated to make toffee "cakes." After cooking, the "cakes" are pounded to make a powdered flavoring which is used in confectionery. Fredy Girardet serves a magnificent **pralin** ice cream in which the nutty toffee provides a crunchy texture and subtle flavor for a vanilla base.

Almonds are also used to make macaroons (**macarons**). These meringue-like biscuits, made from crushed almonds, are very popular in France. They are in turn used in the making of **frangipane**, a lovely custard-cream containing eggs, ground almonds and rum or kirsch. It is used in many elaborate desserts.

More than half the weight of the almond is oil. Like all nut oil, almond oil can go rancid, and the sweetness of the nuts is vital to the success of any dish using them. So almond oil should be kept in the refrigerator.

Amande vert. Soft unripe almonds are picked and sold in May. Enclosed in their seed cases, which are like furry green "plums," they are soft and sour tasting. In Provence local children pick them and eat them, but it's not easy to see why people pay high prices for them at the grocer's.

Amuse-gueules. "Gueule" is an animal's mouth, so these are savory snacks to "tickle your chops." Sometimes such items are called **petits salés**. The Roux brothers, Britain's most successful restaurateurs, who both served their apprenticeship in pâtisseries, specify that these tiny items must be well seasoned and add, "They must be light and not too rich or indigestible. Above all, they must be crisp and fresh; garnish the bases at the last moment. . . . Do not offer too many or too much choice, or you will spoil your appetite for the meal."

In the selection, anything goes. Typical examples are slices of sausage (sausage cooked inside brioche is especially good), cheese straws, miniature pizzas, cheese-filled choux pastry, spicy steak tartare mixtures heaped on toast or crackers, sausage rolls and so on, and so on. All such items should be no more than "bite-sized"—that is, small enough to go into the mouth whole. This is "finger-food": something to be eaten standing up with a drink in hand. Hot amuse-gueules—fried **goujonnette** at *Chapel*, sausage in brioche at *Bocuse*—are now served gratis by most three-star French restaurants when they bring the apéritifs and are eaten at table with knife and fork.

Canapé is loosely used for any small item of food served with drinks. But more accurately, canapés are spreads or anchovies or slices of smoked salmon, and so on, on small flat bases of toast or pastry. Even more strictly speaking, canapés are small offerings of the liver and innards of game birds and are served with them. To replace small rounds of toast, the American food industry invented crackers of the same shape or size. Some of them are convenient and not at all bad when used for canapés, but most are far too salty.

Hors d'oeuvre literally means food served in addition to the meal. Nowadays it consists of a choice of foods, hot or cold and sometimes quite elaborate, that have to be eaten off a plate (while canapés and amuse-gueules can be picked up with the fingers). Hors d'oeuvres are served at the table, usually as the first course. In restaurants it is more usual to offer a selection of food, sometimes from a trolley, so the hot hors d'oeuvre is virtually extinct. What a shame. No matter, at home you are not bound by the restrictions that restaurants obey.

Anchois: anchovy. This small fish was found in the Mediterranean and in both the Atlantic and Pacific oceans in such quantities that it was commonly used for animal feed and even as manure. For most people "anchovies" are dark-brown salty fillets from a tin, and these closely resemble the *garum* that the ancient Romans liked so much. This reddish brown color is a result of fermentation and comes with the salting and storing. A purée of such little fish is called a **pissala**, and when it is baked on a disc of bread dough, together with black olives and a generous layer of onion **fondue**, the result is a **pissaladière**, which is a pizza variation very popular in the south of France.

    Anchoïade is a mixture of anchovy and garlic made into a thick dressing eaten in Provence with raw vegetables as a first course, or spread on toast as a snack with a bottle of the local pink wine. **Tapenade** is a comparable anchovy paste containing also tuna and capers, but black olives should provide the predominating flavor. Salted anchovies used to be on sale from barrels in fish markets but now they are difficult to find.

    Fresh anchovies are small oily fish, rather like sardines, and like sardines they are barbecued over charcoal in many coastal villages of the Third World. Gourmets have always claimed that the European anchovy is better eating and that Mediterranean ones are best of all. Collioure, in France but very near the Spanish border, was famous for its many varied anchovy dishes. **Sauce Collioure**, an anchovy-flavored **aïoli**, was named for this town. Now the restaurants here boast only a **tapenade aux anchois**, a spicy paste of oil and crushed olives with anchovy in the mixture. It is eaten in this region with fresh bread as an hors d'oeuvre. Nearby Port-Vendres has now replaced Collioure for anchovy boats which often return empty. There are not many anchovy dishes to be found now, for the anchovy is disappearing from the Mediterranean, a victim of the devastating pollution this inland sea has suffered.

Andouille: a sausage made from chitterlings—pork tripe and intestines. It is very much like **andouillette** (see below) except that it is smoked. It's also bigger, rather more firm and makes a prettier pattern when sectioned. It is intended to be eaten cold without any preparation. In Vire, Normandy, where the famous **andouille de Vire** is produced, it's served with a sorrel purée. Although I like it, and serve it, I am reconciled to seeing guests leave the sorrel on their plates, for this bitter, lemony-flavored accompaniment remains something of an acquired taste.

Andouillette: chitterling sausage. These sausages made from pork entrails have no equivalent. In France they are relished and are on sale everywhere, priced about the same per pound as good pork loin! A luxury version of the same product is called **andouillette à la ficelle** (made more carefully with long sections of chitterling while the ordinary type are made from smaller chopped pieces and usually include small pieces of pork too) and will cost about double the price of pork loin. **Andouillette de Lyons**, one of the most interesting, is made from a veal and pork mixture. The ones in the **charcuterie** are cooked and ready to be grilled briefly (just enough to color and heat them) and served with potato purée. For **andouillettes grillées au vin de Vouvray** (or any other white wine available) the grill pan (or frying pan) is deglazed with the wine to produce enough gravy to trickle over the sausage.

As a variation on sausage in brioche at least one chef has put andouillette inside a crust and made an **andouillette en croûte**.

Originally from the northern provinces, where the towns of Caen, Cambrai and Troyes claim to have the finest andouillettes in the world, this popular sausage is to be found all over France and varies in quality from shop to shop. To strike a bizarre note, intrepid gourmets report that in the weekly market in Saumur, a town on the river Loire, andouillettes made from horsemeat and eel are on sale.

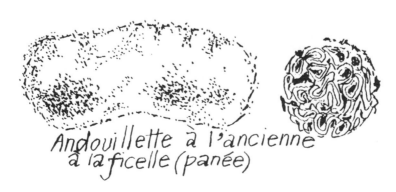

Andouillette à l'ancienne
à la ficelle (panée)

Anglaise: English. Often used to describe simple ways of cooking, such as steaming vegetables or boiling meat. **Assiette anglaise** is a plate of cold mixed meats, sausage and so on. **Crème anglaise**—or more exactly **crème à l'anglaise**—is a delicious egg custard, not at all like the floury sauce that the anglais make from packets of custard powder. **A l'anglaise** also means coated in flour, egg and breadcrumbs and then fried in butter.

Anguille: eel. The Spaniards, the Italians, the Belgians, the Germans, the Dutch and even the British have an enthusiasm for eating eels that the French lack. Like so many other French dishes, you'll find it in cookbooks but you won't often find it on the menus except as a **matelote, cotriade** or in a **terrine.** Gault and Millau, the originators of *Guide gourmand de la France*, said that eel is virtually unknown in France.

Apéritif. The pre-meal drinks associated with this name are strong. They had to be in order to absorb the flavors of the herbs and spices which gave them the curious bitter flavors that people thought must be good for them. The strongest are probably the aniseed-based **pastis,** such as Pernod and Ricard that I drank so much of when I was young and foolish. There are gentler ones—Suze and Chambéry—but a glass of chilled dry white wine is probably the best apéritif of all, better than champagne, I think.

Of course restaurants are keen to sell you a glass of inferior champagne with **crème de cassis** in it and call it a **kir royale.** The champagne is unlikely to be freshly opened or of high quality. So if you are ordering an apéritif in a restaurant, why not look at the wine list and buy half a bottle of white wine (or champagne)? It will be cheaper and better than any "house apéritif."

Appellation d'origine contrôlée (AOC) is a system of regulating the production—and supervising the quality—of certain choice foods: butter, cheese, wine, poultry, etc. In particular, it is applied to the system that controls which vines are planted where, and what may be said on the label about the wine that is made from them. However, the wine business has always attracted a small percentage of rogues; some amiable, some less so. Wine varies in quality and price and it's poured into ships and tanker trucks and sent roaring across the world in every direction. It is foolish to regard the label as a guarantee of quality.

Don't depend upon the government to punish miscreants: the bureaucrats responsible for travel and export are all primarily concerned to avoid any scandal that might damage the economy. However, many vineyard owners want to sell a good wine at a sensible price. When you find a wine that suits your palate and pocket, stick to it. You might have found such an owner.

Armagnac. Although Cognac may be the most famous French brandy, Armagnac is the oldest and for some drinkers the finest. It is produced in the corner of France which is near the Atlantic and Spain. Unlike Cognac, it is made by continuous distillation, and some say that gives it a special softness as well as a distinctive fruity flavor. The best Armagnac comes from Bas-Armagnac, but as with Cognac aging improves its quality tremendously. Armagnac mixed with grape juice makes a powerful apéritif—**Floc**—which only the locals can handle before a meal. If you don't believe me, try it.

Artichaut: globe artichoke, an edible plant of the sort to which we apply that vague term "thistle." In France young ones are eaten raw but not, I hastily add, by me. Larger ones can be eaten leaf by leaf, but I find this a tedious dish. Better to cook artichokes in a big saucepan and discard everything but the heart while they are still hot. The hearts make a luxury garnish and may be topped with foie gras or even caviar. Best of all I like them tossed in vinaigrette while still warm to make my favorite salad.

The most famous artichoke recipe is **artichaut à la barigoule.** This is regional cooking and the dish varies from chef to chef, but usually ham or pork and always mushrooms are included. Some chefs say the mushrooms must be fresh morels because a barigoule is a morel (which most Frenchmen call **morille**). Anne Willan says barigoule should be **farigoule** and is the Provençal word for thyme.

Our Jerusalem artichoke is so named because, like a sunflower, it keeps turning to face the sun; hence its twisted root and its name **girosol**, which became Jerusalem. In France it is called a winter artichoke or **topinambour**, and treated with a distinct lack of enthusiasm. The French say Jerusalem artichokes become sticky and gluey when cooked, which is more likely to be the case when they have been stored. Cooked freshly dug and served with just butter and pepper they are rather good.

Asperge: asparagus. Julius Caesar is said to have enjoyed asparagus with melted butter, but whether this luxury food was eaten before the days of the Roman Empire has never been clearly established. It requires a cool climate and a sandy soil so the theory that it originated in northern Europe seems sound. Waverley Root, the American gourmet and scholar, suggests that it came from the Baltic regions or even the British Isles. Even with cold ground and sandy soil it is not simple to grow, as I know from practical experience. A long time elapses between establishing the bed and getting the first crop, and even then a lot of it might be "sprue": thin shoots suitable only for soup. There is also the matter of judging each year when to stop gathering it and allow it to go to seed. In France they stop cutting it on St. John's Day or Midsummer Day, June 24.

After all the trouble of growing it, cooking it seems simple. The trick is to cook the delicate tips rather less than the hardy stalks so that as much as possible is good to eat. Many chefs like to stand it upright, half-immersed in boiling water, so that the tips are cooked only by steam. This is sound reasoning, although it requires a pan of exactly the right girth for the bunch of asparagus you cook. So I use my very large (Chinese) steamer and cook it laid out with paper or foil

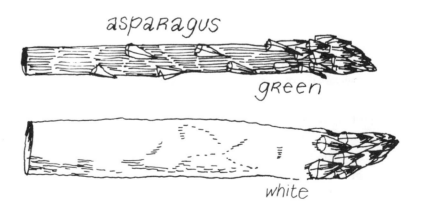

asparagus

green

white

over the stalks to concentrate the heat there. I am a great enthusiast for steaming because it minimizes loss of flavor and vitamins. It also makes it easy to test for hardness and to judge when food is cooked. For asparagus this is vitally important since it's not nice underdone and terrible when cooked too much.

Argenteuil is a town in Seine-et-Oise, where much asparagus was grown. It is used on menus to indicate the presence of asparagus, but **Argenteuil** is actually a variety of asparagus. It has pink or violet tips. There are many other varieties and it is to be found growing wild. Recently the tips of wild asparagus have been seen in the dishes served in top French restaurants, but in my experience they are more decorative than flavorful. Perhaps because French chefs now travel so much, the news seems to be getting around that the white asparagus, from which a tough outer layer must be peeled before cooking, is a fifth-rate vegetable compared with the delicate green asparagus. Don't write and tell me that these are the same plant—one grown above ground, the other buried under the soil—I don't believe it.

Aspic. This is not to be confused with jelly (**gelée**). An aspic is a cold dish: a piece of poultry, fish, lobster or foie gras, and so on, set in a mold and covered with clear sparkling jelly. Confusion comes from the way writers translate such dishes as **aspic de volailles** as "chicken in aspic." An aspic is one of the easiest dishes to prepare but very difficult to prepare perfectly. Flavorful, clear jelly of the right texture, prepared from natural ingredients, is the ultimate test of the skilled cook. The food in the aspic has to be carefully selected, lightly cooked and not kept too long in the refrigerator (or it will be flavorless and rubbery).

Auberge: a coaching inn. Such places were providing food and lodging for travelers long before there were any hotels or restaurants. Nowadays the name is too often a wishful attempt to add spurious glamour to an otherwise dull modern eating place.

Aubergine. Some varieties are white and egg shaped, which accounts for the American name, "eggplant." Many recipes tell you to slice them and sprinkle with salt to get rid of the water, but that advice was

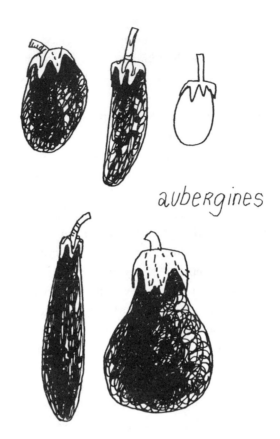

aubergines

originally intended for the coarse, bitter-tasting varieties still to be seen heaped high in the markets of India and the Far East. Even the finest eggplants have little flavor and the texture is so rubbery that they cannot be eaten raw. The best way to eat them is to roast them over an open flame, wash the burnt skin off and mash (or blend) the flesh with good olive oil and garlic. But that's not French cooking.

Avocat. As well as being a French lawyer this is the familiar avocado. Weight watchers take note: although it has the highest protein content of any fruit known, it is 25 percent oil, which makes it a very fattening salad. People who find avocados too rich and cloying with oil and vinegar on them might like them with Worcestershire sauce. Eccentric and un-French, I know, but for me it is the only way to eat them.

Baba au rhum: a sweet bread made with a yeast dough, which is soaked in a rum-flavored syrup before being served. The story is that Stanislas I Leczinski, King of Poland and father-in-law of Louis XV, invented the dish by pouring rum over a *Kugelhupf*—a sweet dough made with yeast—and calling it Ali Baba. Another source[2] says that "baba" is a Russian word for peasant woman and that the 10-inch-high version served in Russia ". . . does have a certain resemblance to the figure of a woman dressed in full sarafan." (My dictionary says a *sarafan* is a long mantle, veil or sleeveless cloak that forms part of the Russian peasant costume.)

The baba is distinguished by having raisins or other dried fruit in it, whereas the savarin is a plain version of the same thing. These yeast and flour mixtures don't collapse when soaked, while an ordinary sponge mixture disintegrates. Babas are baked in individual tapered cylindrical baba molds (also known as **dariole** molds, although the dariole is virtually extinct). Savarins are usually cooked in large, ring-shaped molds, not unlike those fluted ones used for a Kugelhupf, or what the French more often call a **kougloff.**

Bagna cauda: a dip for raw vegetables made from anchovy, olive oil and garlic.

Baguette: a long, thin "French loaf" evolved to utilize France's soft wheat flour. These are difficult to reproduce in a domestic kitchen.

Baies roses: pink "peppercorns." Actually the seeds of another plant, but used like peppercorns in such dishes as **canette aux baies roses** in which they flavor a duckling. The knowledgeable Glynn Christian in his encyclopedic *Delicatessen Food Handbook* says that they are from a plant related to poison ivy. He says they are dangerous to eat and that the Food and Drug Administration has suspended their import.

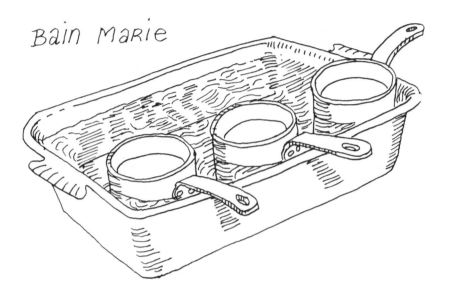

Bain Marie

Bain-marie: a rectangular pan of hot water on a stove top. Saucepans stand in it so that their contents will stay warm but not cook. Sometimes the bain-marie is used for gentle cooking processes (for instance, to cook egg custards, which must not become hotter than about 178°F or the mixture will separate).

A good comparison of techniques is provided when a chef makes scrambled eggs. A chef trained in France makes it in a double boiler and the result is wet and almost like a thick soup. In British or American kitchens it is cooked in a saucepan or frying pan and the dry outer layer is stirred into the wetter parts to provide a lumpier and quite different result. **Cuisson au bain-marie** means to cook something in a water-bath. Such cooking is almost always done with the bain-marie inside the oven. It provides a steamy heat. This method is used to cook terrines and egg mixtures and some cooks like this gentle method for a soufflé.

Ballottine: meat, game or poultry that has been boned and rolled. Such dishes are likely to be elaborate and may be served hot or cold. A **galantine** is the same sort of dish, but it contains a rich filling and is always jellied and served cold.

Bar, called **loup de mer** (sea wolf) in the Mediterranean, is sea bass. This aggressive ocean fish can grow to 5 feet in length and is, like the barracuda, one of the very few fish known to attack humans; thus its name.

Bar comptoir. Not just a bar-counter, a place where simple meals are served. In the days when Paris markets were in the center of the city, it became fashionable for people to come from theaters or nightclubs to eat there in the small hours of the morning. Many of these "bar-counters" served their famous onion soup—a **gratinée** heavily laden with cheese and browned under the grill—to porters and to toffs.

Bardes. Thin sheets of pork fat (**bardes de lard**) are used to protect the outer parts of lean meat, poultry or game while it is roasted. This is called barding. These bardes should always be taken from the outer fat of the pork loin. Pork is chosen because it is—for the chef—the finest sort of animal fat and has the best flavor too. Bardes are also used for lining a terrine or wrapping around fillet steaks.

Baron d'agneau: two legs of lamb and a saddle, all in one piece. The way in which the lamb carcass (unlike beef) is delivered to the butcher whole makes it possible for him to prepare cuts in which both sides remain joined. I love lamb and I follow the general taste in believing that the leg (**gigot**) is the most flavorful cut, closely followed by the saddle (**selle**). When I had the pleasure of arranging a birthday lunch for Eric Ambler I talked to my friend Anton Edelmann, the maître cuisinier at the *Savoy Hotel*, London, and we agreed that a baron d'agneau would be a fitting meal to celebrate such a birthday. The

Savoy gave us Eddie, their most experienced carver, so the baron could be carved at the table-side. It was one of the best meals I have ever had, and was matched by the company.[3]

Barrier, Charles (1916–). Few great restaurateurs are able to sustain top quality for year after year. Outside Paris only *Père Bise* and *Troisgros* come to mind as places where expectations are not sometimes disappointed. Charles Barrier in his well-designed restaurant at Tours was, for a time, a restaurateur to whom gourmets made a special journey. Or as they say in France, not entirely as a joke, "a pilgrimage." Barrier is a loner. He never appears in advertisements or promotions. His critics say he's antisocial; Barrier replies that he is dedicated and has no time for frivolities. He disdains garnishes or food shaped to look like something else, and says he serves only ingredients that people can actually taste. He believes that customers have the right to choose, and if someone wants a well-done duck, Barrier, despite his belief that duck should be underdone, will serve it as required. He feels that because nowadays his customers are mostly people who don't get enough exercise he must give them healthy food. He cuts back on sugar and animal fats. When a newspaperman asked Barrier what advice he'd give to a domestic cook, he said, "Choose only the best produce."

Barrier designed his kitchen so well that even the wonderful kitchen of the *Troisgros* didn't outshine it. It is at least as big as the dining-room, and in the middle, from inside a glass-walled office, Barrier surveyed his realm.

It was in this kitchen that—seeing the bowls of sugared fruit for sorbet making—I remarked to the maître d'hôtel that measuring the proportions of fruit and sugar for a sorbet is a tricky task. The maître d'hôtel and his head waiter began an animated discussion with each other about the hydrometer readings best suited to various fruits. Where but in France would you find two members of the dining-room staff who know that a hydrometer is necessary to the making of a perfect sorbet? Alas, some years later I asked where the maître d'hôtel was and they told me he was now running a taxi service.

Barrier has always been a rebel. He was repeatedly in trouble with the authorities. By the time this book is published who can guess what he'll be doing. But for a time, not so very long ago, he was at the very top of the tree. It was my great pleasure to eat with him then; who knows, his day might come again.

Bavarois. Forget what is so often served under this title; the real thing is the epitome of delicate, creamy desserts. A **crème bavaroise** is an enriched **crème à l'anglaise.** To make it, 1 cup milk and 1 cup thick whipping cream are beaten with 8 egg yolks. After this mixture has been gently cooked in a bain-marie, a little gelatin may be added. Then into it go 4 beaten egg whites and 1 cup whipped cream. When that mixture is chilled and unmolded you have a bavarois. All sorts of fruits and flavorings can be added; for example, Calvados in the custard and applesauce in the middle of the ring to make it **à la normande.** If ladyfingers are put around the mold before the bavarois is chilled, the unmolded result is a **charlotte russe.** Lately trendy chefs have tried to inject a little novelty into bleak menus by using dessert descriptions for savory dishes and vice versa. Thus we find sweet "soups" and savory bavarois. I hope such gimmickry will be short-lived.

Béarnaise: a sauce of the egg and butter group (other examples are **hollandaise, mousseline** and **Colbert**). Vinegar, wine, chopped onion and chopped tarragon are boiled until the liquids have reduced to half their volume. This reduction is strained and egg yolks and butter are whisked into it. This sharp-tasting creamy sauce is served with grilled chicken or boiled fish but is best known as an accompaniment to steak.

Beaujolais: This wine-growing region is a continuation of its more famous neighbor—Burgundy—which stretches from Macon to Lyons. But while the Burgundian wine producers abandoned the Gamay grape (and replanted their vineyards with Pinot Noir), the tenacious farmers of Beaujolais wine—light and fruity and drunk when young—persisted, and their names have become world famous. It is virtually all red: white beaujolais is a curiosity.

In November 1988 **Regnie** became the tenth Beaujolais cru officially entitled to label its bottles with the year of production and its name. The others are **Brouilly, Chenas, Chiroubles, Côte de Brouilly, Fleurie, Julienas, Morgon, Moulin-à-Vent** and **St.-Amour.** These appellations each have their own distinctive flavors, as a tasting devoted to all ten of them will delightfully demonstrate.

Béchamel: one of the most basic of white sauces. A typical recipe would be to melt 2 ounces butter over a low heat and stir 2 ounces flour into it. Cook it for three minutes, making sure it doesn't brown, and you have a **roux.**

Slowly add 2 cups warm milk (with seasoning) while stirring or whisking the butter and flour mixture and you have a béchamel. This is the basis for many sauces; for example, cheese sauce (**mornay**) or **velouté,** and other classic sauces such as **ravigote, crevette, Nantua** and **cardinal.** Add cream to béchamel and you have **sauce crème.** If you add the yolks of four eggs to the béchamel, and carefully fold in their stiffly beaten whites, you'll have a soufflé ready for a hot oven.

Beignet is a type of fritter. Usually these are pieces of lightly cooked food, dusted in flour to dry them off, dipped in batter and fried in deep fat. This is a good way to put some life into leftover vegetables such as cauliflower, carrots or turnips. Fruit beignets are made from apples, pears, bananas and so on. There are other types of beignet that are made from choux pastry and some from yeast dough.

Belgique: Belgium. French cooking is found all over the world, but outside France only in the French-speaking regions of Switzerland and Belgium is it the prime style of cooking. In Switzerland (no matter what may be claimed for Fredy Giradet's restaurant near Lausanne) French cooking is a pale shadow of what is offered across the border. In Belgium, however, the French cooking is reinforced by the heartiness of the northern lowlands and a few culinary tricks that are entirely parochial. Belgian cooking is robust but superb. It can bring new enthusiasm to a generation eviscerated by nouvelle cuisine.

Beurre: butter. When I first moved to the country and discovered that old Essie, my nearest neighbor, made butter, I begged for some. She eventually spared me a little and I went home to the warm home-made bread I'd baked and tried it. It was terrible: slightly rancid and very salty. I was to discover that quite a lot of country butter is just as bad. (As an aside, let me say that rancid tastes seem not to offend country people in the way they disgust "townies." In Spain and Portugal many people prefer their olive oil slightly rancid.) Nowadays I stick to commercially made butters.

In France only foreigners eat butter with their bread and it's never served with cheese. Cheese is made to stand alone; a fine cheese doesn't need anything but bread and wine. Butter is for cooking. The great Fernand Point said that the secret of good cooking was "the finest butter and lots of time."[4] Of the mass-produced butter in Europe, some of the best comes from Holland, Denmark and Normandy, where Isigny butter is famous. In California I buy Knudsen's sweet butter, which is as good as any I've tasted. Australian and New Zealand butters are excellent when first made, but eaten in Europe the necessary storage requires salt as a preservative and rechurning lowers quality. When in France try Echiré, which is the best French butter I've yet found. The salting of butter dates from times before commercial refrigeration. Butter properly stored, and sold when still fresh, needs no salt. Wherever you are, buy unsalted butter; it's almost always fresher and of higher quality than the salted kind.

Clarified butter is prepared by the chef—or more likely a junior assistant—to improve the flavor and appearance of dishes containing butter. As the butter is heated to above the boiling point of water, the water in it is driven off as steam (the butter bubbles and sizzles). After that, a white froth (whey proteins) forms and should be skimmed from the surface. The hot butter is then carefully poured into another container so that the white sediment (milk proteins and salts) sinks to the bottom and is left behind. Don't heat the butter enough for the sediment to turn brown or your butter will have the scorched taste that clarification is designed to eliminate.

Beurre blanc. A rich and delicate warm butter sauce made by beating butter into a reduction of chopped shallots, white vinegar and white wine. It originated in the Anjou region, where the local wine was used. It was served with pike (**brochet**) and mullet (**mulet**), both of which desperately need some help to make them appetizing dishes. Beurre blanc goes well with **quenelles**, with whitefish and with salmon too. It's one of those things that, like soufflés, is regarded as being difficult to make. In fact it is simple to prepare, and at home we use it when there is no fish stock in the freezer to make the sorrel sauce that is the perfect accompaniment for almost any fish.

There are variations on this useful sauce. Herbs, such as basil, can be immersed in the vinegar during the reduction. The chef at the *Bourgogne Restaurant* at Cluny uses red wine and shallots as the base. It is served with fresh escargots and he calls it **beurre vigneron.**

Beurre Colbert is a dressing which is served unmelted on roast meat, steak or chicken. A tablespoonful of glace de viande is mashed into 4½ ounces of softened butter and a teaspoonful of lemon juice. A little finely chopped parsley and tarragon are stirred evenly into the mixture, and you have beurre Colbert, and very nice too.

Beurre meunière is butter warmed in a pan with a squeeze of lemon juice. It is used as a sauce for fish and certain vegetables. For instance, **sole à la meunière** is sole floured and fried in butter before having the beurre meunière poured over it.

Beurres composés are (cold) butters used for garnishing hot dishes, for stirring into soups or even for basting during the cooking process. There are many of them and they are made by beating chosen flavorings into softened butter. Try it with garlic, anchovy, mustard or onion juice. At *La Côte St. Jacques*—his three-star restaurant in Joigny—Michel Lorain makes truffle butter to serve with asparagus tips. The most commonly found example is called **beurre maître d'hôtel** and is flavored with lemon juice and chopped parsley or other herbs. It is perfectly disgusting when put upon a good steak, but being cold it can usually be scraped off and discarded fairly quickly. Far more useful is **beurre d'escargot.** This is butter into which finely chopped shallots, crushed garlic and parsley have been mixed. It's used to fill snails' shells, but is very good put upon the tiny cultivated mushrooms, which the French call **champignons de Paris**, before cooking them for a few minutes in a hot oven. Use as an appetizer or first course.

Beurre manié is butter mixed into uncooked flour. It must be left at least 30 minutes before being used to thicken sauces, soups or stews. The flour absorbs the butter so the result doesn't taste floury.

Beurre noir is a misnomer for butter which has been heated to a brown color well short of black! The danger of burning is lessened if the butter is clarified before use. The result is poured over fish (particularly skate) or brains immediately before serving, or served alongside.

Bifteck. This is a very vague term found on French menus to describe any piece of meat that the chef considers your teeth can handle, including chopped or minced beef. It should be regarded with suspicion. **Bifteck haché** is beef that has been put through a grinder, or chopped by hand. Until quite recently the use of the meat grinder was forbidden in the kitchens of good restaurants because of the way that juice was squeezed from the meat by the grinding process, so losing flavor. Often a slice of fillet steak was chopped at the tableside by a waiter using two sharp knives. Served raw, with raw egg yolk, capers and onion, such finely chopped beef was called **Bifteck à l'américaine.** **Bifteck à la tartare** was the same without the egg yolk but with a tartare sauce. Lately, under the influence of American and other foreign visitors, tartare has come to mean chopped or minced raw beef served with a selection of flavorings mixed at the table as desired by the customer.

Bigarade: bitter orange or **orange amèrc.** It also means a sauce or dressing made from the juice and peel of bitter (Seville) oranges, sometimes with caramel and sometimes with alcohol (curaçao, Madeira or port) added. This dressing is used only with duck, in particular duckling, for it is said that the ducklings in France are at their best for eating during the rather brief time when the Seville oranges are available. It is this bitter flavor of the Seville orange that, contrasting with the fattiness of the duckling, gives an authentic **caneton à la bigarade** its distinctive flavor. So when the great Henri-Paul Pellaprat made his **canard à l'orange** he artfully added a little lemon juice to add bitterness to its taste. It took Raymond Thuilier of *L'Oustaù de Baumanière* to invent the remarkable **caneton aux citrons verts**, a very sharp-tasting dish employing limes.

Bise, the family. Paul Bocuse once said that, taking everything into account—the food, the cooking, the service and the setting—*L'Auberge du Père Bise* at Talloires on Lake Annecy is the greatest restaurant of all. As a child Louisette Bertholle, co-author of *Mastering the Art of French Cooking*, regularly went there on holiday. The exuberant James Beard said, "My favorite restaurant in all of France is *L'Auberge du Père Bise* . . . a family affair of three-star magnitude." Waverley Root, the American author of *The Food of France*, put it "at the head of the French restaurants from my own personal experiences in recent years." It has been my favorite since I first visited this wonderful place in the 1950s.

The restaurant is named after Marius Bise, whose father had started it and whose brother ran *Le Cottage*, a rival establishment in the same village. The time of the proprietor chefs had not yet come. Marius was a larger-than-life figure who dominated the dining-room and spent his time with his customers. But the gastronomic fame of *Père Bise* came from his wife, Marguerite Bise, for she ran the kitchen and created dishes that are still on the menu. It took Marguerite and Marius only two years to get three stars. Such quick promotion today is unheard of, and so is the recognition for a woman chef. It seems that in 1931 the Michelin staff were bolder, and in every way more discerning, than they are today. And yet perhaps not, for now this kitchen again has a woman chef: Sophie Bise, the granddaughter of Marius, is working alongside Gilles Furtin, who has worked here for many years and took over the kitchen after the tragic death of François Bise.

During his time here François, the son of Marius, ran the kitchen on strict and systematic lines. I remember standing in the kitchen one morning at about 5:30. François was not there. The young chef making the croissants weighed and measured everything with such care that it was hard to believe he'd done the same thing every morning for countless months. Even the time for kneading the dough was specified as "10 mins. for each kilo of flour." No preparation for the yeast; all ingredients assembled and kneading starts. I have used these rules ever since.

L'Auberge du Père Bise is still remarkable for the way in which it is run. Pluck it from its magnificent lakeside and mountain setting and it could take its place in Paris alongside such sophisticated establishments as *Taillevent*. This is extraordinary, for outside Paris the grand restaurants all share that grotesque ambience that Jacques Tati created for M. Hulot. But there is no hint of Disneyland at *Père Bise*, no plastic beams or fake fireplaces, no tin swords or phony candelabra, for Madame Charlyne Bise (the lovely widow of François) is a perfectionist. To help her she has the youthful and energetic Michel Marucco, who, it is hard to believe, has been the maître d'hôtel here since before François took over. To these two hard-working people the *Auberge* owes its rightfully earned place at the top of any list. And they prove my contention that a really fine restaurant is run from the dining room. The chef must be a tactician who can win the fierce sudden battles that rage at the stove; but the war is won by nerve, conviction and consistency, and the long-term strategy is decided in the dining room. Madame Bise—with Michel as her chief of staff—has won her place as the greatest strategist in the gourmet's world.

Despite the formal décor, *L'Auberge du Père Bise* is a place to relax. Service is friendly but exemplary. No one will ever ask you to put on a necktie or climb into a jacket. On warm days lunch, and dinner too, is served outdoors so that diners can enjoy not only the ever-changing light upon the mountains and lake, and the **omble** that is fished from it, but also the clean and wonderful air. Such is perfection.

Bistro: a cheap eating place. Expect paper napkins, carafe wine and plastic table tops and simple plats du jour dishes. Nowadays inverted snobbery induces restaurateurs to call their exclusive and expensive establishments bistros.

Blanchir: to blanch. A process of precooking or preparing food by putting it into boiling water. Almonds are prepared for skinning in this way and so are tomatoes. The water should be kept as hot as possible. Boil it hard so that the skin comes off immediately, before the flesh cooks.

When vegetables such as **haricots verts** are served in the home or restaurant it is the normal procedure in France to cook them partly rather than fully. Again, the water must be at a fierce rolling boil all the time. For this reason when vegetables or pasta are boiled you need a very big pot of water; otherwise the (cold) vegetables bring down the temperature of the water. When almost cooked the vegetables are put into ice water (with plenty of ice) to bring their temperature down as fast as possible. When quite cold the vegetables are drained and if necessary dried with cloth or paper. This cooling process is called "refreshing" (**refraîchir**). To prepare the vegetables for serving they are typically warmed quickly in a pan with hot butter.

Blanc-manger. Forget those brightly colored, flour-thickened, artificially flavored, unappetizing splodges of sickly sweet dessert that masquerade under similar names in Britain and America. The real thing is made with cream and real vanilla and a little gelatin. Sometimes almonds are used as flavoring. My mother-in-law, Freda, makes a delicious blanc-manger using 2 cups of cream (**fleurette,** not **crème fraîche**) and 2 cups of milk with 4 ounces of sugar and 1 ounce of gelatin. For flavoring a whole vanilla bean is used. This can be put in a blender with the milk so that there are tiny flecks of it in the final result.

Blanquette. A stew exactly like a **fricassée** except that it is started by putting the meat or poultry in water and bringing it to the boil (while a fricassée is started by frying). Lamb, veal or chicken are all commonly used for such dishes, but the chicken must be skinned first. (In a fricassée the chicken skin is fried to get rid of the excess fat, so the skin can be kept on for the finished dish.)

Blette, sometimes called **carde**, is chard or Swiss chard. Closely related to beets, both green leaves and white stalks are eaten. Chopped, it is the

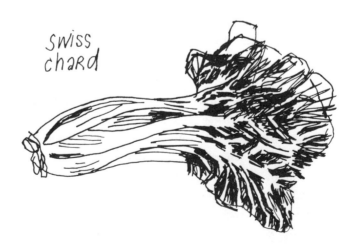

SWISS
chard

filling for **tarte au blette**, a popular snack sold in Nice markets. The white stalks need more cooking than the leaves, but "poor man's asparagus" they are not. The green leaves are more tender and don't shed much water when cooked (in the way that spinach does), so you are likely to find those artful French making spinach quiche from the green leaves of blette. Served as a vegetable blette is rather boring, but butter and pepper liven it up a little. Or, with cheese sauce, it can be made into a gratin.

Bocuse, Paul (1926–). Arguments about whether this man is the greatest chef in the world are fruitless, but none of his contemporaries would deny that he is the style-setter and the number one chef in France. And this position doesn't depend upon his determined self-publicity, and his commercial attitude to drinking and eating in all its aspects. Bocuse is to be found on wine labels, on TV commercials, magazine covers, and running restaurants in Osaka as well as Tokyo. No wonder his enemies complain that he is not always to be found in his own restaurant.

Bocuse was an apprentice under Fernand Point at *La Pyramide*, Vienne. For his generation of chefs a period at *La Pyramide* was the first step to fame and fortune. After further service in Paris kitchens, he returned to his father's war-damaged little hotel outside Lyons (nine tables and nine bedrooms). Despite the problems Paul Bocuse gained a Michelin star in 1961. By 1965 he had three stars, Michelin's greatest accolade. He'd absorbed the neighboring restaurant and the establishment was called *Paul Bocuse*, its name proclaimed by a huge electric sign on the roof. Since then he has gone on to win not only culinary awards but the Légion d'Honneur and the opportunity to supervise a famous lunch for the President of France, an occasion for which he created the **Soupe aux truffes Élysées**. The dish is an interesting insight into both his authenticity and his flamboyance: a simple chicken consommé is poured upon truffles and foie gras, and surmounted by puff pastry that the heated air makes into a golden dome.

Julia Child says Bocuse was "very macho, fun to be with and very amusing."[5] Provoked perhaps by his critics, he is an outspoken man who denounces nouvelle cuisine and blames much bad restaurant food on architects who make commercial kitchens smaller and smaller. He scorns the cuisine minceur such as that of Michel Guérard; such dietetic meals are, he says, like opera without the orchestra. Give him a chicken from the yard and a leek from the garden, he says, and he'll produce a fine meal. This emphasis upon the fresh quality of simple ingredients is typical of the chefs who came from Point's kitchen. They are, of course, reflecting Point's rediscovery of the opportunities of peacetime after the rationing and hunger of wartime occupied France. Nowadays, it has become one of Bocuse's gimmicks to take wide-eyed food writers to the market. This has endorsed the myth that "real chefs" buy their food in person each morning.

The *Bocuse* restaurant is close to Lyon, the acknowledged world capital of eating. The markets—including the superb farmer's market on the Presque île—and more notably the traditions of that region, are evident on every *Bocuse* menu. This is why the *Bocuse* restaurant rightfully retains its place as one of France's top ten restaurants. Many famous—and still acclaimed—restaurants serve only a parody of the food that earned them their stars. *Bocuse* is not the restaurant it was in the 1960s; the passion and the anxiety that contribute so much to making a good restaurant a truly great one are no longer there. But Bocuse is an honest man who wants to give good value, and for me a visit to his restaurant has always been an exciting and rewarding experience.

Boeuf is beef and at one time it dominated the menus of France. This was especially true in Burgundy, which is France's most important beef-rearing region. (Charolles, Burgundy, is the home of Charollais beef cattle.) In their heyday, such restaurants as Fernand Point's *La Pyramide* at Vienne, and Alexandre Dumaine's *Côte d'Or* at Saulieu, gave pride of place to beef dishes. But prime-quality beef became more and more expensive. American nutritionists railed against it and nouvelle cuisine derided it as unfashionable. Now beef has been relegated to a lowly position on the totem pole of fashion. Pierre Troisgros is one of the few great French chefs who express undiminished fervor for beef. (A surprising enthusiasm for a man who created what is probably the world's most famous fish recipe: **escalopes de saumon à l'oseille Troisgros**.) Pierre Troisgros has always been interested in beef and chooses **pot-au-feu** as a dish which he particularly likes to cook and to eat. He takes personal charge of the selection and preparation of meat for the restaurant of the *Hôtel des Frères Troisgros* at Roanne and confides that if he hadn't become a chef he would have become a butcher. Of course, French butchers possess technical knowledge and skills beyond those found in other countries and no doubt the invincible Troisgros would have become the very finest of them.

Great beef recipes are at the heart of French cooking but less familiar to those tourists who know only the cuisine of the summer months. Winter in the Burgundy wine country provides the mighty **boeuf à la bourguignonne**, as well as the **daube**, and the **estouffade**. Even the **hachis de boeuf à la Parmentier**—chopped beef topped with potato purée—served to my children at their Provençal village school smelled delicious.

More than one maître d'hôtel told me that steaks are something that the kitchen keeps for foreigners—specifically for Americans— who don't like French cooking. That is defeatist talk. I like beef in all its many variations: even steaks—the **entrecôte**, the **contrefilet**, the **filet mignon** and **tournedos** given their classic sauces, have a respected role in traditional French cooking, and I remain uncon- vinced by the prejudice against beef on health grounds. A cut of beef is little more fattening than any other protein. In any case, it seems to me that a visit to a grand restaurant is not the time to be counting calories or measuring your waistline.

Boeuf au gros sel. Perhaps the most important thing to remember about this menu description is that it is *not* salt beef. It is beef (and vegetables) cooked in the style of a pot-au-feu. The gros sel is coarse sea salt and is served alongside it, or sprinkled upon it. **Boeuf haché:** beef minced in a grinder or finely chopped. In France it is usual for the butcher to let you select a piece of meat and then put it through the grinder for you. This is rather better than buying mysterious mounds of fatty mixture from a tray. So ask your butcher to do the same thing. **Bifteck** and **bifteck haché** are other names for it. **Boeuf salé** is salt beef. Shoppers should not buy such meat at random from a butcher, as the odds and ends of unsold meat are consigned to the brine tub. It's better to select a piece of meat and ask the butcher to salt it for a prescribed time (about three days will probably be sufficient). French cooking makes very little use of salted meat. Is this because for most of France a milder winter made wholesale slaughter and salting unnecessary? Or is it that French cooks can't bear the waste that comes when the cooking water has to be discarded?

Boeuf bourguignon is braised beef (preferably rump) in one piece or cubed. It is cooked in red Burgundy, and some chefs would marinate it in the wine for 6–12 hours first.

Bombes. Dating from the times when bombs were spherical, and hidden under the cloaks of men with long beards, these ice-cream concoctions are made of layers of contrasting flavors and colors placed inside a spherical mold. With ice-cream machines and other gadgets it's easy to make ice cream at home, so if you prefer ice cream made from fresh fruit without artificial coloring or flavoring, make it yourself.

Bonne femme: housewife style. A menu term with no consistent meaning beyond "simple cooking."

Bordeaux is a seaport city on the Garonne river in south-west France. This whole region became an English possession when Henry II married Eleanor of Aquitaine in 1152. It remained English for three hundred years! During that time it became a great trading center and the red wines—which the British call clarets—began to rival those of Burgundy. The most important grapes are the Cabernet Sauvignon and the most important vineyards are in the Médoc—a strip of land about fifty miles long and six miles wide—on the left bank of the Gironde, which produces some of the finest red wines in the world.

The Sauvignon Blanc grape is used in both dry Graves and sweet Sauternes, but the white wines of this region are not as celebrated as the reds. Back in 1949, half a dozen wine experts formed "The Bordeaux Club" and met regularly in London, Oxford or Cambridge to reaffirm their delight in the wines of this region. Significantly they soon dropped the condition that the white wine must be a Bordeaux. "Faithfully in turn we tried all the châteaux with great or not so great names, but frankly we found they were boring us to distraction," said Harry Waugh,[6] a famous wine expert and a founder of the club. "One evening in fear and trembling, a member (I forget who it was) suggested a relaxation of the rule and it was acclaimed with both relief and enthusiasm!"

It is curious that the French, who persist in using the old pre-revolution province names for other districts, have no name for this one. "Aquitaine" is long since renounced and **"bordelaise"** (once used as a district name) is now used only to describe sauces and dishes. So we are forced to call this region, that takes in Poitou in the north and the Landes in the south, and stretches along the banks of the Charente, Dordogne and Garonne rivers, "the south-west," or simply say Bordeaux.

From the Charente region comes not only Cognac but also what most chefs consider the finest butter in France and yet—as is so often the case with luxury foods—local people here do not use much of it; they sell it. Here everyday cooking is mostly done with oil, usually adding lots of garlic.

The people of this region, like the Burgundians, say that the better the wine the better the cooking, but this is a region of good simple rustic eating rather than the grande cuisine of the more easterly parts of France. Significantly the menu description **à la bordelaise** has no reliable meaning. There are no famous cheeses around here. The goat, which survives on even the poorest coastal strips, provides some unusual goat cheeses for those who like them. (Personally I find most goat cheeses a bit too salty.) But lucky visitors arriving here at the right time will find such foods as the vineyard snails, local Pauillac lamb, mushrooms (particularly **cèpes**), eels (baby ones in winter), lampreys, **langoustines** and Marenne oysters to be as good as any they have tasted. For the extravagant, there is foie gras from the Landes or perhaps truffles from nearby Périgord. It just happens that all those regional specialties are amongst my favorite foods. If they are not items you crave, there are always the mighty Médocs.

Boucherie: butcher's shop. In France the boucherie is usually open on Sunday morning and closed on Monday. Meat is officially graded, with **qualité extra** at the top, then two grades of **choix**, and **fourth grade** used only for **charcuterie**. Unlike those in some countries, French butchers' shops sell pork as well as lamb and beef. Some larger towns, especially in the north, have charcuteries where pork and cooked pork products are sold, but my part of France—Provence —sells such things in the butcher's shop. Here are good pork sausages and such delicacies as **rillette, boudin** and **tête de veau.** Perhaps it is the prevalence of braising in closed pots that has given France such highly skilled butchers. My local man can bone and roll a shoulder of lamb while continuing to serve customers with other items. It's an education to watch him working.

Boudin noir is a pork blood sausage, which is called black pudding in Britain and blood pudding in America. Such sausages have existed ever since men first began to eat pork. In Scotland oatmeal is added; in England and Ireland onion, herbs, nutmeg, pepper, allspice and pork fat. Always matte black on the outside, most regions of France, Spain, Germany and northern England, and many other countries too, produce a variety that they claim is superior if not unique. I find the French boudin so distinct from the others that it is like a different dish. My wife does not like boudin except in France, for here it is soft and delicately flavorful. The town of Nancy is famous for its boudin, but many regions have their own individual styles which vary greatly. In the south most butchers stop making them when summer approaches and start again in September. This indicates the lack of preservatives and accounts for the fine flavor.

Beware when cooking them because the French ones are soft and the skins burst very easily. In France boudins are usually served whole

Boudin

because they are so difficult to slice. They should be grilled, or gently fried, just enough to warm them through. Applesauce—or better still well-caramelized sliced apple—is the favored accompaniment, with mashed potato.

In the north the winter solstice was the traditional time for slaughtering and eating fresh food ravenously, before the few lucky animals to be spared were brought inside, and the surplus food dried and pickled. So Christmas Eve (specifically the meal after Midnight Mass) was most associated with boudin. Nowadays factory-made boudin is eaten all year round. Much commercially made boudin (and in Britain and America it's very difficult to find any other kind) tastes of little but black dye, excessive salt and pepper and chemical additives. However, some butchers in France still manufacture their own and even our local supermarket in France sells quite good ones. Fine boudin is worth searching for; it's delicious hot or cold.

A type on sale in Nice is called **boudin niçoise** or, as I saw one marked in a shop, **vrai trulle niçois à mylace.** On a menu such special local boudin is called **trulle.** They are very rich—too oily for my taste—and contain rice, crème fraîche and blette. They have to be poached rather than fried. Another unusual variety is the **boudin Antillais** which is flavored with cayenne.

Boudin blanc. Although I am very fond of boudin noir, there is really no comparison between that and the delicate and subtle boudin blanc. This is a very special sausage made, according to local recipes, from chicken or pork, although the very best ones are made from brains, veal and cream, and usually contain egg so must be cooked gently. Unlike the boudin noir, boudin blanc is really only available in France, and only at Christmas time when it is traditionally served after Midnight Mass alongside the boudin noir. Make the most of it; it can be delicious. Devotees, and there are many, might consider a journey to Munich, where the similar—but blander—*Weisswurst* is on sale all year long.

Boudin de volaille. This is not a sausage; it's a fancy misnomer for a chicken forcemeat (the mixtures vary considerably) which is put into a mold and gently cooked in a bain-marie before being turned out and fried in egg and breadcrumbs. The resulting concoction is served hot with **sauce Périgueux** (demi-glace with truffles) or with

sauce suprême (chicken stock with butter and cream), the first of overwhelming flavor and the latter extremely rich.

Bouillabaisse is of course the saffron-flavored fish stew that Marseille claims as its one and only contribution to France's gastronomic glory. The complete selection of fish required for a bouillabaisse that will satisfy the purists is no longer easy to acquire anywhere along the coast of the ever-more-polluted Mediterranean. It includes **chapon, fiélas, loup, rascasse,** red mullet, **rouquier, saint-pierre,** sea perch and whiting, as well as conger eel and shellfish such as **langouste** and crab. It is quite a shopping list. The stew is started with tomato, onion and lots of olive oil, and is cooked rapidly, the fish being added according to how much cooking they require and the whole thing taking no more than 15 minutes in all. An unusual, if not unique, aspect of this dish is that it is boiled—a violent form of cooking that fish is not normally subjected to—and this emulsifies the oil and water to thicken the resulting stew to its characteristic consistency. This probably accounts for the name **bouillabaisse,** which means "boil down."

Bouillabaisse is usually served in two dishes (as is a pot-au-feu), one containing the fish, the other the broth. Some of the fish, tiny crabs for instance, are there just for flavoring and can't be eaten; at least I've never tried to eat one. The broth is poured over chunks of bread that have been baked crisp. Sometimes **aïoli** or **rouille** —powerful mayonnaise made with raw garlic, paprika and cayenne—is served too. It is stirred into the broth.

At *Restaurant Bacon,* Cap d'Antibes, which is famous for its bouillabaisse, the fish served in the broth included **vive** (weever), **lotte** (monkfish), **rouget-grondin, rascasse** and **turbot.** The broth was made from many other fish. They serve rouille and croûtons (with raw garlic to rub on them).

The cook should remember that if the fish is tasty and the broth thin the bouillabaisse will be a failure, but if the fish is tasteless and the broth flavorful you will be acclaimed.

Whether or not a real bouillabaisse actually needs the full selection of fish, or whether it should simply be made with whatever swims into the net or what is to be found on the slab in the market, is fiercely disputed. Even in Marseille **bourride** is available and bourride is poor man's bouillabaisse with only the cheaper fish in it. And to what extent are those fish stews made from the fish of other waters comparable? Can a bouillabaisse be made in Boulogne? In Grimsby? In New York? In Los Angeles? I don't know, but the fact that so many attempts to prove it are called bouillabaisse must be a tribute to the chefs of Marseille.

There are plenty of other sea-fish stews in France: **cotriade** in Brittany, **chaudrée** in Poitou. Inland there are stews of river fish and lake fish. None of them is quite like bouillabaisse. Dare I say some of them are better?

Bouillabaisse borgne or "one-eyed" bouillabaisse, also known as **aigo sau d'iou**, is a leek, onion and garlic soup cooked with white wine, potato and chopped, skinned tomato and flavored with thyme, bay leaf and saffron. Towards the end of the cooking time, eggs—one per person—are poached in the soup. It gets its name by being served in the manner of a bouillabaisse; that is, the broth is poured upon a chunk of bread while the egg and vegetables are served on a separate plate. It's much better than it sounds.

Bourride is a variant of bouillabaisse; it also comes from the south. No two people agree on what it contains, but the consensus is that the fish are smaller and cheaper than those in bouillabaisse—so certainly no shellfish—and instead of thickening by boiling, it's thickened with egg yolks added just before serving.

Bouilli. The French have many recipes for beef, vegetables and so on, poached gently in water—**pot-au-feu**, for example. In common parlance, both in England and France, this is called "boiled beef" and the meat of such a dish is called **boeuf bouilli.**

Bouillie (porridge) is a mixture of milk, sugar and starch into which the cook beats egg yolks and butter. A bouillie of this sort is one of many ways to begin making a soufflé.

Bouillir: to boil. We often see this word used to describe any process of cooking in very hot water. Such temperatures are crucial to the cooking process, as some foods (for example, those containing albumin) will harden, separate and spoil if too hot. The French are careful to distinguish between **frémir**, when the surface of the water is shivering at about 180°F, and **mijoter,** when bubbles are rising to the surface. When the French say boiling—bouillir—they mean a turbulent rolling boil. Such high-temperature water is necessary only to cook pasta, to reduce the volume of a liquid, and to cook those vegetables that will not be damaged by the turbulence. The unacceptable loss of flavor and vitamins into the water will persuade the wise cook to steam foods rather than boil wherever possible. When cooking salty foods, or when salt has been added to the cooking water, remember that salt water boils at 224°F.

Bouillon: the liquid from the stock pot or the liquid from a **pot-au-feu.** This "soup" is not clear enough to be called **consommé,** which has to be of excellent color for use as jelly. It is one of the many problems of making fine consommé that most of the ingredients that produce flavor also produce cloudiness.

A **court bouillon** is quite different. It's a liquid flavored with herbs, vegetables and sometimes wine or vinegar, used for poaching fish, brains, sweetbreads (or meat or vegetables). The court bouillon is used to put flavor into food and so reverses the previous process. A typical court bouillon would consist of 7 cups water in which 2 onions, 2 carrots, a very small wineglass of white wine, 6 peppercorns, a bay leaf and a bouquet of herbs (thyme, parsley and celery leaf) have been simmered for about 20 minutes. At *Baumanière* M. Thulier told me he liked the court bouillon to add a distinct, sharp flavor to the fish and he uses not only vinegar but lots of lemon and orange juice. *See also* **Fumet**, page 106.

Bouillon is a dish that gave its name to the places that sold it. (Café and restaurant did the same.) But nowadays there are no more bouillons in which we can comfortably sit. The last one in Paris, the *Bouillon Buci*, in rue de Buci, closed in the 1950s.

Boulangerie: baker's shop. It will be closed on Monday but open Sunday morning. If it's combined with a pâtisserie it might be open all day Sunday, for that is the big day for French cake eaters, and not many French cooks make their own cakes. Even today in France a surprising number of country people do not have an oven. Traditional French cooking is done in a closed pot in the fireplace. No home-made bread or cakes in France. No roast meat either. French housewives buy fresh bread daily and so do the rest of their shopping daily too. This absence of ovens is surprising to the British, for whom the Industrial Revolution provided cheap cast-iron ovens that even the poor could afford. In the warmer regions of France where constantly burning fires were unnecessary, the baker's shop would cook food for a small fee. Thus dishes that required long slow cooking in the dying embers of the bread oven take their name from the baker's wife and are called **boulangère.**

Bouquet garni: a selection of herbs bound together—sometimes held within two ribs of celery—to flavor soups or stews.

Bourgogne. Burgundy. If, when here, you forget that Burgundy was once a dominion that challenged the power of France itself, a Burgundian will remind you. Most Frenchmen, and certainly all Burgundians, would tell you that their wine, produce and good cooking are unchallenged. There is plenty to support this claim. While the menu description **à la bordelaise** is somewhat vague, **à la bourguignonne** immediately conjures an image of a large piece of beef cooked in good red wine. Here are the world's most full-bodied and elaborate red wines, and here is Charolles, which gave its name to the famous Charollais beef that Frenchmen (denied the pleasures of Angus or Texan beef) eat with delight. And here is Dijon mustard to help it down.

This region has been noted for wine since 50 B.C. The Chardonnay grape is a legal necessity for the white Burgundy wines, which are exquisite. The Pinot Noir grape is used to make the complex red wines that vary so much from place to place that a man could spend a whole life comparing them. And some men have. From these vineyards come also the best **escargots** I've ever eaten, and here is Bresse, from which comes incomparable—and incomparably priced—poultry. It is a region that produces food in unrivaled variety and abundance and yet—like that other great wine district, Bordeaux—no fine cheeses are made here. Why? For once I have no theory.

I first came to know this area in the summer vacation of 1950 when, with a group of students in a broken-down Alvis motor car, I was stranded just outside the wine-producing village of Aloxe-Corton. Luckily the breakdown occurred on the outgoing journey, so we had enough money to buy food, and we had a huge tent in which to sleep. The local villagers were sympathetic and took us under their collective wing. I was a keen photographer and poked my nose everywhere in the way that photographers do. I believe we got to see life in a small rural French community as few foreigners did at that time. Whenever I see Aloxe-Corton on a label I remember it all with great affection.

Burgundy has for a long time had the greatest concentration of luxury restaurants anywhere in France. These restaurants sustain the high standards of the local food producers and demand better and better supplies. Yet to explain the position that Burgundy enjoys as a gourmet paradise one has only to look at the map. Long before the construction of the autoroutes, the frantic inhabitants of Paris came through Burgundy en route to the sun. The growing popularity of motoring in the years after the First World War produced hotels and restaurants that catered to the growing numbers of affluent motorists. The only road came this way, and Burgundy was the halfway mark.

Bourride. A fish soup resembling the American chowder. And like a chowder there are many versions, from those with clear broth with tomato to the cream style. In the port at Nice, *L'Ane Rouge,* a restaurant well known for its bourride, serves a version which includes **lotte** (monkfish), **grondin** (gurnard), **loup** (sea bass), **vive** (weever) and mussels. They are served alongside the garlicky fish stock into which quite a lot of cream and egg have been beaten to make a rich thick soup. It comes with grated cheese, **rouille** and toast. I was told when eating one that bourride (unlike bouillabaisse) must never have saffron in it.

Boyer, Gérard (1945–). Boyer comes from a family of restaurateurs. His grandparents came from the Auvergne to start a restaurant in Paris. His father, Gaston, had a restaurant in Reims and, after Gérard had served his apprenticeship and come back from working as a chef in *Lasserre,* he took him into partnership. The restaurant was called the *Chaumière.* It was on the outskirts of the city, it was easy to park the car and I ate well there. And the prices were low. By 1979 it had earned the coveted three stars of Michelin. This was quite an achievement; being notorious for its disappointing food and restaurants, the Champagne region was not an easy place for an ambitious chef to work.

It was a local champagne producer—Xavier Gardinier of Lanson and Pommery—who had the idea of renovating the magnificent Château des Crayères and its fifteen-acre garden in the middle of Reims, and making it into one of the finest hotel-restaurants in France. It has provided Gérard Boyer with an opportunity to show that he is one of the most notable and skilled chefs working today. I like to eat there still, but no one could say the prices are low.

Braiser corresponds to the English word brazier, a metal container for burning coals or charcoal. When I was young every hole in the road was attended by a nightwatchman who sat before a glowing brazier. In olden times birds, rabbits and even hedgehogs were braised; wrapped in clay and cooked in the braise or embers. In France it now means to cook in a **braisière**, a covered pot, kept at a heat just above the boiling point of water so that very small amounts of stock poured into the pot provide it with a moist heat. It used to be buried in the glowing embers of the fire. Nowadays such pots usually sit on the stove top. But many braisières have ridged tops to hold pieces of hot coal or wood.

Brandade: dried salt cod—**morue salé**—reconstituted with olive oil and garlic, and sometimes tomato too, to make a winter dish popular in Provence and Languedoc. This can also be made with **morue sèche** (hard yellow items from Iceland that are widely known as stockfish). Brandade should be approached with caution unless you like salty wet Kleenex.

Brasserie. Originally this name signified a place where beer was brewed and sold. French beer is mostly from Alsace and so most brasseries served Alsace food—choucroute, sausages and so on—with the beer. After the Franco-Prussian War in 1870 large numbers of refugees from Alsace and Lorraine (now occupied by Germans) came to Paris.

Some started brasseries. Such establishments soon became meeting places where poets, writers, politicians and others with a lot of spare time on their hands sat around drinking. The idea became popular and so, when restaurants set aside a room apart from the slow formalities of the dining room, it was called the brasserie of the restaurant. It was for travelers, families with children and businessmen. Nowadays it's an ever-open place, where food and drink—anything from a glass of Alsace beer, wine and sandwich to a full meal—are available all day long from breakfast to late dinner. Such places will provide you with a cup of coffee in the middle of their lunchtime rush and give you the daily paper with it. A brasserie will be pleased if you go there for half a dozen oysters and stay to write your memoirs or fill in your crossword or your tax return. I'm afraid it says a lot about Britain and America that restaurateurs use the name of such excellent establishments but provide no more than a ghost of the facilities.

Bresse is a region of Burgundy to the northeast of Lyon. Its most famous son was Fernand Point. Here also are raised a white breed of poultry generally considered to be the finest eating of any in the world. The chicks are fed on ground corn, powdered milk and buckwheat. For most of their life they run "free range" and then for the final month they are restricted and fed on rice and milk. After slaughter they are prepared for the kitchen with great care. Each bird is given a red, white and blue label with the farmer's identity number. In effect the quality and sale of Bresse poultry is controlled as carefully as is French wine.

Running along the western edge of this region is the main route from Paris—and the Channel ports—to the south. This route has always been liberally provided with luxury restaurants with chefs, and clients, willing to pay very high prices for the very best ingredients. Although there were other places where chickens were raised with equal care—Le Mans, for example—inevitably Point, and other local restaurateurs, served this poultry. Nowadays almost every top French restaurant uses Bresse chickens. French families cook them for special occasions, but some people feel that the price of such poultry—in my local shop a Bresse chicken costs five times as much as a supermarket bird—will eventually mean the end of this luxury production.

Bretagne or Brittany is, like so many other district names in common use, that of a former province. I lived in Erquy, a small town on the north coast, for a short while, back in the 1950s, and I have to say that it was then a gastronomic desert. There were no outstanding restaurants and charcuterie was unknown. (When I served some local people a simple **terrine de porc** it was regarded as a notable achievement.)

Since then Brittany has been transformed with vast investment programs and government subsidy. It is a bustling place with ugly new buildings everywhere and new motorways to link them. But Brittany has been created by history, a region of poverty and poor harvests, a place where many sons traditionally went to sea. The poor land and harsh weather did not encourage the farmer to grow wheat. Bretons were nourished on hardy rye and the buckwheat that elsewhere was fed to horses, cattle and poultry. Instead of wheat bread there was rye bread and buckwheat porridge, buckwheat pancakes and boiled buckwheat pudding (**kik a'farz**). The omnivorous pig—salt or fresh— remains the most popular meat.

Even today no eating place in the whole region gets a Michelin top award. There is no fine cheese, local butter is mustard yellow and unpleasantly salty, and there is no good local wine either. Once you've sampled the **galettes de sarrasin** (buckwheat pancakes), the **kouign-amann** (a rich buttery loaf), **far Breton aux pruneaux** (a batter pudding with prunes) and the ill-defined fish soup called a **cotriade** you will have virtually exhausted Brittany's unique cuisine. But that doesn't mean that present-day Brittany is a disappointing region in which to eat. Although boundary changes have deprived Brittany of the great town of Nantes, the ducks and ducklings from there are still as good. The lamb is excellent. **Gigot aux haricots à la bretonne** is a tasty combination of lamb grazed on the salt flats and dried white beans, which are a staple food of Brittany.

But the Breton is a seaman and this is a region where the wise visitor eats fish. Everything is to be found in the market: lobsters, spiny lobsters, crabs, scallops, periwinkles, shrimps and some of the best oysters in the world. In the places of high tides, some might even find an **ormier** or ormer (known as abalone in America and *awabi* in Japan), which is becoming rare and expensive everywhere in the world.

Additionally there is freshly landed whitefish from the English Channel and the Atlantic. From Brittany's ports come two thirds of France's tinned fish: sardines, mackerel and tuna from the Azores or Biscay. All of France relishes Brittany's seafood; curiously the average Breton does not share this enthusiasm. Seafood is for the tourist.

Brie is in the département of Seine-et-Marne not far from Paris. It is also a large fermented cheese. While resisting the temptation to write about the vast subject of French cheeses, some are too important to be left out. Brie, for instance. It is said that Talleyrand, at the Vienna Congress of 1814, proposed a tasting of world cheeses at which a **Brie de Meaux** was declared the winner. Whether the story is true or not, this particular type of brie is still considered one of the very finest. **Brie de Melun** is a strong, well-ripened variety which varies from other bries in that its mold formation is not induced by added *penicillium candidum* powder.

    Brie en brioche is a dish I first encountered a few years back. It consists of a ripe brie, weighing about 2 pounds, wrapped in brioche dough (made from 3 cups flour, 6 large eggs and 6 ounces butter). The dough-wrapped cheese is cooked in a 350°F oven for about half an hour and served two hours later while it is still warm.[7] I cooked one, and it was a notable success, but I didn't follow M. Pépin's suggestion of serving it at the end of a dinner. It is quite a formidable offering and better suited as the centerpiece of a light lunch. For a smaller result try it with a camembert inside the dough. This dish is, of course, very like **saucisson en brioche**, for which cervelas, cotechino or any other good meaty sausage is cooked inside brioche dough. It is sliced and served as an **amuse-gueule.**

Brioche. Rich bread from yeast dough, the original recipes used large proportions of beaten egg and butter. Although most commonly found as individual breakfast bread rolls—**petites brioches**—it is made in larger sizes for slicing and many other shapes too. It's also used for other sweet and savory dishes. It can be used for beef fillet in pastry, and to wrap all sorts of other items such as cheese or sausage. The classic brioche mold is a fluted, open-shaped, tinned-steel device that encourages the dough to rise and spread to the traditional shape,

Kougloff tin

Brioche tins

Dariole mold

Savarin

but other tins can be used. Unlike its rival breakfast treat—the complex **croissant**—the brioche is simple to make and is especially delicious when eaten warm from the oven.

The recipe we use is a simple one. Mix ½ ounce of fresh yeast or ¼ ounce of dried yeast into 2 cups flour. Add 2 beaten eggs, a teaspoonful of sugar and ½ cup of melted butter. (The butter must not be very hot.) Now add some tepid water until you have a sticky messy mixture. This must be well beaten. We use the dough hook on an electric mixer but many cooks prefer to do it with just their fingers. At this stage many recipes suggest the addition of a spoonful of brandy. I've never found much flavor difference in the final result if it's omitted but possibly it helps the rising. Let the dough rise for at least two hours. If more convenient, leave it overnight. When ready, fill small tins and place them in the oven to cook at 400°F for about 15 minutes.

When brioche is used for wrapping beef fillet, sausage, salmon or whatever, it has to be made with less egg and butter. Loaves made from this less rich dough are called **pain brioché**, not brioche.

Brochet: pike. A savage freshwater fish, it is regarded as virtually inedible in Britain because of its odor and its slimy appearance when freshly caught. The intrepid French gourmets have long declared this their favorite for making those delicate dumplings called **quenelles de brochet**. If you want to try it, the pike is caught from May until the end of the year. However, these delicate dumplings don't have to be made with such exotic fish; other whitefish make superb quenelles and although cod quenelles sound rather spartan they are excellent. I'm not very enthusiastic about whirling, chopping machines, but this is something they do very well. Whatever kind of fish is used, any such dish depends upon a carefully made sauce, such as the ones made with cream and white wine and, if possible, fish stock too.

Brouillade. Scrambled egg is called **oeufs brouillés.** Finely chop or thinly slice some black truffle into the egg and you have **oeufs brouillés aux truffes**, widely referred to as a **brouillade**, any Frenchman's favorite dish. It was my friend Quentin Crewe who saw the way in which Raymond Thuilier at *Baumanière* artfully slipped a spoonful of **sauce hollandaise** into his version of this dish. The next time I get my hands on a truffle I'll try it. Eggshell is porous and eggs will absorb the flavor of anything stored nearby. So maybe I'll put my truffle in a tin with the eggs overnight and get a flavorful brouillade free of charge.

Brousse or **Broussa:** a delicious fresh unsalted cheese made from goat or sheep milk. It is widely available from supermarkets and from individual producers, such as the man in Nice market from whom I buy. The wet version is eaten with sugar as a dessert; the drained one—rather like ricotta—is usually served with bread but can be stirred into hot pasta.

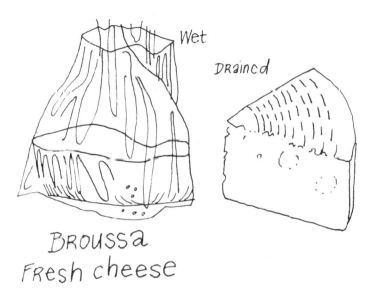

BROUSSa
FResh cheese

Brut means crude or raw, a word found on champagne labels to mean that very little sweet grape sugar has been added to it. Piper-Heidsieck Brut Sauvage has no sweetener. Other unsweetened champagnes have **Brut non dosé** on the label. I like them. Beware of the word **sec**, or dry (which on most wine labels indicates a dry wine), for it's used on the labels of champagnes that are comparatively sweet.

Café: coffee. The finest coffee beans come from the arabica plant, and the rest from the robusta, which most of the newer coffee-growing regions offer. Although introduced to Europe in the sixteenth century, the Arabs had known it for centuries before that and in Ethiopia the arabica plant still grows wild. The Dutch took the plant to Holland—and this was the first coffee to grow outside Arabia—and then to their colony, Java, and the French to Martinique.

The British planted coffee in Africa and the West Indies, Kenyan and Jamaican coffees being particularly finely flavored. Really good arabica grows slowly on tropical uplands and provides subtle-tasting expensive coffee. Robusta, a smaller bean yielding more than twice the caffeine, gives a stronger, more bitter drink.

An Englishman living in South America invented soluble coffee, which is getting better and better every year. Soluble coffee has already been brewed before being sold (the inventor noticed the powdery residue on the spout of a silver coffee pot he was using and went on from there). **Café decaféiné** or sometimes just **déca** is coffee from which most of the caffeine has been extracted. It is sold in beans as well as in soluble form. In France it's sometimes called **faux café.** Some extraction methods use harmful chemicals that might upset you more than caffeine. The water method of extraction is preferred, so look for that on the label. **Café au lait** is coffee served with milk, usually hot frothy milk. It's sometimes called a **crème**, or **un grand crème**. In France coffee is served with milk at breakfast time, and black thereafter. In Paris the espresso machine has now taken over and produces **café express.** A very strong one is called **café serré. Café glacé** is iced coffee; if topped with whipped cream (or ice cream, or both) it's called **café liégeois.** Less well known is the term **café allongé.** This "extended coffee" is ordinary coffee diluted with a little hot water to make it more like American-style coffee. **Café noisette** is nut-colored coffee, which is to say that a small amount of milk has been added. **Café complet** is coffee served with milk and bread or toast. The tourist will get croissants and brioches, butter and jam with it too. In other words, this is a continental breakfast. A **bossu** (literally humpback) is a small cup of coffee to which a generous shot of Calvados has been added. **Mocha** or **moka** refers specifically to Arabian coffee and to anything flavored with it. Sometimes it means a coffee and chocolate combination.

Calvados: a spirit produced from distilled cider. Normandy is usually regarded as the original home of this drink and the source of the best. One estimate said that there are about 800 farm distilleries in Normandy but only 50 or so produce Calvados for sale, which I suppose means that Normans drink a lot of Calvados. Appellation rules have been in force since 1966 and grades go from plain old **eau-de-vie de cidre** up to superb **Calvados de Pays d'Auge.** When the label says **Vieille réservé** it means more than four years old, **VSOP** more than five years old and **Napoléon** (and certain other names) more than six years old. But some drinkers prefer the younger ones, which although harsher are more fruity in flavor. Calvados is becoming more and more popular, as is evidenced by the way that big companies have been buying up the Calvados manufacturers. Even if you travel around Normandy, it's not easy to find Calvados from a small independent distiller.

Camembert. Not just a great cheese of France, it is manufactured all over the world. This soft fermented cheese, always associated with Normandy and William the Conqueror, originated in the Pays d'Auge (from where we get **Livarot** and **Pont l'Evêque**). Camembert is best from October to June. There is not much sign of cheese in the little village of Camembert these days, but the nearby village of Livarot still makes cheese and even has a *Conservatoire des Techniques Fromagères Traditionelles* and there is plentiful farmhouse production nearby. The **Fourme du Cantal** is another great cheese of France. It is a large yellow cheese not unlike Cheddar. Originally from the Haute Auvergne in central France, it is now commercially made, and sold all over France.

Canard: duck. The Rouen duck is probably the finest served in France. It is traditionally the one that goes into the silver duck press at the Tour d'Argent in Paris to produce the famous **caneton rouennais à la presse.** For this the carcass is pressed at the tableside to make a sauce which is poured upon the cooked duck breast. The Rouen duck is killed without bleeding, which means the flesh is deep red in color and strong in flavor. Some gourmets prefer the ducks from Nantes. These **canetons nantais** are smaller, sweeter and distinctly milder in flavor. In southern France we find Barbary ducks (like America's Muscovy ducks) from which the livers are used for **foie gras de canard,** but the flesh of the Barbary (sometimes called **canard d'Inde**) is not very good to eat. The Barbaries are crossed with Nantais or Rouennais ducks to breed table birds and also for foie gras ducks. A **caneton** is a small male duck and a **canette** a small female duck.

Caramel is the delicious toffee-like substance that the cook produces when sugar is heated to a brown color but not burned. The result is what Carême called "monkey's blood." Caramelizing, **caraméliser**, is a very important chemical change that takes place when foods containing sugar are heated. When we heat onions or carrots we see them change drastically. The onion no longer irritates the eyes, carrots soften and the sugar in them browns. The vegetables produce appetizing smells and flavors. This same complex process provides the well-done outside coating on roast meat and barbecued foods. It begins at temperatures somewhere about 320°F. The exact chemistry is not yet fully understood, but of course you can't get water or steam to these temperatures, so boiled or pot-roasted foods don't caramelize.

    Crème caramel is a dessert that I have seen on menus everywhere from Okinawa to Damascus. It's an egg custard cooked—and then served upside-down—so that it has a caramelized sugar coating. It can be delicious, but is often quite awful. The most common faults are rubbery texture, wetness and bubble holes in the custard. These are all signs that the egg mixture became too hot: it separated to make the wetness and boiled to make the bubbles. Oddly enough the French call it not crème caramel but **flan.**

Carême, Marie Antoine (1784–1833), was the founder of classic French cookery. Some say he must have been the greatest chef who ever lived. Born into poverty and abandoned by his family when ten years old he got a job in a cookshop and went on to become a pâtissier. He worked for Talleyrand (Napoleon's Foreign Minister) and for Britain's Prince Regent during a period of great social change, when newly invented "restaurants" were beginning to serve food as good as that in private houses. He worked for the Czar in Russia and for the British Ambassador in Vienna.

    Carême liked the dishes of the cold buffet—such as **chaud-froid**—and did much to make them elaborate and prestigious. His written recipes are long and meticulous but his observations, about British tastes in food, the competence of his fellow cooks and the strenuous work in the kitchen, are pithy and amusing. "The charcoal kills us but who cares, the shorter the life, the greater the glory." He died in bed lecturing a student who'd brought him food, "Yesterday the quenelles of sole were very good but your fish was not good. You didn't season it enough. Listen, you must shake the casserole . . ." and with one hand held aloft shaking an imaginary casserole he died. Today Carême's egotistical writings will provide many entertaining moments for anyone who has ever worked in a professional kitchen, and for those who are interested in such slavery.

Carré: the ribs or "'rack'" of an animal, usually lamb or mutton. Sometimes separated into chops, these racks make fine roasts. In this case the fatty meat at the end of the rib bone should be removed or "Frenched" before cooking.

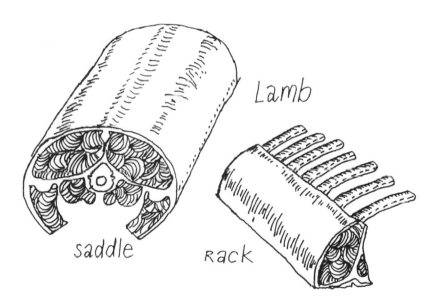

Carte is what we call a menu, a restaurant's priced list of available dishes, although some patronizing and pretentious establishments hand out unpriced menus to ladies, to "guests" and those judged impecunious or innumerate.

In France the word **menu** means the set—or limited choice— meal offered at a fixed price. Sometimes wine, service and tax are also included. In Britain and America this is called **table d'hôte.** This name came from the old cookshops that provided hot food to take away but had a table where those who were in a hurry could eat on the premises.

A la carte refers to dishes ordered from the list of individually priced dishes and not from the set-price menu.

In France regulations demand the display of a carte outside the restaurant. These will not only provide details of what is available and how much it costs, but indicate other things about the eating place. A crisp, clean, dated notice will often mean a clean, well-organized kitchen from which comes fresh, well-cooked food. Look for simply described traditional French dishes and regional dishes too. Pretentious "poetic" menu descriptions of "artistically" arranged food usually mean poor value.

Cassoulet. Probably only **bouillabaisse** excites the passions of the disputatious in the way that this bean and meat stew seems to do. But these arguments are more usually between cookbook writers than between cooks.

These bean stews are all fatty. They are winter dishes from the cold regions of France, particularly certain parts of Languedoc in the south-west. Have you ever been there in February? It's not an experience that readily slips your mind. The cassoulet is a combination of white haricot beans and fatty pork. From place to place other ingredients are added to make it a local specialty. It is usually made in a big earthenware pot and cooked in an oven (or over the embers of a fire), for there is not enough movement of the liquid to prevent burning if it were put on a stove top.

I suppose the **cassoulet de Castelnaudary** is the most famous. The recipe calls for different types of pork cuts as well as local ham and sausage. Pork skin is included for flavor. (In France, with no tradition of roast meat, there is no pork crackling. Pork skin is used as a flavoring in stocks and stews.)

The **cassoulet de Carcassonne** adds mutton to the pork. I have never eaten such a combination and have no urgent desire to do so. The **cassoulet de Toulouse** adds goose. This should not be precious fresh goose but **confit d'oie** (preserved pieces of goose). Although only the Toulouse version has goose as an ingredient, a cassoulet is not considered worthy of the name unless goose fat is used in the preparation. The confit d'oie is largely goose fat, of course. Most local versions of this dish include various local sausages, some of which have a strong flavor.

A cassoulet is mostly beans with the other ingredients added according to what is available. Even in France pieces of chicken are often used instead of goose. When almost ready for the oven—where it will spend many hours—a final layer of breadcrumbs is placed on top. Stock and lots of fat are added until the fat reaches those breadcrumbs. This is an important factor in the authentic recipe. It ensures that the fatty breadcrumbs go brown and crisp by the time the cassoulet is served. (Exactly this technique should be used to brown and crisp the top layer of potato in an Irish stew.)

Caviar. The eggs of the sturgeon are perhaps the most expensive food normally and widely eaten. There are several kinds of caviar, but roughly speaking the larger the eggs and the lighter gray their color the more expensive they are. Beluga caviar is graded 0 to 000 from dark to light. Most caviar comes from the USSR and Iran, which are on opposite sides of the Caspian Sea, but in France a sizeable amount of caviar is French! It comes from the Gironde. This is a little advertised fact because Frenchmen prefer to think that their caviar comes from more distant places. In America caviar is obtained from a species of sturgeon fished in the Tennessee River and off the coast of Georgia and the Carolinas. It is much cheaper than imported caviar. (Cheaper still is the roe of the paddle fish, which is fished in these waters and is very like caviar.) The keluga is a type of sturgeon that swims in the Amur River of northern Manchuria. The caviar from it is very like beluga from the Caspian. This Chinese export looks all set to gain a place in the top-quality caviar market. The expense of caviar is partly due to the difficulty of storing and transporting it. Long-term storage is at 36–38°F. It keeps about two weeks in a domestic refrigerator, then becomes bitter. Experts advise buying it in closed tins of the size you'll finish at one sitting and serving it on ice. Vodka or champagne is usually considered the right thing to drink with caviar, but a carefully chosen still white wine might be even better.

In the Caspian the sturgeon are fished twice a year, in March and October. It takes about a month for the resulting caviar to reach the dealers. One remarkable expert at a blind tasting of caviar went into gastronomic legend when he pulled a face and said, "I never could stand the autumn catch from the Volga."[8] When I asked him about this, he said that the rains bring mud, and industrial effluent, into the river, and this affects the fish. The spring catch is fresh and clean tasting.

Céleri: celery. A strongly flavored vegetable eaten raw as an appetizer, made into soups or used as a flavoring. Sometimes it is cooked and served as a vegetable. More interesting, **céleri-rave** is the edible root of a variety of celery. It is tough, but has an excellent and subtle flavor. Thus it is usually briefly cooked and then cut into matchstick-sized **juliennes** before being mixed with mayonnaise and served as a salad vegetable. Sometimes this celery root is served as a purée.

Chambré: the temperature of a normal living-room, but not the warm temperatures that central heating has brought. Some foods are best when served at room temperature and so are most older red wines, but the acidity of newer reds makes them taste better when cool. Butter must be chambré before it can be spread. Frozen pastry must be chambré before it can be rolled. These latter two items can be effectively made ready by a few seconds in a microwave. Some (including reputable wine experts) say red wine can be chambréed and even "aged" in a microwave, but I have never had the nerve to try it, out of respect for both my wine and my microwave oven.

The temperature of food should be taken into account when estimating cooking time. A large piece of meat from the refrigerator will take longer to cook, and will cook less evenly, than it will if allowed to stand in the kitchen for two or three hours before the meat is cooked. Before I get an irate letter from some eagle-eyed health inspector let me add that the meat should be covered to reduce any risk from bacteria. Frozen food should first be left to thaw out in a refrigerator rather than at room temperature.

Champagne: Usually blended, this sparkling wine from a small region around the valley of the Marne gets its bubbles from carbonic acid left in the bottle after the final fermentation. The story goes that the process was invented and developed in the seventeenth century by a monk named Dom Pérignon. This fermented wine—dryish because two fermentations use up the grape sugar—was always sweetened and often served as a light drink for the dessert course. It was in the mid-nineteenth century that a British buyer asked one of the producers—Perrier Jouet—if he could taste some champagne without this injection of sugar syrup, or **dosage.** He liked this drier flavor and soon most of the champagne supplied for sale in the U.S. and British markets were **Brut,** which means with very little of the sweetener. **Brut non dosé** means no sweetener at all.

The British and Americans drink a full-bodied **brut** champagne as an apéritif, while the French stick to their sweeter versions and serve them late in the meal. There are many arguments about the quality of champagne. Prices vary greatly. Members of the Syndicat de Grandes Marques de Champagne—Bollinger, Krug and Roederer—produce some of the most expensive and prestigious champagnes, but some lesser known, cheaper champagnes are excellent and are worth seeking out. The district of Champagne is widely said to be the only wine-producing region of France to have mediocre cooking and poor restaurants, although *Les Crayères* (the château at Reims where M. Boyer cooks) provides a notable exception to that judgment.

Champagne stories abound, but one of my favorites is that during the 1920s Mr. E. Berry Wall came to the bar of the *Paris Ritz* each day at 4 P.M. to drink a brandy snifter of hot champagne that was always prepared ready for him.

No matter which champagne you drink, its most tenacious and most effective enemy is detergent. Glasses washed in a dishwasher will retain traces of chemical even after another half a dozen careful clean-water rinsings. The detergent will of course affect the flavor and the bubbles of any champagne it encounters. The better the quality of the detergent the more effectively it ruins your champagne.

Champignon: fungus. Molds, smuts and rusts are fungi. So are yeasts and **champignons comestibles** such as mushrooms. They have no chlo-

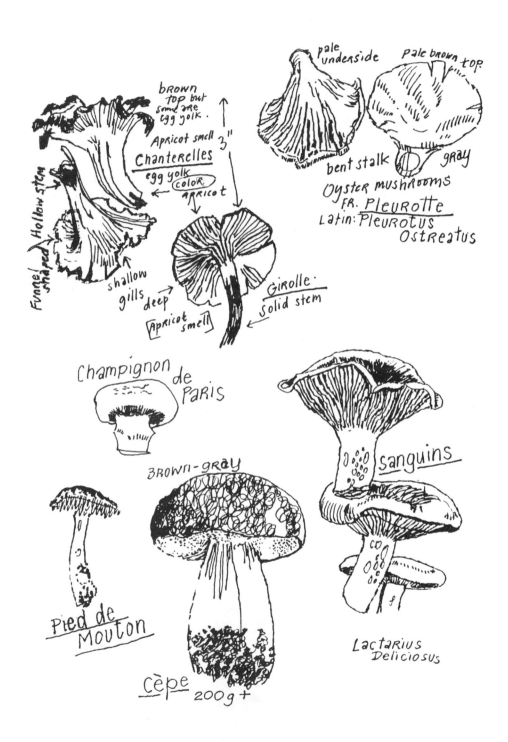

brown top but some are egg yolk.

Apricot smell 3"

Chanterelles

egg yolk (color)
apricot

Funnel shaped Hollow stem

shallow gills deep

Apricot smell

Girolle · Solid stem

pale underside

pale brown top.

bent stalk gray

Oyster mushrooms
FR. Pleurotte
Latin: Pleurotus Ostreatus

Champignon de Paris

brown-gray

sanguins

Pied de Mouton

Lactarius Deliciosus

Cèpe 200g +

rophyll, so they can't use sunlight to manufacture carbohydrates the way other plants do. They have to plunder their nourishment from organic materials living or dead. And many fungi need no light. As far back as the seventeenth century the French were renowned for their appetite for this strange food. A visitor to Paris in 1698 wrote, "The French delight in nothing so much as mushroomes; of which they have daily, and all the Winter long, stores of fresh and new gathered in the Markets."

Mushrooms provided a convenient source of food—and vitamin D—during the Napoleonic Wars, and the caves outside Paris contained 1,000 miles of mushroom beds. But how to choose which ones contain nothing more lethal than vitamin D? Mrs. Beeton's advice—to put a sixpence in the cooking pot and see if it turns black —is no good at all, and might well have caused more fatalities than Jack the Ripper. The only practical way to be sure is to get an illustrated book written by an expert.

In France the many different varieties are hunted, cherished, cooked and discussed endlessly. Even the same mushrooms vary from district to district because, as Darwin told us, geographical separation brings eventually an origin of species.

Cèpe (*boletus edulis*). Brownish gray top; its sponge-like underside has tiny pinholes. White stem. They can be up to 8 inches, and I've seen even bigger ones. Found in autumn until late November (they finish earlier than most of the others) in woodland clearings. These are amongst the most flavorful mushrooms we eat. Good for drying. Avoid if spores are pink or red.

Chanterelle (*cantharellus infundibuliformis*). Funnel-shaped with hollow stalk. Ragged rim and texture is limp and floppy, almost like thin rubber. Apricot smell. Egg yolk color, the tops are brownish gray. Measures anywhere from 1 to 5 inches. Grows near beech trees late summer onwards. Avoid if brown and without ragged rim: this might be the *paxilus involutus.*

Girolle (*cantharellus cibarius*) is frequently confused with the mushroom commonly called the chanterelle for it has roughly the same shape and size and also smells faintly of apricot. But the girolle never has dark tops; it is all the color of apricot (while the chanterelle is a lighter shade and more the color of egg yolk). Also, the girolle is firmer and its stalk is solid (not hollow).

Sanguin (*lactarius deliciosus*). Rich brown color with pronounced gill lines. Caps sometimes hollow-shaped like a chanterelle, but if possible choose the ones that are not hollow-shaped and you'll have more of that strong beefy flavor. These are often the best buy in the market.

Pleurotte (*pleurotus ostreatus*) or oyster mushroom is a pale pearl gray. Its cap is never circular, and its stalk is bent, because it grows in bunches on the sides of trees. Today it is cultivated and is among the cheapest of the "exotic" mushrooms.

Morille (*morcella esculenta*). There are many varieties of this curious morel mushroom with its egg-shaped honeycomb head. Some experts say it is related to the truffle. It is found in late spring. The flavor is excellent and it can be dried.

Although there is no reliable rule by which to judge which mushrooms are poisonous, one reference book (*The SAS Survival Handbook,* by J. Wiseman, Collins Harvill, London, 1986), written by a very experienced instructor at The Survival School, says that the fungi growing on the sides of trees and stumps may be leathery but are not harmful.

In the vegetable and flower market in Nice, one stall sells only mushrooms. At the time of writing these are the prices. The prices show the relative value of the different kinds. No morilles were on sale at this time (autumn).

Champignons Paris 2.80 FF per 4 ounces
Champignons Rose 3.50 FF
Pleurotte (cultivated) 9 FF
Chanterelle 10 FF
Sanguins Auvergne 25 FF
Cèpes 29 FF (Dried ones were 140 FF per 4 ounces)
Girolles 40 FF

Chapel, Alain (1937–). Too young to know the amazing Fernand Point under whose direction most of France's many present-day star chefs served, Alain Chapel worked at Point's *La Pyramide* after the old man died. Like so many of his contemporaries, Chapel subsequently became a proprietor chef (as compared with Point's generation of proprietors who ran their restaurants and employed their chefs). After experience in other restaurants Chapel went back to his father's one-star restaurant *La Mère Charles*, at Mionnay, not far from Lyons. By 1973 he'd gained three stars, Michelin's highest rating, and was calling his restaurant *Alain Chapel*.

I sat down with Chapel and his friend Paul Bocuse at Chapel's kitchen table when the new Michelin, giving Chapel his third star, was published. At that time I would say that Chapel's restaurant was serving the best food available at any price in France. Bocuse said the best meal he'd ever eaten was prepared by Chapel. But consistency of excellence is a goal that few men in any walk of life achieve. He admits to the difficulties he faces in a small kitchen with a small staff—for he will take no apprentices—and talks of having to win a race to be champion of the world twice a day.

It is difficult for any proprietor chef to handle the constant problems that arise minute by minute in dining-room and kitchen. The old-time style of restaurateur sat down with his clients and had a far better opportunity to hear what the customer liked and disliked. Any proprietor chef who spends too much time in the kitchen can lose touch with the people for whom he cooks. Perhaps this difficult job demands too much of any man. And only the boldest of customers will wish to complain of the cooking to any chef-patron.

Breakfast at Chapel's is a communal joy: in a large light room those clients lucky enough to spend a night in the well-furnished bedrooms sit together at a refectory table. But alas I have seen this social exchange become a post-mortem when customers found the previous evening's meal anything but magnificent. Running a restaurant means catering to the wishes of many different palates, and different personalities, and this provides a constant and difficult "race." Chapel is a somewhat melancholy fellow, deeply hurt by unjust criticism. I wish him only well; there is no doubt that given a little more luck and more imagination applied to the restaurant dining room rather than the kitchen, Alain Chapel could be the greatest chef in France.

Chapon. A castrated cockerel or capon specially fattened for the table is, many chefs and gourmets believe, more delicious than any game bird: pheasant, partridge, plover, wigeon and so on. The chapon, tender and juicy, is particularly suited to roasting. In Carême's time **foie gras** was the fattened liver of the chapon rather than of geese or ducks. Carême's foie gras recipe mixed the liver with butter, eggs, mushrooms and breadcrumbs to make what he called a **pain de foie gras.**

But recently in Britain—and probably elsewhere too—the "chapon effect" is being obtained from hormone implants. I regard this as an undesirable development. Hormone treatment of meat and poultry is something which all consumers should watch warily.

In Provence **chapon** is a slang word for a crust, a toasted or fried finger of bread flavored with olive oil and garlic (and sometimes vinegar too). These delicious tidbits are stirred into the salad solely to give it added flavor, but in my family they are gobbled up greedily.

A **chapon** is also a dark red fish with a speckled harlequin pattern of great beauty. This **rascasse rouge**, a variety of scorpion fish, is cherished throughout Provence. At one time it was a mandatory constituent for **bouillabaisse**, but nowadays it's far too rare and expensive to go into a fish stew. The *Restaurant Bacon* (a luxury restaurant in Cap d'Antibes that specializes in fish) reserves chapon on special orders only. Waverley Root, the American gourmet and food writer, said he'd buy and eat all the chapons his Villefranche fish shop could supply.

Charcuterie: a shop where pork, and, more specifically, cooked pork products are sold. Charcuterie is also the term for terrines, pâtés, game pies, headcheese, various aspics, hams, cooked chicken, quiches and so on, sold in such shops.

Charlotte. When a **bavarois**—a very rich cream custard—is cooled in a container lined with ladyfingers or **génoise** cake the result is called a charlotte. Carême invented it, although his original recipe specifies "green pistachio biscuits" and he insisted that the bavarois must be put into the container less than an hour before it is served, which leads me to say that he must have had a damned good refrigerator, especially when you remember that, at this time, Carême's dishes were made as "take-aways" for the great private houses of Paris to which he catered. He called his creation **charlotte parisienne.** Nowadays we find variations such as **charlotte au chocolat** (beloved of chefs because the presence of the chocolate makes it set more firmly) and **charlotte royale** flavored with kirsch.

It is always served cold. Ideally the bavarois should be thickened with egg and not gelatin. If gelatin is used, it must be kept to the barest minimum. It is the taste and texture of gelatin that make most charlottes less than delicious.

The apple charlotte—**charlotte de pommes**—is very different although equally delicious. It was invented by an unknown chef in the reign of England's George III and named for the Queen. For this a special metal pot called a "charlotte mold" (which is recognized by the little handles it has to help the turning-out) is lined with fingers of generously buttered bread. The mold is filled with chopped apple and put into a hot oven. The object is to make a crisp caramelized crust around cooked apple. It should be served hot with a warm apricot sauce, although in England cream and custard are usually served too. The important thing is to choose apples that will not turn wet when cooked.

charlotte mold

Charollais: a breed of cattle originally from Charolles, Burgundy. This whitish-colored animal produces average to very good beef despite the fact that it's slaughtered later than most other breeds. It is this added age that makes the steaks chewy if not tough. The people who like it—yes, there are some—say it has a good flavor. And for decades Charollais have been imported into America for breeding, and sometimes for meat. But in my opinion it falls far short of Aberdeen Angus or almost any American beef cattle. Even Bocuse was forced to admit that Texan beef was comparable to any anywhere, which is quite an admission for a man who provides relentless publicity for France and its exports. The Charollais's shortcomings are to some extent offset by the skills of French butchers, who are the world's best. But France is a country more renowned for **boeuf bourguignon** than for its **bifteck.** Charollais beef may be a reason for this.

The amazing success of the Charollais as a breeding animal and especially its use by artificial insemination for cross-breeding is due to the way that it converts animal food to beef at a very fast rate without adding too much fat. This is the beef farmer's dream. There are other French breeds capable of similar miracles. Amongst them there are the *Limousin,* which can endure the hard winter of the Massif Central, the *Maine Anjou* and the *Blonde d'Aquitaine,* which has been known to add as much as 4 pounds to its weight per day! The popularity of these beef cattle comes from the demand for lean meat, rather than meat marbled with streaks of fat. Undoubtedly supermarkets which provide a chance for shoppers to sort through transparent packs, without a knowledgeable butcher to give advice, has contributed to this fad. It's an acknowledged fact that purebred Aberdeen Angus beef—now virtually disappeared—marbled with fat has a flavor a thousand times better than any of the French breeds of beef. It is also a fact that many of the people who know this go out and buy the leanest meat they can find.

Chateaubriand (or Châteaubriant), François-René de (1768–1848) was a novelist, poet and politician, but he got into the history books—or at least onto menus—by the simple device of employing a chef who grilled for him a very thick slice of fillet of beef suitably garnished with potatoes (**pommes de terre château**) and a sauce. Technically this steak is sliced at a point where the fillet branches. Only one such steak can be taken from a fillet, and it is flattened before being cooked. Nowadays the potato and sauce are often forgotten and the steak might turn up as an **entrecôte**. Unfortunately for M. Chateaubriand's memory this steak is now widely referred to as **un Château.**

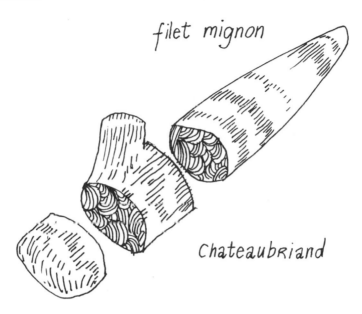

filet mignon

chateaubriand

Chaud-froid: literally hot-cold. This is a rather spectacular method of preparing cold poultry and meats for the table. The piece of food, or sometimes a whole bird or joint, is first coated with a heavy, clinging, warm, light-colored sauce (this is the "hot"), then a clear jelly coating is applied (this is the "cold"). Between these two layers the chef applies tiny decorative pieces of food—truffle, cooked egg or tomato—to make a glittering decoration. It is difficult to do well: don't try it unless you are a trained chef or you feel like a challenge. It seems likely that this dish evolved from the way that leftover cold cooked chicken pieces look so attractive coated with their own gravy and jelly.

Chaudrée: one of the many fish stews that abound around the coast of France. This one, from the neighborhood of La Rochelle, used to have eel, plaice and sole, cooked with white wine, butter and garlic. Now the price of sole has produced more modest chaudrée recipes.

Chef: chief or boss. The **chef de cuisine** is in charge of the kitchen. He or she hires the kitchen staff, helps to decide on the menu and in any sort of argument, no matter what they tell you, the chef is likely to prevail even against manager or proprietor. Except when the proprietor calls himself a **chef-patron**. In a very large restaurant the chef is called the **maître-cuisinier** and will have many chefs including perhaps a banquet chef working under him. The importance of sauces in French cooking is evidenced by the fact that the **chef saucier** who makes them is usually the second in command (although some master chefs have an assistant called a **sous-chef**). The other specialists in a big kitchen include the **chef poissonnier**, the fish chef, who cooks the fish and makes the sauces for them. Even in a smaller kitchen the stove and oven, storage and preparation area for fish are kept separate from everything else.

The **chef potager** makes soup. The **chef entremetier** is in charge of the vegetables and egg dishes, and in some kitchens, the desserts too. But more normally the **chef pâtissier** prepares the desserts and ices as well as any hot **amuse-gueules**, special celebration cakes and so on. The **rôtisseur** is in charge of grilling, deep-frying and roasting meat, but there are specialist restaurants where they employ a **friturier** who does only deep-frying, and a **grillardin** who gives the necessary minute-by-minute attention to such special equipment as turning spit or charcoal fires. The **chef cafetier** is now rarely seen, which is why it's often so difficult to get a cup of coffee at the end of your meal. He used to be the man who prepared coffee, infusions and other teas, and chocolate drinks.

The **garde-manger** has the vitally important task of looking after the larders and cold rooms (or refrigerators in smaller kitchens) and prepares cold dishes such as pâtés, terrines, aspics and all cold dishes of poultry and game. It is usual in a kitchen to provide specially high quality ingredients for cold dishes (the pastry for cold pies is cut before that for the hot ones).

All these chefs are known as **chefs-de-partie** and in a big kitchen you'll find **chefs tournants** who take over from any of them when they have time off. Last and least there is the **commis chef**, the chef's helper, the lowest form of kitchen life. I know, I was one. A busy chef might have three or four such slaves.

Chèvre is a goat, **chevreau** is a young goat. (But **chevreuill** is venison.)
No longer much favored as a source of meat, the goat is still a blessing
to the poor farmer. It will nourish itself upon bare soil and rock,
survive precipitous rocky land, desperate winters and still produce
enormous amounts of milk. So much milk that many sheep farmers
keep them to feed motherless lambs. Much goats' milk goes to make
cheeses. These little round cheeses are often called **crottins,** which
means dung or turd, and are hard with a strong salty flavor. Home-
made ones are likely to be milder, sweeter and more flavorful than
commercial goat cheeses, many of which go for export. In Provence
our local goat cheese is **poivre d'Ane**, a simple product smothered in
dried savory. Further away, near the Alps, there is the other extreme,
a **bosson macéré,** which goes through an elaborate process with
alcohol, herbs and olive oil. Lately it has become fashionable for
restaurants to serve warmed goat cheeses with salad. Warm up your
own goat cheeses; it's cheaper.

Chocolat. Chocolate was a delectable luxury that the Spaniards discovered
in Mexico. The French encountered it in the Spanish Netherlands.
Some say that it was Louis XIV who found his wife, Maria Theresa,
secretly drinking it. In any case it reached France sometime about the
middle of the seventeenth century and was at first regarded as a
medicine. It has been a luxury ever since and the finest chocolate
productions are likely to remain so, for chocolate is grown and
harvested only in the most miserable equatorial climates. Like most
oils and fats it requires careful storage. Cocoa powder, cocoa butter
and sugar are the only ingredients in the high-quality bitter chocolate
which the chef uses. In the kitchen the slightest variation in temperature or humidity can make even an expert's work go badly wrong. I
know; I saw a famous chef give a demonstration away from home and
watched him battle against it. In a way the demonstration did show all
of us what a demon substance it can be. It also made me appreciate
the skills of cooks who create fine chocolate desserts. Swiss and
Belgian chocolate are the best in the world. The U.S. mass-produced
chocolate is not far behind. British chocolate is poor. French chocolate
is limited by the way the government forces the manufacturers to use
second-rate cocoa beans from former French colonies. There is hardly

any need to add that chocolate is suspected to be a cause of migraine and that for some people it is addictive.

For most French children, and many adults too, chocolate is hardly worth eating unless it's accompanied by a piece of dry bread. For anyone who has not sampled this unlikely sounding combination I recommend it highly.

Chou is cabbage. **Choucroute** is shredded white cabbage, salted and preserved by the lactic acid which comes with the fermentation process. This method of preserving cabbage through winter has been known for centuries. It provided sorely needed vitamin C for various peoples of Europe. It remains popular because it is so conveniently available in jars and tins. I have tried to pickle my own cabbage but without success. It is hard work. Don't write and tell me how to do it; I've given up.

No matter what anyone tells you, the choucroute from jar or tin needs rinsing to get rid of the strong, salty, acid flavor. Drain it and then put it in a closed pot with lightly fried onion, juniper berries, bay leaf and some herbs to your taste. I add a glass of dry white wine. Some like raisins in it and my father-in-law insists upon plenty of potatoes too. Four hours in a very low oven is not too long; six hours is even better.

Long a favorite food of Germany and Austria, sauerkraut one-pot (*Eintopf*) combinations became popular in France's Alsace region where they were all called **choucroute garnie**. The traditional recipe calls for the pickled cabbage to be cooked with smoked pork, ham pieces, Strasbourg sausages (rather like frankfurters but made specially for the choucroute garnie) and **cervelas** (a pork sausage with a touch of garlic). Boiled potatoes and stewed lentils are sometimes served alongside it. That's the authentic recipe, but if you take my advice you'll modify it drastically. Smoked and salted meats do not go well with pickled cabbage; use milder fatty meats, chicken, duck, goose or even lamb, and choose sausages that are not salty.

Chou farci is stuffed cabbage and one of France's favorite winter dishes. If a Frenchman says **farci** he means chou farci. How you start depends upon what type of cabbage you have. A tight-leafed cabbage might need scalding to open the leaves up. A very tight-leafed cabbage demands the drastic course of wrapping the farce leaf by leaf like cannelloni or even cutting it into slices and using it as layers in a pot. But it's best to have one of the loose-leafed type of cabbages. Wash it without breaking it up, then stuff a minced pork stuffing (even better if flavored with chopped fried onion, herbs and whatever you like) down between the leaves. Tie it firmly to hold it together—some chefs wrap it in a piece of muslin or cheesecloth. Put it in a closed pot with enough stock to make steam, and cook it gently on the stove top for at least 2 hours (the pork must be cooked through), and an extra hour's cooking doesn't spoil it. It is sometimes served with a simple tomato sauce. This is a fatty dish; keeping the meat lean spoils it. My own version uses a spicy smoked sausage in the farce and buries a split pig's foot under the cabbage. In the Auvergne, leftover chou farci is roughly chopped and warmed up with stock (or even water) to make **soupe au farci.**

Pâte à choux is hot-water pastry that is piped into shape while still warm, like icing onto a cake. Best known as the **éclair** or the **profiterole,** or cheese-filled appetizers. Such pastry puffballs are stuck together with caramel and assembled to become a tall pyramid (the **croquembouche**) or the **St. Honoré** that was at one time the Frenchman's traditional birthday cake. Now my local patissière tells me birthdays are celebrated with "American style" layer cakes.

Cidre (cider) was known in northern France in the eleventh and twelfth centuries. Its popularity varied from place to place and from time to time, but it had the advantage that the apple would grow where the vine would not and that, unlike beer, cider did not require the grain that was sometimes badly needed for bread. When the taste for "burned wines" spread through Europe, cider was distilled to make Calvados, a drink that challenged the finest brandies. *Le distillateur ambulant*— a man pushing a huge wheeled contraption—is available to transform cider into the magic beverage without mentioning his visit to the taxman.

Civet: game stew—hare and venison are favored ingredients—with mushrooms. The sauce is dark and rich, with red wine as its basis and blood added at the final stage of cooking. Such dishes (using blood) must be cooked at low temperatures, below about 180°F, or the albumin will curdle. A **coq au vin** is a type of civet.

In the weeks before Christmas these stews, thickened with blood, are a favorite winter dish in France. Typically, a shop in the rue Meynadier, Cannes (a little street of notable food shops), offers in November huge dishes of ready-cooked civet. Side by side there are trays of stewed venison, rabbit, hare and of pork, as dark and shiny as bitter chocolate. Further inland even the little village butchers will have ready-made civets on display.

Clafoutis is a thick batter pancake from Limousin. The original had black cherries in it, but other fruit is substituted when there are no more cherries.

Cognac is grape brandy made from white wine and produced in the Charente region, where the wonderful Charentais melons are grown. Originally the craft of distilling wine to make "burned wine" or brandy was promoted by the desperate search for a medicine that would cure the plague. But soon any medicinal qualities became secondary. The rival distillers of Armagnac and Cognac were lucky to find themselves near plentiful woodland that was needed for fuel and casks. Their local wines suited the long and difficult process that it then was, and with the convenient routes of navigable waterways to transport the finished product these brandies became famous.

Soon the demand became so great that people north of the wine-producing regions began distilling from grain. They made gin, vodka, schnapps and whisky. The northerners welcomed cheap stimulants that kept the cold out and provided "'Dutch courage" for soldiers going into battle. But the French brandies kept pride of place; drinks to be sipped and appreciated by the wealthy.

Confit means preserved. (**Confit d'oie** means preserved goose.) It is not a dish served at table. Poultry, duck or more often goose, cooked and potted with their own fat, with air and water virtually excluded, will keep for a long time. The goose and duck used are often the ones slaughtered for **foie gras**. Such birds are usually rather tough and the pieces from the confit pot are best used for **cassoulet** or other long-cooked dishes. Nowadays confit d'oie and **confit de canard** are widely on sale in attractive-looking pots and jars. They are expensive. Don't buy them unless you are particularly fond of tough, flavorless poultry. Make your cassoulet from something more tender and flavorful.

Confit also means fruit or vegetables in sugar, alcohol or vinegar. **Confiture** is jam or preserve and can be whole fruit preserved in sweetened alcohol.

Consommé is clear soup based upon strong broth made from meat or poultry or game. It is extremely difficult to make the result both strong and clear. I'd say making a good consommé is one of the ultimate tests of an expert cook.

A **consommé double** is a strong broth that will set to a light jelly suitable for jellied soups. Usually it is flavored with lean meat. To make a firmer jelly for aspic, calf's foot (or something similar) is needed.

Contre-filet is a high-quality cut of beef. It is the sirloin boned and without the fillet part. Steaks can be cut from the contre-filet or it can be roasted.

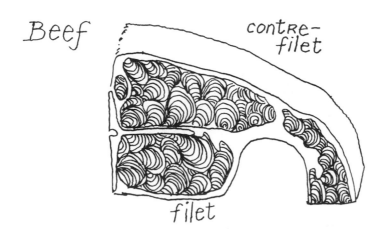

Beef
contre-filet
filet

Coq au vin. This recipe evolved as a peasant's way of preparing the tough, sinewy old cockerel for the table. Such elderly birds, sometimes 9 pounds or even bigger, needed marinating overnight in the red wine with which they would later be cooked. A genuine coq au vin does not have to be a cockerel; any tough old boiling chicken will do, but a genuine coq au vin must have the chicken's blood used to thicken the gravy. The blood is added at the last minute and, as the albumin in it will curdle if boiled, the pot must be off the boil and the contents gently stirred while this final thickening process is completed. Before nouvelle cuisine this dish was often prepared at the table-side, finished with brandy and flamed. Forget it! Order coq au vin today and you'll get a mouthful of battery hen plonked upon a puddle of sauce and delivered on a big floral plate.

Coquille St. Jacques is the flamboyant name the French have given to the scallop, whether it is the large *Pecten maximus* fished from the Atlantic or the smaller, sweeter but (in my opinion) less flavorful *Pecten jacobaeus* from the Mediterranean. (There are other scallops, the most common being two small species which the French call **pétoncle** and **vanneau.**) That remarkable food scientist Harold McGee tells us, "As a consequence of their very different muscle

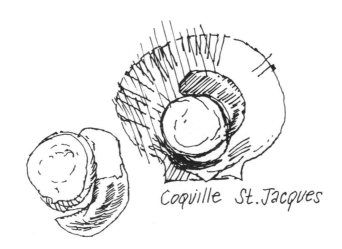

Coquille St. Jacques

organization, fish and shellfish constitute a special category of meat. Because their connective tissue is fragile, the muscle fibers short, and their fat content relatively low, they generally should be cooked as little as possible, only to the point that the muscle proteins coagulate."

Of course the Japanese serve them raw, and very nice too. So all these little bivalves need is to be warmed through, perhaps in some cream and melted butter. I slice the white part into coinlike discs, cook them gently for two or three minutes and toss the orange coral in at the very last moment. It is difficult to go wrong, but somehow restaurant cooks find ways to make them inedible. So buy them fresh in their shells, rinse briefly under the cold tap and cut away the edible white and orange with your kitchen scissors. Scallops are best in winter—slice thin, warm them through and eat them. Even deep-frozen ones are not too bad, but let them thaw in the refrigerator; on no account microwave them.

Corse: Corsica, a mountainous Mediterranean island 114 miles long and 52 miles wide, over 100 miles away from the southern coast of France. I was there one September and still remember the sudden chill that came each afternoon as the sun disappeared over the mountains.

It is the birthplace of Napoleon Bonaparte, a savage landscape and a perfect place for anyone who wants to "get away from it all." This seldom being my desire, I became so desperate in Corsica that I bought a ticket for a boat trip without asking the destination. (I landed in Morocco but that is another story.) Over the years much time and money has been spent to promote Corsica as a fashionable holiday place. But Corsica seems neglected by writers interested in French food and cooking. The *Guide Michelin* inspectors, usually somewhat generous when awarding stars in regions devoid of them, have difficulty finding establishments worthy of their single-star rating. My time in Corsica provided no evidence with which I could challenge the *Guide*'s verdict.

Côte: chop of pork, lamb or mutton taken from the loin and containing the most delicate meat (the fillet and the "eye"). A **côtelette**

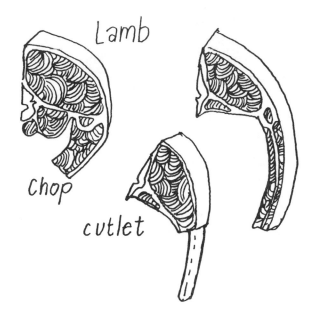

(cutlet) is a longer-boned, less meaty chop taken from the rack. For restaurant service the côtelette bone is bared before being cooked.

Cotriade: a fish soup from Brittany sometimes miscalled a **bouillabaisse.** Cotriade is a vague description for a simpler dish. Any Atlantic fish goes into it and usually potato too.

Coulis. In theory a coulis is a thick purée of meat, fish, vegetable or fruit. Sometimes it's used in the menu to describe thick soups or sauces. But nowadays it more often arrives as a thin, saucelike purée of raspberries served cold with desserts; for example, raspberries, strawberries or ice cream.

Coup de feu. In its literal sense (a blow of fire) this is a way of describing the browned outside of overcooked meat, but in kitchen parlance it means the work of serving a meal. The associated expression **mise en place** means the preparatory work before the meal service.

Couper: to cut. Mastering this basic skill is likely to occupy a large part of the apprentice cook's time. Every restaurant kitchen has enormous amounts of onions, potatoes and carrots that have to be prepared.

Consistent size is needed if the items are to cook evenly. Odds and ends would come out scorched and burnt.

I was taught to cut **juliennes** to measure one-eighth of an inch in cross section. Cut these into sections to get dice, **des.** But the French don't measure in inches as I soon found to my cost. My next boss wanted his julienne of potato to make the French fries that are called **pommes frites pailles** (straws) or **pommes frites allumettes** (matchsticks). He was furious. For him a julienne stick measured half a centimeter square. He was right, and the standard French slicing machine, the **mandoline,** has its blades set to that measure. But I also heard finely shredded orange peel and **céleri-rave** described as julienne. Those chefs called the larger-size sticks **bâtonnets.** From that time onwards I knew that a julienne was anything a chef wanted it to be; that's why he's called "chef."

Courgette. No matter what it says on the back of that expensive packet of seed, a courgette or zucchini is a hideous old squash. Picked when small, 4 to 5 inches long, it is a fine and versatile vegetable, good eaten raw in salads. Some restaurants like to have them with the flowers still attached. Sometimes the flowers are served still attached to the cooked vegetables and sometimes the flowers are used to wrap around mixtures and then deep-fried. Steam them whole—don't overcook—or do what a chef in Bavaria showed me last year: slice finely and stir briefly over a high flame with cooked chopped onion. Serve still a little crisp.[9]

Court bouillon: a flavored cooking liquid which is used to cook meat, fish or vegetables. Sometimes the white court bouillon—or **blanc**—serves the purpose of whitening certain food and keeping it white. Lemon juice is usually the bleaching agent and melted fat is in the blanc. This forms a thin layer over foods which darken when oxidized (salsify or artichoke hearts, for example) and keeps the air from turning foods dark. (*See also* **Bouillon.**)

Couscous is a complex combination dish from North Africa—Algeria, Tunisia and Morocco—widely eaten throughout France (in the way that Indian food is eaten throughout Britain and Mexican food everywhere in America). The basis is crushed semolina wheat which is steamed in a special steamer (**couscoussier**). To the grain are added pieces of mutton, chicken, carrot, onion, turnip, beans, chickpeas, and so on. A broth is served separately; so is a fierce cayenne and cumin sauce called **harissa**. Alas, it is one of those ethnic dishes that gets better as it loses its authenticity. I don't particularly recommend the real thing except as a sociological experience.

In France hot **merguez** sausages are often included in the couscous but I've never seen these included when I've had couscous in Morocco, Tunisia or Algeria, and I suspect this addition is French in origin. The cooking of the wheat is a lengthy and tricky task, but packets of pre-cooked couscous wheat are on sale in shops everywhere: Los Angeles, Tokyo and London. It is simple to prepare and delicious. It makes a splendid winter dish and I find it particularly good with roast duck.

Couteau: a knife. My first job on my first day in a professional kitchen was filleting sole. I was lucky; it sometimes takes months before you get near the real work. I quickly learned the difference between a filleting knife, **couteau filet de poisson** (medium width and springy), for getting fish off the bone, and a boning knife, **couteau de saigner** (narrow blade and less flexible), for getting the bone out of a leg of lamb, and so on. Filleting knives and boning knives all have very sharp pointed tips. Many boning knives have a notched handle to provide a tight grip because they are wielded in every direction during the de-boning process.

A general-purpose knife—a chef's knife, **couteau de cuisine**—may be used for everything from slicing salami and cutting cabbages to chopping parsley. Use the chef's knives of whatever size that you find best. Choose a heavy blade and hold it well forward (thumb and forefinger joint gripping the metal of the blade). A chopping knife must have a deep "heel" to the blade so you don't keep banging your knuckles on the chopping board. Cold meat, ham or cold turkey is best sliced with a ham knife, a 10-inch-long flexible-bladed knife with a rounded tip.

Hot meat and poultry are more usually carved with a slicing knife, **couteau du tranchelard**, which has a stiffer, broader blade. Nowadays I find more people buy meat in large sections, and save

chinese cleaver

chopping knife

Butcher's knife

Filleting knife
(flexible)

Boning knife

money by dividing them up as required. For separating the muscles of a leg of veal, or simply cutting a fillet from a sirloin, a proper butcher's knife is useful. (I have done many such jobs using a carving knife, but my fingers were frozen by the time I'd finished.) A butcher's knife has a large wide curved blade and a good grip to protect the fingers.

With so many French chefs plundering the Orient for new ideas, it was inevitable that the thin-bladed Chinese cleaver should be seen in French kitchens. The technique of using one has to be learned by experience, but nowadays I find even small fiddly jobs, such as cutting up chickens, can be done with it. Despite its similarity of shape to a butcher's cleaver, and its name, a thin-bladed Chinese cleaver should not be used for heavy chopping and cleaving. For such chopping buy a butcher's cleaver or **couperet de cuisine**. Get the heaviest one you can comfortably handle. Since it doesn't have to be sharp, a stainless one is convenient. I have such a knife, but to tell the truth it is not much used.

Almost every kitchen has a bread knife in use every day so it is particularly sensible to have a good one, although I find the electric (circular-bladed) slicer very good indeed. It even cuts fresh soft bread. Electric knives are also good for such jobs. Good kitchen scissors are also useful for cutting the rinds from bacon and chopping herbs. Having scissors in the kitchen discourages anyone from using your kitchen knives for cutting string and so on. Lastly have a very good quality, high carbon sharpening steel (**fusil**) with a large guard, because a poor quality steel won't make much of an edge on a good knife. For any knife a ceramic sharpener is better and harder than steel: for stainless knives a ceramic sharpener is essential. Get a white one; on these, the gray streaky deposits will show you how effectively the steel edge is being truly taken down. Remove the gray streaks from the sharpener with steel wool or Brillo pads. If there are no gray streaks, your ceramic sharpener isn't doing a good job on the knife. American ceramic sharpeners are excellent and cheap. The ones I've seen in Europe—including some sold as ceramic-coated steels—are expensive and ineffective, but perhaps I haven't searched hard enough.

Many chefs remain faithful to the old-fashioned carbon steel blades. They can be made razor sharp and keep their edge, but must be kept clean and dry between use or they will rust and ruin. Nowadays the manufacture of high-quality stainless steel knives has reached a stage at which (for a price) you can have the best of both worlds: sharpness and a material that resists salt, acid and water. One chef working out in the remote countryside persists in using old-fashioned carbon steel knives because they are much easier to sharpen. Although stainless knives can be kept true by a few strokes on the steel or ceramic every time the knife is used, when they need resharpening—as every knife does two or three times a year—they have to be done by a professional. A super-hard stainless steel blade doesn't yield to the sort of stone used for carbon steel blades, so some chefs provide themselves with diamond sharpeners.

Look for a "full tang"—a blade that goes right to the tip of the handle—they are usually stronger. Riveted handles are now obsolescent because health regulations demand sealed handles that provide no chance of hidden bacteria. In my experience German knives are incomparably the best. I particularly like the top-grade ones from Henckel.

On my visits to California I look in to see Fred Wieser of Standard Cutlery (9509 Santa Monica Boulevard, Beverly Hills, California). He is world famous for his knowledge of knives and their manufacture and says Wüsthof (Trident) are as good as Henckel if not better. He says the very finest knives come from Friedrich Herder's Constant Factory, Solingen. Herder's knives are not milled; they are hand ground so that the whole blade (side) is a subtle curve all the way to the cutting edge. But Fred adds a caution: "Most chefs lack the knowledge that makes the high prices of such superb knives worth the extra cost" and encourages chefs to buy only one such super knife until in use the difference becomes evident. "Then some chefs come back and want a complete set." Fred says we should never put any knife in a dishwasher.

There are many different knives, all with a special purpose. A really good set of knives, and a sharpener, should be a cook's priority and come before mixing machines and other equipment. My family spends so much time in rented apartments that we have assembled our own "kitchen kit." It consists of a ceramic sharpener from Colorado Ceramics (via Fred Wieser) which I can use on any blunt knife I find, kitchen scissors, a zester, a peeler, two small knives for vegetables, a six-inch Henckel chef's knife, a Chinese cleaver and an eight-inch Herder general-purpose knife that is used for anything requiring its razor-sharp edge. All chefs have their own knives and when you work in a kitchen you soon learn that taking a colleague's knife without permission can bring immediate and sometimes violent retribution. Buy yourself some fine knives and look after them.

Couvert: a place setting; wine glasses, cutlery, plates and linen, or a charge for the cost—breakages, washing, laundry and so on—of such a setting. A brasserie or bistro where the table tops are bare and the napkins paper should make no cover charge.

   Although at home, as in many restaurants, we may take a sneaking pride in setting out many knives and many forks, together with gravy spoons and bread plates and their knives, the great French restaurants are more likely to set out the simplest possible cover—one knife, one fork and a gravy spoon. The waiter replaces the setting before each course is served.

Crémant is a semi-sparkling wine.

Crème. "Un grand crème" is the way a Parisian orders a large cup of coffee with frothy milk. A **crème à l'anglaise** is a custard. But such custards are made from eggs and milk and cream rather than from yellow-colored powders (as is still done in Britain). **Crème pâtissière** is a heavier, flour-based egg "custard" which is used as a layer under the fruit when making tarts. This layer seals the pastry against juice, holds the fruit high to improve appearance and is delicious to eat. It is called a pastry-shop cream because tarts in a pastry shop might go many hours before being sold and eaten. The restaurant chef doesn't use the cream because his creations are made for each meal service and eaten immediately. Thus with his tarts the underlay can be fruit (for example, chopped apple).

   Crème pâtissière is also used as a filling for éclairs and other pastries. A **crémerie** is a shop selling dairy products—in the case of my local one they sell wine and pasta too—sometimes combined with the cheese counter of the **fromagerie.**

Crème fraîche: cream containing lactic acid and other fermentations. Once upon a time cream was obtained by skimming from milk which had been allowed to settle. Such cream, containing harmless bacteria, developed a flavor almost as complex as good wine. The taste varied from district to district and even from farm to farm. Cream was something to relish. Then came the separating machine: no bacteria, no flavor, but convenient and cost-cutting for the farmer. Crème fraîche is not produced by the traditional methods but it provides a hint of what real cream tastes like. People brought up to expect tasteless cream sometimes find its sharpness unpleasant.

When first purchased, crème fraîche is rather sweet and the fermented taste develops if it is kept for a week or so. It has a very high butterfat content so chefs use it to thicken sauces (which ordinary cream will not do). Some use it because it will boil without curdling, although I find almost any cream will do that. Crème fraîche is mostly used for savory dishes. **Crème fleurette** is a thinner cream used with sweets, fruits, desserts and coffee. Mix it with superfine sugar and a trace of good vanilla to make **crème chantilly.**

Crème pâtissière cooled, cut into fingers, rolled in egg and breadcrumbs and then deep-fried is called **crème frite.** A little cream used to deglaze the pan in which meat or fish, or even vegetables, have been fried is used as a sauce and gives the result the title **à la crème**. It's an excellent way to give a final polish to an otherwise ordinary dish.

Crêpe: a very thin pancake like the wrinkly fabric of the same name. To make them, an egg and flour batter mixture is cooked on both sides in a frying pan, using the minimum of oil, to produce a dry steam finish. A pan kept for such egg dishes should be wiped thoroughly to clean but never washed. A crêpe can be served wrapped around jam or cooked apple, or be part of a more complex dish which is later grilled or baked. The most famous dish of this sort is **crêpes Suzette**, for which the crêpes are reheated with butter, sugar, the juice and grated zest of an orange, plus curaçao. For many years it was said that Henri Charpentier—a *commis de rang* or assistant waiter—at the *Café Royale,* Monte Carlo, was serving crêpes to the Prince of Wales (the future King Edward VII) when the sauce caught fire. Keeping calm, as a good waiter must, he continued to flip the crêpes into the flaming mixture. The dish was thereupon named after the lady accompanying the Prince.

But when Charpentier died in 1961 his claim was contested. More than one authority said crêpes Suzette were invented by M. Joseph (who ended his career at the *Savoy Hotel,* London) for an actress, Suzanne "Suzette" Reichenberg.

In Brittany large buckwheat crêpes—**crêpes au blé**—are sold in special eating places—**crêperies**—and wrapped around almost any food that comes to mind. Anyone trying to reproduce them must know that these specialties are made from a rather heavy batter across which a "knife" is wiped to skim the batter and thus make them thinner. In America the pancake originated with a heavy cornmeal batter made with hominy grits and yeast, and still today an American pancake is a small thick disc also made with a heavier batter mixture.

Crépine is a lace-like caul (a membrane enclosing the paunch), which provides a quick and convenient way to make sausages; you just wrap them up like little parcels. Such items are called **crépinettes.** It is also used to wrap the meat mixtures that make terrines. Crépine has a wonderful flavor and the fatty content occurs in the right place: the outside of the meat that is being cooked. Even in France butchers are reluctant to sell crépine. Perhaps they think their sale of sausages will suffer. Often they will sell crépine that is too heavy for wrapping. To see what the real thing is like, buy a crépinette and unwrap it.

Croissant: a crescent-shaped breakfast roll. This masterpiece of the baker's art is made from yeast dough layered with butter. Since the dough

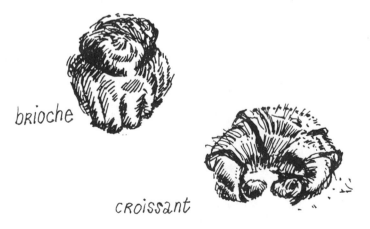

brioche

croissant

needs warmth and the butter needs cold this combination demands careful attention. Nowadays there are cabinets which change the temperature at measured intervals so that the baker can get an extra hour in bed. But only big bakeries can afford such sophisticated machinery. My wife discovered that hard wheat flour is essential to the process, so I imagine all French croissants are made with imported flour.

Croque monsieur: this should be a ham and cheese sandwich dipped into beaten egg (for just long enough for the bread to absorb the egg) and deep-fried. Too often it's the label affixed to a prefabricated, plastic-wrapped sandwich that has been zapped in a microwave oven. Try making a real one.

Croquette is made from finely chopped chicken, fish or vegetable, which is bound in a heavy sauce and well coated in beaten egg and breadcrumbs before being deep-fried.

Croûtons are small cubes of bread fried or toasted, sometimes flavored with garlic. They are stirred into salads or sprinkled upon soups just before serving.

Cru: growth. A strictly controlled classification of the best vineyards of Bordeaux and Burgundy.

Crudités are small pieces of vegetable served raw as an appetizer (usually to accompany drinks). Strips of carrot, turnip, green pepper, cucumber, celery, beans, radishes and so on are sometimes beautifully trimmed and cut and presented like a flower arrangement.

Aïoli is a popular accompaniment; so is an **anchoïade.**

Cuisine: the kitchen or the style of cooking. Most Frenchmen agree that there are at least three kinds of French cooking.

Haute cuisine is the cooking of the court, and of grand houses, which is to some limited extent available now in the best and most expensive restaurants. This is the cooking of delicate flavors and refined ingredients. Rich ingredients predominate: cream, butter, foie gras and so on, but no garlic or unusual local produce.

Cuisine bourgeoise is the ordinary, "middle-class" home cooking available throughout France. Yes, but what is it? Some years ago the food correspondent of *Le Monde* was reviewing a Paris restaurant: *La Grille* in rue Montorgueil. The restaurant had old-fashioned décor with its original zinc counter, lopsided wood paneling and little pigeonholes for the napkins of regular customers. The proprietor described his menu as **cuisine bourgeoise.** It included salt pork with lentils, pig's trotters Sainte-Menehould, grilled pork, **entrecôte marchand de vin** and **coquilles** Bercy. That is **cuisine bourgeoise** and it's what I like.

Cuisine paysanne (or **cuisine régionale**) is rough and strong tasting. It is the heavy food needed by agricultural workers. It uses whatever the peasant can find: wild fruits and seasonal vegetables. It uses game, eels, frogs and other unusual regional ingredients. It goes without saying that there will be tough cuts of meat, chewy fowl sometimes made tender by local wine. It often involves long cooking times.

Cuisine minceur. Michel Guérard, a famous chef who works in a health spa, invented a style of cooking for dieters which uses little or no flour, cream or fat. Of it Bocuse said, "I'm also against what people are calling cuisine minceur these days. Michel Guérard is a good friend of mine, but there is no way you can make a good **blanquette de veau** with cottage cheese instead of cream."[10]

Nouvelle cuisine, as everyone knows, is a pernicious gimmick by means of which tiny amounts of food are arranged "artistically" on large plates in the kitchen before being brought to the table. This saves money by using smaller portions of the ingredients. It also saves the cost of skilled dining-room staff who could prepare food at the table-side according to the wishes of the customer. The arranging of food out of sight of the customer leads to all sorts of unhygienic happenings; for example, food is dropped on the floor and carelessly handled by people who don't wash their hands enough. As Julia Child said, "It's so beautifully arranged on the plate—you know someone's fingers have been all over it." Nouvelle cuisine is good for chain-restaurant accountants; bad news for the customer.

Recently there has been a reaction against nouvelle cuisine. This feeling that France's great tradition of cooking cannot be thrown away in favor of decorated plates has been fueled by the invasion of fast food. Hamburgers, fried chicken and ribs are rapidly becoming the standard fare of young French people. Now concerned chefs and restaurateurs are returning to traditional hearty French dishes. The name **cuisine de grandmère**, granny food, is attached to the new movement. Whether it recovers lost ground only time will show.

Curnonsky, Maurice-Edmond Sailland (1872–1956) was called "the prince of gastronomes." He was not a chef; he was a critic. There is no doubt that his fame, and the adulation he received, were due to the immense power he wielded. A word from him could make the fortune of a restaurateur or damn a chef to oblivion. The Michelin tire company sponsored his gastronomic writings in a newspaper column which he signed "Bibendum." Terrified restaurant managers kept tables empty just in case he showed up without warning. His most famous book, *Le Trésor gastronomique de France*, has now become no more than a curiosity. His life shows how much of "the art of cookery" is transient fashion. But he was certainly correct when he said, ". . . you do not invent a new dish by pouring fish soup over a sirloin nor yet by smothering a jugged hare in peppermint."[11]

Darne: a thick slice of fish that is cut right through to include the bone. A **filet** is a piece of fish removed from the bone.

Daube is not just a fancy word for stew; it's a particular type of stew made in a **daubière**—a pot of iron, stone or tinned copper— with a well-fitting lid. It's usually richly flavored and made with beef or strongly flavored game that has been larded with fat and marinated in wine. Such marinated meat is not fried or browned; in fact the meat and wine marinade are usually all put in the daubière together. If available, the blood is also added. Such dishes must be cooked very slowly. The lid of a daubière has no vent in it; in fact often the lid is sealed to the pot with pastry. The heat must therefore be kept below 212°F or the steam generated will blow the lid off!

Long ago the daube was often served cold, gleaming under its own jelly. In Nice, and that region of France where Italian ideas infiltrate the kitchen, the remains of a daube are mashed to make the traditional filling for the local style of home-made ravioli.

Decant, as everyone knows, means to pour off, to transfer wine from a bottle to a decanter. The purpose is to leave the sediment in the bottle. To do this, wine should always be stored label upwards and gently put upright before decanting. One expert said it should remain upright for twelve hours; another said two hours was enough. This sequence will get all the sediment into one corner of the bottle and if you decant it, or pour it, label up (as you always should), all the sediment will be left behind. Have a light behind the bottle while pouring so you can stop before the sediment comes rushing out.

So much for the uncontroversial aspect of decanting. When and if to decant are more vexed questions. I have asked many experts whether all—or only some—wines should be decanted, and found little or no accord. Some say that even the cheapest plonk will benefit from the aeration; others that only vintage wines (with heavy sediment) should be treated this way. I regret therefore that I will have to leave the decision to you.

Déglacer. The word **glace** doesn't refer only to ice encountered in drinks in summertime, and on ponds in winter; it is used also to mean glaze as in the icing of cakes and cherries (**cerises glacées**). So when you've been frying chops or steaks, and the pan is left with a layer of caramelized juices, you might want to deglaze it; that is, stir a little stock around in the pan to make gravy. Wine can be used instead of stock, but in this case the wine must be boiled until it's reduced to about half its volume or else it will be too acrid for most tastes. Sometimes such gravy is too fatty to be taken straight to the table. Take the fat off it—**dégraisser**—or serve it in the special twin-spouted jug called a **maigre-gras**, so that it can be poured with or without the oily top layer. The easiest and most efficient way to remove fat is by making it cold, but there are many gadgets that will remove most of the fat from warm liquids.

Demi-glace or half glaze refers to a stock that has begun to thicken. It is arguably the most important sauce in the French chef's lexicon, but it is never served. For demi-glace is degreased and slightly thickened rich stock (**fonds brun**) to which tomato (for coloring) and **mirepoix** have been added. It is used to make other sauces. For instance: **sauce italienne, financière, madère, poivrade, lyonnaise** and so on.

When the fonds brun has been used to make demi-glace, the beef and veal bones are not thrown away. More water is added and simmering begins again. But this second, and less strong, stock is eventually reduced down until it becomes a dark-brown sticky mess that sets into a jelly or rubbery consistency. It is called **glace de viande** and is one of the most valuable flavoring substances a chef can have on hand. Over the years there have been many commercial compounds of this sort on sale but none anything like the real thing because of the expense involved in making such a protein-rich substance.

Déjeuner. Jeûner means to fast. So literally déjeuner means to break the fast or breakfast. Artfully the French have managed to arrange some eating before breakfast so déjeuner now means lunch. So what about **dîner?** In medieval times those who were rich enough to eat big meals ate the biggest one of the day at about 9 a.m. Since then the main meal has been served later and later. One book (*Description of England,* William Harrison, 1587, 2nd edition) says the English had only two meals per day and describes the variations in mealtimes. Harrison says that until then many people had eaten four times a day and admits somewhat disdainfully that there were still ". . . here and there some hungry stomachs that cannot fast till dinner time."

Now, he says, nobility, gentry and students have dinner at 11 a.m. and supper between 5 and 6 p.m. Merchants, especially those in London, a shade later: at noon and 6 p.m. Husbandmen "dine at high-noon as they call it, and sup at seven or eight." Out of term, he says, university scholars dine at 10 a.m. "As for the poorest sort they generally dine and sup when they may, so that to talk of their order of repast it were but a needless matter."

Today most people eat between 7 p.m. and 9 p.m. But is it dinner? In France, as in Britain and Ireland and other places too, people who eat their main meal at midday call it dinner (dîner). In

France's rural areas the evening meal is often called **la soupe** or **souper** (supper). If a Frenchman asks you to join him for a potluck meal (a most unlikely possibility, may I add, since the French are reluctant to invite people into their homes, especially for an informal meal), he would say, *"Venez manger la soupe avec nous?"* This association of soup with evening meals means that many chefs of the traditional school do not believe that soup should be included on any proper lunch menu.

Demi-tasse: a small coffee cup appropriate to servings after lunch or dinner; the coffee is usually offered without milk. In France breakfast cups—sometimes bowls—are large and the coffee comes with milk.

Des: dice. For cutting vegetable strips *see* **Couper**, page 72.

Digestif. I suppose it was some public relations man who found this lovely name for powerful shots of alcohol consumed in the middle of the meal (nowadays often poured upon a water ice) or at the end of it. Delicious they may be; aids to the digestion they are not.

Moutarde de Dijon. Dijon in Burgundy is where France's most popular mustard is produced. Its flavor comes from the addition of unripe grape juice (verjus). Our word "mustard" comes from "must," which is unfermented grape juice. **Moutarde de Meaux** contains whole seeds (*brassica alba*), so is more pungent. Bordeaux mustard is another distinctive one—darker and milder—containing wine. So is **Florida** from the champagne area. These are basic types, but of course there are an infinity of variations with herbs and other flavorings added. Mustard is used for making sauces and for salad dressings.

Double consommé is an old-fashioned term for a consommé because a **bouillon** was called a **consommé blanc.**

Pommes duchesse are the sort of garnish that so often gets a restaurant a bad name. Does your heart sink when you see mashed potato piped around the serving platter? Mine certainly does. But it doesn't have to be so awful. Into each pound of steamed and puréed potatoes (for which a "ricer," an old-fashioned device like a big garlic crusher, is simple and super efficient) put a big spoonful of butter, fresh grated nutmeg and a beaten egg yolk. Stir well; in fact beat it to make it light and fluffy. Put through a pastry bag while still warm and decorate to your heart's content, or better still, serve it as it is.

Du corps. This is how a chef describes the body, the texture of a sauce, stew or soup. Whether it will cling to the back of a spoon is the usual test. But we are not talking about flour and water; we are talking about the body that comes from such things as gelatin and collagen, which are found in abundance in certain protein foods: for example, calf's foot, veal knuckle, tripe and oxtail.

But let's hear from the professionals. For sauces the Roux brothers' favorite thickening agents are (1) reduction or thickening of gravies over a high heat; (2) adding butter or cream piecemeal; (3) shellfish coral, blood or foie gras; (4) egg yolks; (5) mashed vegetables (for example, those cooked round a roast). Less favored by these famous cooks are flour, arrowroot or potato starch.

Dumaine, Alexandre (1895–1964) made his *Côte d'Or* at Saulieu a mecca for gourmets, who literally came from all parts of the world. Unlike Fernand Point, "Alexandre le Grand" remained always a chef and was only truly happy working in his small kitchen with his four assistants, a very small kitchen staff for such a place. And Dumaine didn't just stroll around offering advice and criticism; he cooked. He distrusted flavorings of any kind, preferring to depend upon high-quality ingredients. His **poularde à la vapeur** (steamed chicken with truffles) was typical of his most famous dishes. It had to be ordered twenty-four hours in advance.

Eau is water, and the French, like the Californians, prefer it from bottles. Spring water gains mineral content as it passes through the earth's varying layers: iron, calcium, magnesium, sulphates and chlorides. They say there are over one thousand suitable spring **sources** in France and fifty or so brands of water. Recently, in France, my family staged a blind tasting of such waters. Of the sparkling waters Badoit (slightly alkaline) was top for taste and Vals did well. Perrier, by far the most expensive, was only preferred by those who liked its fierce fizz. Of the non-fizzy waters we found so little variation in taste that it was not worth rating them. The French themselves like Evian from the Alps, which is the biggest selling brand. It's very low on minerals and is favored for babies' diets because it is pure and neutral. Contrexéville is slightly alkaline with magnesium and sulphate. It has a laxative and diuretic effect and dieters prefer it. Vichy from the Allier valley is too salty for my taste. Vittel contains iron for those who want iron. Some cooks use these bottled waters for making pastry or pasta.

Eau de vie means the water of life just as whisky comes from the Gaelic for water of life. Alcoholic spirits can be distilled from almost any organic matter from apples to woodwork. These drinks range from fiery vodkas to the most delicate **framboise**, which is made from raspberries and is one of my favorites. **Poire** made from William pears can be superb, as can **marc**, which is distilled from crushed grapes and skins after wine-making. Some wine-makers produce only a small amount of marc and keep it for their personal use. Others have made marc into big business. Some of these marcs are aged in oak and turn a dark color, and are not then called **alcools blancs.** There is a marc from the champagne grapes, various Burgundy marcs and a fashionable **marc de Gewürztraminer** from Alsace. These alcools blancs are known all over Europe. *Kümmel* and *aquavit* come to mind, as does **kirsch**, which is made from the cherry crop in many countries. French kirsch is particularly good because it has the crushed kernels in it to give a distinctive flavor that the others don't have. Kirsch is used in the kitchen more than any of the others.

Échalote: shallot, a small onion-like plant that is sometimes unobtainable in America and neglected in Britain. In France the shallot is regarded with great respect. It is said to taste of garlic but to be far more easily digested than onion. French chefs use it in reductions of wine, the first step in making many sauces. It is also used raw as a garnish, but is not so good when fried.

My memories of it began in wartime when it was a substitute for onions which were usually scarce. Whether it is milder, sweeter or more flavorful than the ordinary onion I can never really decide, but it's much more fiddly to peel and chop so I don't use it as often as perhaps I should.

Éclair: a small hollow pastry made from **pâte à choux.** They are filled with flavored pastry creams or chestnut purée. Only rarely do the French fill them with cream as is done in other countries.

Écrevisse: crayfish, a small freshwater shellfish to which the French are passionately devoted. By that I mean they eat them at every opportunity. There are countless ways of cooking them and many country restaurants have live crayfish in tanks and baths. It is not to be confused with the **langoustine** (*nephrops norvegicus* or scampi or Dublin Bay prawn) which is a salt-water crustacean and looks nothing like any kind of prawn!

For me the difficulty of distinguishing between the two is not that they look alike—they don't—but the fact that the stubby little *écrevisse* looks like a sea creature and the long slender pale pink langoustine looks like something you might find in a fast-running stream. One of the most famous recipes for crayfish is the **gratin de queues d'écrevisses** served at *L'Auberge du Père Bise* at Talloires. For this, onions, shallots and garlic are cooked till soft in olive oil and then

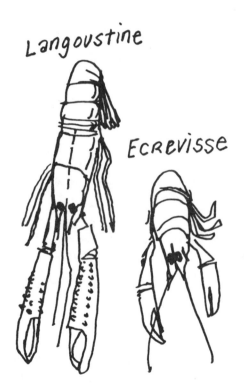

Langoustine

Ecrevisse

tomatoes are added for a few minutes. The crayfish are cooked in this "sauce" for 15 minutes. Then the crayfish are shelled, the "sauce" is reduced and strained and cream is added. Finally the sauce is put over the crayfish tails, a very small amount of Gruyère cheese is sprinkled over them and some sliced truffle. They then have a few minutes under a brisk heat to color the topping. No wonder it's been on the menu for so many years.

Émincé: sliced, not minced, for which the French use **hâché.** Cold cooked meat toughens and dries when reheated. But if thinly sliced (émincé) leftover meat is coated with hot sauce (mushroom, tomato or something more luxurious), it is called an émincé. Sometimes a chafing dish is used to keep the plates and serving dish hot. The best advice you can have about émincé is to avoid it. However, a certain three-star restaurant in the south of France has found an artful variation on the émincé. They freeze raw salmon—a terrible thing to do except in extreme circumstances—and are then able to cut paper-thin slices from it. The slices are put on a very hot plate and covered with a generous amount of a sauce hot enough to cook the salmon. In the interests of science I tried it; it was not nice.

En croûte: in a crust, food cooked inside pastry. The most famous such dish is the **loup de mer en croûte,** for which Bocuse puts lobster mousse on sea bass and wraps it in pastry that is elaborately decorated to look like a fish, complete with fins, gills and scales. Chapel calls his version **bar en feuilletage.** Chopped or puréed fish can be added to fillets instead of mousse.

En croûte often refers to meat as well—usually a fillet of beef or a boned leg of lamb—wrapped in puff pastry or brioche and served hot. No matter what your cookbook says, the meat or fish should start off raw. The art of it is to cook both pastry and meat just right. Serving your guests warmed-up meat is not worth the effort. **Filet de boeuf en croûte** is easy. Wrap the beef fillet in flaky pastry; cook it for 45–50 minutes at 400°F the first time you do it. A fish weighing 5 pounds will require about the same cooking time. The length of the fish or beef doesn't matter; the girth must be the deciding factor. Vary the timing on subsequent occasions according to how you like that result.

Getting a leg of lamb small enough to cook right through before the pastry burns is difficult. In France, where the milk of the ewe (**brebis**) is used for making cheese, tiny lambs are sold for meat. The metric system has encouraged chefs to think of a leg of lamb in terms of a kilo of weight. Such a leg will cook inside the pastry. You'll need to find a special supplier for such a lamb. For a variation on such en croûte dishes try using lattice pastry—you'll need a special roller to make it.

En espalier: fruit trees when splayed flat on a wall or trellis frame. This style of growing is the traditional method in France, and has been for hundreds of years. It gives the gardener access to the fruit and exposes it to maximum sunlight. Thus it provides high quality sweet fruit.

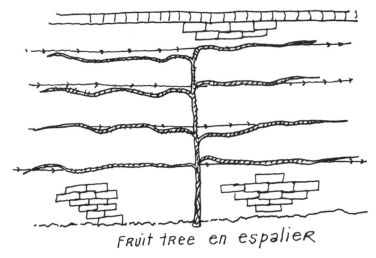

FRUIT TREE en espalieR

Entrecôte. Literally this means between the chops or ribs and some experts insist that this must be a slice of rib steak cut from the meat between the rib bones. Whether or not it ever meant exactly that, it nowadays refers to any steak from the rib or loin, if not from the cheaper rump or **rumsteak.**

Entrée: entry. This is one of those misnomers that should have been dropped decades ago. At one time it described the course that came after the fish and before the main course, which was probably a roast. The entrée was a specially garnished dish, a display of skill of the sort that Carême so liked to make. In Britain and America entrée remains now as an awkward word for the main course. In France, however, where a meal often includes a course between fish and main dish, it still has its original meaning. In that case the entrée is likely to be offal (variety meats), a filled pancake or an omelette.

Épaule: shoulder, a flavorful but bony joint, tricky to carve. An **épaule d'agneau** and **épaule de mouton** are well suited to the pot roast, the Frenchman's favorite style of cooking. But the French chef wants it boned and rolled. The preparation of such boned meat is a good example of the skills of French butchers. While he bones it my local butcher in France will even ask me if I want the mutton shoulder **roulée** for an oval-shaped pot or **en ballon** for a round pot. He knows how I'm going to cook it—the average French butcher's knowledge of cooking enables him to give you exactly what is needed—and he knows that fitting the meat to the pot can be important. Ask him to fill such a boned piece with forcemeat and he'll oblige. He'll even do it with forcemeat that I've made myself. There are limitless variations. An **épaule de mouton à l'albigeoise** is stuffed with a garlicky forcemeat of bread and pork liver. Other variations specify cooking the meat on a bed of red cabbage (**chou rouge à la flamande**) or with white beans. Such dishes are always served well done and sometimes cold. In any case it will be necessary to skim the fatty juices before serving. (Lamb fat has poor flavor and is never used in the kitchen.) Alternatively prepare a sauce separately.

Épicerie. Although the name means a spice shop, an épicerie sells groceries. **Alimentation générale** is another sign for the same kind of shop.

Escargots: snails. The most sought after is the white Burgundy snail, which is light brown. They feed in the vineyards. A smaller kind—**petit gris,** which are darker brown and sometimes called **cagouilles**—are just as good. In fact there is a lot of arrant nonsense talked and written on the subject of snails. Most of the European varieties are equally good to eat; it's the preparation of them prior to cooking that makes such a difference. To prove this point, an old friend living in England has prepared and cooked garden snails for me and they were excellent. She was certainly making a valid point, because recently—during a time when snails were at their best—I had dinner at a very famous restaurant in Burgundy. Snails, said the menu, were a specialty. We ordered them and got canned snails, which are rubbery and not worth eating. So much for the widely advertised "great chefs of Burgundy." If you like snails, find a little family restaurant where the local French eat and nouvelle cuisine has not yet supplanted real food.

Usually snails are baked in their shells with a dab of **beurre d'escargot** in each one. But in Burgundy they sometimes combine them with **chanterelle** mushrooms. People who say that the melted garlic butter tastes better than the snails are usually those who have not tasted fresh snails.

The French eat about 2 billion snails each year and about one-third of these are imported from Turkey and eastern Europe. In 1982 the French parliament passed a law that such snails could enter France only at places where the customs officers had "snail testing machines" to make sure the snails were alive and healthy. The imports mostly go to the Jura, where they are cooked and prepared.

Escoffier, Auguste (1847–1935). Although he worked mostly in England, and left the *Savoy Hotel* amid a scandal, Escoffier was honored by the President of France, who made him an officer of the Legion of Honor at a banquet held in his honor at the *Palais d'Orsay*. Escoffier was a man of passion and boundless energy. Today he is remembered for the dishes he created for the famous personalities who came to eat his food—**salade Tosca, pêches Melba, tournedos Rossini** and **poularde Derby**—but his influence went further and wider than that. He reorganized his kitchen staff into co-ordinated teams under **chefs de partie** who specialized in sauces, fish or cold foods and so on. He changed the noisy hell of the kitchen into relative quiet and calm. He simplified recipes and standardized them so the same dish could be produced again and again. To save the delicate feelings of the *Savoy Hotel*'s lady customers, he called frogs' legs "nymphs." He dealt a final blow to the medieval **service à la française** that Carême liked so much. For this, selections of food built to architectural heights were displayed beforehand and offered batch by batch. Escoffier delighted in the **service à la russe**; food was brought to the table course by course as it is today.

Estaminet. This sign seen painted on buildings in old photos of Flanders in the First World War meant that it was a café where smoking was permitted. Now that smoking bans are spreading we might see the sign put back into use. But don't look for me inside.

Estragon: tarragon, a strongly flavored and delicious garden herb. When I first gathered it from my newly acquired garden I found the crop quite tasteless. It was not until a French visitor told me that I was growing "Russian tarragon," a flavorless look-alike, that I planted some tarragon from France and tried again. Eureka! Tarragon is used in sauces and salads and to flavor vinegar, but if you use it only for chicken tarragon it will still be worth the trouble of growing it. There are many recipes. The chicken can be boiled, pot-roasted, roasted or sautéed. Pot-roasting is particularly good. For **poularde à l'estragon**: put a handful of tarragon inside the chicken and more round it. Cook your chicken in a tight-fitting closed pot, and add a chopped onion and a glass of dry white wine. It will need an hour (15 minutes more for a big chicken) at 375°F in the oven. Test it for tenderness. If you are using a boiling fowl it will take much longer. Add stock from time to time if it gets too dry. The pot must be kept steamy. In any case end up with at least a cupful of juice. Stir in a cupful of cream to make the sauce. Carve it up and serve it. Wonderful; I can almost smell it.

Étoile: a star, and three stars is the *Guide Michelin*'s top accolade. There is an ever-growing list of three-star restaurants in France. These are establishments which Michelin's famous guidebook declares are worth a special journey. But is the journey worthwhile, and more to the point is the food worth the high prices?

It is difficult to maintain high standards of cooking and service. Any newly starred restaurant buzzes with excitement. Every customer is treated like a Michelin inspector, but as the years roll on, the enthusiasm wanes. The staff grow waxy-eyed and even the Algerians in the kitchen are bored with arranging small pieces of food on the huge brightly patterned plates. What was once a grand restaurant becomes a food factory. A profitable food factory. Through it come the tourists, weary and disheveled, their faces set in the same expression of stony endurance that is to be seen in the lines that shuffle through Westminster Abbey and the Taj Mahal. They are for the most part elderly foreigners, without much experience of the French, their language or their cuisine. The Japanese drink brandy with their escargots; the British admire the pommes frites and ask about the curtains; the Americans want iced water and the Germans want Tabasco sauce. They all stare at the plastic menus and note that they are too big to tuck into pocket or handbag. They read the "chefspeak" of menus where the meals begin with bavarois and end with a soupe, and are secretly resolving what they will eat the moment they get home. Here and there one spots a native or two, celebrating an anniversary and wondering at all the red plush and weathered gold cherubs that have appeared since their previous visit a few years ago.

Apéritif? May I suggest the specialty of the house: a fizzy wine, very like champagne, with crushed frozen blueberries stirred into it; we call it **Kir Carême,** who was, as you know, a famous French chef. It tastes very expensive: just right for a special occasion like this. Oh, yes, I speak English. I used to work in Detroit. *Menu dégustation*, madame? Just a small portion of all our specialties, one after the other for fifteen courses, pausing only for a tobacco-flavored sorbet? The wine list is too long, sir? What about this short list of wines? Overpriced, yes, but they all bear our famous proprietor's name on the exotic-looking highly colored label. Have you seen the display of cookbooks at the cash desk? Signed copies always available. If you're staying the night in one of our super-luxury suites we'll have your name inscribed too. And while you're buying our proprietor's cook-book, why not take a silver garlic press or a gold corkscrew, or one of these lovely wristwatches; the hands are little knives and forks? Send the folks back home this crafted wooden box of truffles or a bottle of our very special olive oil with caviar in it. Make the most of it, every-one. Read the menu carefully; for only ten dollars you can take it home with you. You don't like the food? But look, sir, every seat is taken—all major credit cards accepted—and few of these lovely people will come back next year, if ever. Three-star restaurants, you see, are worth a journey. Even Michelin doesn't claim them to be worth more than one.

Étuver. A l'étuvée means a style of cooking in a tightly closed—or sealed—pot, with very little moisture. Temperatures must be kept below 212°F and this suits foods cooked in butter (which otherwise might burn). Delicately flavored garden vegetables, leeks, celery and even peas are cooked like this, but so is the hearty pork and bean stew that the people in Languedoc call an **estouffat.**

Faire chabrot is the homely habit of pouring a little red wine into the final few spoonfuls of soup and then drinking it by holding the bowl up to the mouth.

Faire revenir means to give flavor. Cooks often use it to mean browning meat in a pan before cooking it in a pot or in the oven. It's one of cookery's most widely prevalent myths that such a technique will seal in the juices; it won't. Meat will shrink when heated and the juices inside will emerge, as does water from a squeezed sponge. There is no way to seal juices into meat, but the next best thing is to dry the juices as they appear on the outer coating of the meat—some cooks lightly dust meat with flour—and to cook the meat as little as necessary. Never baste meat as this washes the dried juices away. Use a trivet to keep the meat off the bottom of the cooking pan, and let the hot air get to it. (Basting poultry is okay because the skin prevents a loss of juices.)

Faisan is pheasant, a most beautiful game bird, slow-flying, noisy and easy to shoot. It is found all over Europe (and in the northern United States, although the southern states are too hot for it). It was much prized by the chefs of long ago because they used its feathers in their food arrangements. But, like most game birds, it is inclined to be rather tough and flavorless, especially if eaten fresh. That's why chefs hang it for three weeks, and lard it carefully, to give it flavor. (In French the word **faisandé** is used to mean high and gamy tasting.) Sportsmen will of course eat it and relish it, but sportsmen will eat almost anything.

Farce, as well as meaning something comic like a practical joke, also means stuffing or forcemeat. In France this is not something to joke about. It is likely to be a pork and veal combination marinated overnight in a little wine or brandy. Breadcrumbs and beaten egg—not very much of either—are added before use. Sometimes such a mixture would have game in it. The same mixtures are used for terrines and stuffed cabbage. Others—some including such things as truffles—go into fish, quenelles, chickens, boned pig's foot and ravioli.

Farine: flour. There are many sorts—rye, corn, buckwheat and rice—but wheat flour is the most versatile ingredient known to man, which is why our civilization flourished on it. Wheat flour is a complex food and there are many varieties. **Farine de gâteau** (cake flour) is a soft wheat flour and **farine de blé** is made from hard wheat varieties.

You can go on cooking for many years without being affected by the differences in flour. Then the mystery of a series of failures is solved—suddenly and magnificently—by changing the one you use. That's how it was after my wife had spent two years trying to make the perfect croissant, and succeeded when she tried hard flour.

Flour deteriorates when stored. This especially applies to whole-wheat flours because the wheatgerm turns rancid. Keep flour in a cool dry place and buy it in small amounts. **Fleur de maïs** is cornstarch, a finely ground flour made from corn. It is used mostly for thickening sauces because it is less likely to get lumpy but arrowroot (the French also call it arrowroot from the American Indian word *araruta*) works better.

Fève. This large pale green bean is one of the earliest crops to appear in my garden. In Britain it's called a broad bean, in America a fava bean. Its pod is inedible. It's not very good dried (and it goes brown), although the dried variety is widely consumed. Even when young and fresh it is less than delicious. When it is large and mature some cooks remove the outer layer of the bean, but by that time the garden is offering better things.

Filet: the tenderloin, or what in America is called a beef fillet, the choice muscle of beef that is found alongside the **contre-filet** (which is sometimes called the **faux filet**). From it are taken many luxury quality steaks: tournedos, chateaubriand and so on. The pointed end provides the **filet mignon.** A whole fillet can be roasted at 400°F for 45 minutes (being without fat it might need barding). But when the orders arrive in your kitchen you might need to remember that **un filet** is a piece of fish taken off the bone.

Fine is brandy distilled from wine. **Fine champagne** is such a brandy coming from "La Grande Champagne," which includes the towns of Segonzac, Jarnac and Cognac. In France it is served in tiny tulip glasses, but a balloon glass is a necessity for drinking a really good brandy.

Fines herbes: mixed herbs finely chopped, usually consisting of parsley, chervil, chives and tarragon. But in an **omelette fines herbes** you'll usually find only chopped parsley. Not in mine you don't.

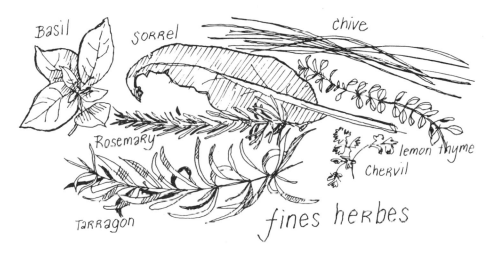

Flageolet. For some folk beans are beans but the French are choosy. The **haricot blanc** (*phaseolus vulgaris*) is a light-colored seed but varies in size. The flageolet is a sub species regarded as the finest of these. It is green in color and turns paler when cooked. In France it is considered an essential accompaniment for many lamb or mutton dishes. Out of season try the canned or frozen ones: they are better than the dried varieties.

Flambé means flamed. It is said especially of a dish that is flamed at table-side: steaks, kebabs or crêpes. I used to sneer at people who ordered such dishes, but I have long since changed my mind. In fact any restaurant providing table-side service gets my immediate attention. And dishes that are prepared at your table-side are more likely to be the way you want them, whether it is something flambé or your steak tartare being mixed to your order.

Flamiche. When a quiche containing leek has a pastry top, making it into a pie, the French call it a flamiche.

Fleuron. A small shape, usually a crescent, of puff pastry used as a simple garnish on such things as a fish and sauce.

Foie is liver. Generally speaking, veal liver is considered superior to any other sort except perhaps **foie gras.** Ancient Egyptians knew about foie gras; at least they knew that force-feeding poultry provided delicious liver. But in France it was considered a rural dish fit only for fat peasants until Louis XIV developed a taste for it. In America there is no foie gras produced because of a law that forbids the forced feeding of ducks or geese. But in his book about the Dordogne James Bentley has comfort for those foie gras eaters who ask if it's cruel. Where he lives he sees the ducks and geese come willingly to be force-fed on the warm corn. The corn makes the liver a bright yellow (as it makes the corn-fed chickens). The season for foie gras begins in September, but sometimes the sellers hold back until Christmas is near.

Nowadays chefs in France are newly interested in foie gras and use it widely as an ingredient in their dishes. It appears on steaks or warm and in a bed of salad. At the *Espérance* restaurant at Vézeley, Marc Meneau's head waiter proudly boasts that the foie gras croquettes will "explode in your mouth," and they do!

When served in France foie gras is left until late in the meal. But in Britain and America—and in foie gras producing regions too—the foie comes to the table first. That's a much better way. James Bentley says that in the Dordogne the idea of eating salad with foie gras is considered bad because the vinegar in the dressing clashes with it and also conflicts with wine. (Wine is not usually served with a salad course.) Michel Guérard serves foie gras with vinaigrette in his **salade gourmande.** After trying it you might decide that those people in the Dordogne know their foie gras.

When the season arrives, whole goose livers are sold at big auctions in market towns in the three great foie gras-producing regions of Périgord, Alsace and the Landes. Go one Saturday morning in December, January or February to markets such as the one in Thiviers, Périgord, and you'll find an array of raw livers. The experts will choose one weighing a little over 1 pound rather than the biggest. Cooking them is a task for an expert, for there is a big investment at stake in each one. My system is to slice the liver into "fingers" and flash-fry them for about ten seconds each. The fingers are put into a terrine with some suitable jelly. Then a half-pound weight is put on it overnight. Anton Edelmann at the *Savoy Hotel,* London, suggested this method, although his own recipe marinates the liver first and seals the fingers with a rich reduction which the menu calls "marbled." An overcooked goose liver loses much of its delicate flavor and texture, so it's a great pity that the canning process requires too much heat. The real thing is fresh and pink and undercooked at the center. There are good shrink-wrapped ones on sale at some French airports. Most of these are imported from Israel, but Eastern Europe—Poland, Hungary and Czechoslovakia—is discovering that it can be a hard currency export. Duck livers prepared in the same way—**foie gras de canard**— have a slightly different flavor and are marginally less expensive.

Cans bearing labels **pâté de foie gras** must by law contain 80 per cent goose liver, **mousse de foie gras** over 55 per cent. The remainder is almost entirely fat so canned foie gras is easy to spread, and some chefs use it in sauces. (I knew I'd find something good to say about it.) **Foie d'oie** is not foie gras; it's the liver of an ordinary goose. But **pâté minute** (chicken livers cooked for one minute in boiling water, drained, then mashed with melted butter) is more delicious than any foie gras from a can. It is a chef's trick to use goose fat—which is available in cans—to cook duck's liver or chicken liver.

Fondue. This useful type of vegetable dish, and ingredient, is little known outside France. A vegetable such as chopped leeks is cooked gently with a little water, or stock, and butter (or oil or lard or goose fat) so that it becomes thick and on the way to becoming a mess. You'll have to keep the lid on as much as possible and add a spoonful of water from time to time because the fondue will be ruined if it starts to fry. The silky texture characteristic of a fondue is due to the emulsion made by the final traces of water and the fat.

You can do it with leeks, onion, carrot, celery or tomato (peeled and seeded). Herbs can be added as flavoring. Or use a combination, as is done when making **ratatouille.** Fondues like these are served with plain foods such as poached fish, poached chicken or omelette. A fondue of chopped shallots moistened with red wine is often served with red meat (for example, steak) in the Bordeaux area. If serving the fondue cold, use oil rather than fats that harden.

Fougasse: a flat oval loaf shaped to have holes. In Normandy it is sometimes made with eggs and butter. It may be flavored with cheese, orange or pieces of anchovy. I like the one with olive flavor. It can be eaten alone or with cheese. It dates back to the Middle Ages and mention of it can be found in Rabelais's *Gargantua*. Nowadays a Paris baker[12] makes a light flaky fougasse with a type of croissant dough from which yeast is omitted.

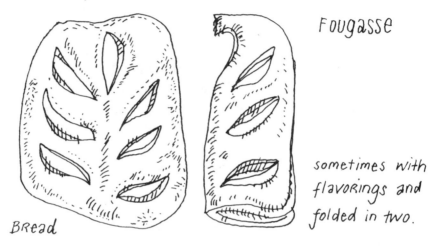

Fougasse

Bread

sometimes with flavorings and folded in two.

Four: oven. It was England's Industrial Revolution that made its cooking so different from that of its European neighbors. For the Industrial Revolution gave the British cheap cast-iron stoves and iron pots and pans too. In France the oven was something only seen in grand houses, pastry shops and restaurants. I lived in the Dordogne as a young man and not one of my neighbors had an oven. Their pot-roasts and stews cooked in pots buried in the embers of an open fire. Bread was bought from the baker. Even today in France there are few Sunday roasts or even home-made cakes. Britain, on the other hand, became a land of cakes and pies, home-made bread and roast beef.

But the oven has brought an end to true roasting: cooking in the dry radiated heat of an open fire. The heat of a small domestic oven is moist, steamy heat. If you are at a restaurant with a large open grill—there are many in France—you have a chance to taste what roasted food should be like. Restaurant ovens are becoming more and more complex; some will provide steam, dry heat or smoke at the touch of a switch. Thus a turkey could be started in steam, then crispened in dry heat and finally smoke treated.

Framboise: raspberry. They grow in cool damp woodland with adequate sun, which is why the ones I grow in Ireland are so delicious. Scotland too is noted for them. In France they grow best in high cold places with plenty of rain. My crop comes in July and the season is far too short. Freezing destroys almost everything I like about them, but a compote of mixed red fruit, including raspberries, freezes well.

Frangipane: pastry cream. It is like **crème pâtissière** but more elaborate, for it contains butter, sugar, eggs, flour, alcohol and ground almonds, or crushed macaroons. The resulting mixture is like a thick marzipan-flavored egg custard. It is used under a layer of fruit in a fruit tart, or as a filling in its own right. The remarkable **gâteau de Pithiviers** is a flaky pastry pie filled with such a cream to which a trace of rum has been added.

    When this cream is used in an open fruit tart the fruit is distributed so that the frangipane is well in evidence. The lovely **tarte de pommes à la Normande**—with sliced apples arranged like spokes, and half buried in the frangipane—is a notable example. In this case the frangipane contains Calvados, which gives the tart its name. Watching Jacques Pépin make a pear tart I noticed the frangipane in it had ground almonds that had been browned in the oven. This gave the resulting tart he calls **poires Bourdaloue** a lovely extra flavor. From then onwards I always toasted the almonds in my frangipane. Fruit tarts can, of course, be made without cream supporting the fruit, but in this case the tart must be eaten very soon after coming from the oven. For that reason restaurant cooks are less likely to use these pastry creams because restaurant food is made for immediate consumption. Pâtisseries (shops) do use them. Frangipane made without sugar and almonds is used as a rich stuffing for fish and poultry.

Frémir: to tremble or shiver. It's the way the chef describes the almost imperceptible movement of water that reveals the right temperature for poaching.

Fricassée. The French chef regards chicken skin as unpalatable unless the fat is removed from it. So when making a chicken stew he'll either remove the skin or he'll lightly sauté the chicken to melt the excess fat out of its skin. A stew for which the meat or poultry is first lightly fried is called a fricassée (and thus some chefs use the word fricassée to mean **fricassée de poulet**).

To continue, the fat in which the chicken (or meat) is cooked is discarded and the pan deglazed using a little wine. It is simmered in stock, and when done the liquid is thickened by the addition of cream and egg yolk. A **blanquette,** on the other hand, is a stew (often of lamb, mutton or veal) for which the meat has had a preliminary five minutes being poached in water. No frying.

Frites means only one thing: **pommes de terres frites.** These fried sticks of potato were invented in France (hence the name French fries). In Britain they are called chips. The wafer-thin slices of fried potato that are called crisps in Britain are called chips in America and France.

Friture is deep-frying. French chefs do not fry in the styles of the rest of Europe or America. In France there are two distinct methods. **Sauter** is to cook in a frying pan or skillet using very little fat (thus the food can be made to "jump" without splashing hot fat). In friture the food is completely immersed in fat.

For friture the food is coated with preparations that will prevent the food from escaping into, and so dirtying, the frying fat. These coatings are made from flour, beaten egg and breadcrumbs or various types of batter. When the sealed package is subjected to the sudden heat of the deep fat, two things happen: the outer crust cooks and caramelizes while the water inside the package turns to steam and cooks the contents. Excess steam is forced out of the package and rises through the hot fat in the shape of bubbles. The chef watches the fat and when the bubbling subsides gets ready to remove the food.

The same sort of process happens whenever food is subjected to the high temperatures of cooking in fat, even in sautéing. Whatever you are doing, the choice of what fat or oil to use is vitally important, not only because of its flavor but because of the very different burning temperatures.

Butter 278°F
Beef suet 356°F
Lard or chicken fat 392°F
Vegetable oil 480–520°F
Olive oil 554°F

These figures are theoretical and given for interest only. They are *burning points* and the chef should stay well away from them. Also remember that impurities are always present and these impurities will always have lower burning points than pure fat. Refined lard is more pure than any chicken fat and so the chicken fat burns more readily. Butter taken straight from a packet will burn more quickly than clarified butter.

In a professional kitchen, thermostats make sure the cooking oils stay below 400°F and most kitchens use frying oils that have been specially designed for deep-frying. They have additives such as stabilizers and antioxidants that give them "high smoking points" and prolong their life.

If you regularly deep-fry, it is well worth buying a thermostatically controlled electric fryer. In any case look for a stainless steel or chromium pan (some metals have a bad effect on the oil). If the oil foams or smokes it is spoiled. It is unhealthy to use it. Buy an oil that is suited to high-temperature frying and discard it as soon as its color darkens.

Fromage is cheese, mentioned on these pages from time to time but too fattening to tackle at length. In the mighty eighteenth-century *Encyclopédie,* **Roquefort** was declared Europe's greatest cheese, with **brie, maroilles** and **Gruyère** competing closely. Hard cheeses were less esteemed, being regarded as suited to the poor.

But the English had already staked their claim. Long before the *Encyclopédie,* Daniel Defoe, somewhere between *Moll Flanders* and *Robinson Crusoe,* declared Cheddar to be "the best cheese England affords if not that the whole world affords." It was fighting talk, and by 1973 France had started a *"fromage appellation d'origine contrôlée"* to certify which cheeses were made by traditional methods. Less than 20 percent of annual production was approved.

Fromage frais is fresh cheese, unfermented drained curds. It comes in varying creaminess. The plainest one, **fromage blanc,** was selected by Michael Guérard to mix with various vegetable purées to make a substitute for the classic cream sauces when he evolved his cuisine minceur. For those less dedicated to losing weight it is often served with cream and sugar as a dessert. It is delicious. A **fromagerie** is the shop where cheese and associated dairy products are sold. But those don't include **fromage de tête,** which is jellied veal or pork made from the flesh of the head of the animal (headcheese).

Fruits de mer: a convenient menu term that describes any seafood available. The plateau de fruits de mer that I am right now in the process of demolishing (*Chez Jacky* at Riec sur Bélon in Brittany) is formidable. I find crabs, **langoustines, écrevisses,** oysters (**plates** and **creuses**), clams (**amandes, verni** and **palourdes**), whelks (**bulots**), cockles (**coques**), and shrimps.

Fumet: a flavored liquid based on fish, meat or vegetables. The most common sort—**fumet de poisson**—is made from fish trimmings. Fumets may be used for poaching food (for example, a whole fish) but are usually made in stronger versions by reduction, as an ingredient for sauces.

My wife starts a fumet by sweating a chopped onion, a chopped carrot and three or four chopped mushrooms in olive oil. Then she adds fish, fish bones and trimmings. Fish heads are particularly good. (Some chefs warn that oily fish, such as salmon, are not suited for a fumet, but we frequently include salmon heads and trimmings and find the flavor excellent.) Add water and a big glass of dry white wine. You need at least 4½ pounds of fish to 1 quart of water. Bring to a boil and simmer for no longer than 30 minutes. Strain the liquid, discarding the bones and fish. Perhaps I should add that every cook has their own method. For instance, my wife considers mushrooms indispensable, while other people regard them as an optional extra.

Galantine is a cold meat or poultry preparation. Bone and skin a chicken. Inside it put a rich filling of pork and veal, adding sliced truffle, egg and breadcrumbs. Wrap the boned chicken around the filling and tie it securely. Poach it in stock (preferably stock in which a calf's foot has been cooked) for two hours so that the pork is cooked right through. Cool the chicken under a weight and clarify the jelly. The dish is served cold with the galantine set in the jelly or with the chopped jelly used as garnish. This galantine is a simple version of the sort of dish that Carême delighted in making. A galantine can be made from other meats—boned veal shoulder or flank—but it always has a rich stuffing. Fish can be used but rarely is. Galantines are always served cold. A **ballotine** is cooked in the same fashion from the same sort of meats or poultry, but it has no stuffing and can be served hot.

Galette: a large Breton crêpe made with buckwheat flour. Filled with anything from cheese to sardines, they make a perfect snack. The crêperies of Brittany have now spread throughout Europe and America too. The galette is thin: the heavy, eggless batter being distributed over the griddle by means of a wooden blade. This blade is one of the secrets of successful galette making; the other is to keep the batter thin enough to spread widely. If you don't do this, you'll never make them successfully. That splendid and sagacious lady Anne Willan says that the buckwheat ones are for savory fillings and wheat ones (using egg in the mixture) for sweet fillings. Spread with butter and rolled up they go well with coffee at breakfast, as I was shown in Brittany.

Galette des rois: cake of the kings, a rather dull bready cake containing a small (inedible) souvenir for one lucky diner. Add a little ceremony, which traditionally ends with someone buying wine. South of the Loire it comes complete with a crown. It is served on the evening of Epiphany or Twelfth Night (January 6), which is a big celebration in France. Never declining a chance to celebrate, it's an excuse for a special dinner in my home too.

Garbure. The bitter cold of the Pyrenees has provided the cuisine of that south-west corner of France with some robust dishes. None are more hearty than garbure, a thick garlicky soup with vegetables and sausages, pork and boiling fowl, or a piece of **confit,** according to what is available. Often it is served in a ritual that includes separating the broth from the meat, or making some of the pot's contents into a cheese-topped gratin.

Garçon or rather **garçon!** is what waiters are called in Hollywood films and strip cartoons. In real life customers usually say "**Monsieur**."

Garde manger: a larder or pantry, but also in the jargon of the restaurant the name given to the chef who is in charge of the staples, and of the refrigerators for meat, poultry and fish. In fact, he's in charge of the butchery too and sees to the hanging of the game, and the preparation of fish. As if that isn't enough, he's also responsible for all food that will be served cold.

Gaufre: waffle. The Belgians or the Dutch invented this item, which has been street food ever since streets existed. In case you've never had one, it's made from batter dropped into hot oil. Sometimes a metal mold is used. After a moment's frying they are drained and sprinkled with sugar.

Gelée: jelly. Clear jellied broth made by poaching collagen-rich protein such as calf's foot. It must not boil or the stock turns cloudy. Curiously, present-day professional chefs shy away from this process. A two-star chef, Jean Crotet, said his **terrine de pigeon en sa gelée à l'ancienne** was called ancienne because the jelly was made from calf's foot in the old-fashioned style.[13]

Potage Germiny is an unusual soup which combines lemon-flavored shredded sorrel with chicken broth, into which egg yolk and cream have been whisked. It was created by a chef named Duglère at the old *Café Anglais,* now long closed. Sorrel is more widely available than it used to be. Try it. It is one of my favorites.

Gibier: game, any wild animal that is edible and a few that are not. The French Revolution deprived aristocrats of the sole right to hunt and fish. This gave peasants a chance to eat meat and fish to an extent they'd not enjoyed previously. One could almost say that regional French cooking dates from this time. In contrast to the elaborate and delicate recipes of the court these country ways of cooking produced strong-tasting hearty dishes that suited the laborers in the fields. Nowadays more and more game animals are being bred for food. Such animals are not tough and muscular the way they are in the wild, so a new series of recipes is being evolved for them. In France and America game is more likely to be eaten fresher and rarer than it is in Britain. When the exponents of nouvelle cuisine listed the commandments of that perverse creed, one rule stated that game should not be hung. They were not of course referring to real wild game, much of which would be quite inedible if cooked fresh; they meant farmed game. Wild game served rare presents a real danger of parasites that can be passed to humans. Better to cook it right through.

Girardet, Fredy (1936–). It was Curnonsky who coined the expression **cuisine improvisée** when classifying styles of cooking. Fredy Girardet prefers **la cuisine spontanée** and so named his recipe book. Fredy Girardet learned cooking from his father, who owned a rather bleak mansion in a suburb of Lausanne, a mansion that has now become one of the most famous restaurants in the world. At one time Girardet was more interested in soccer than in cooking, but a client took him to Burgundy, where he discovered the pleasures of good wines. A generous vineyard owner—Jacques Parent—befriended him and took him to great restaurants such as *Bocuse* and *Troisgros*.

Girardet is said to have been inspired with "the revelation of modern cooking" during the weekends he spent in the *Troisgros* kitchens. From that time his life was changed. Unlike Bocuse, Vergé and Guérard—who scamper round the world, cooking and opening restaurants and being photographed—Girardet prefers to stay at home. He says a patron-chef's first duty is to his clients.

Girardet's restaurant is sometimes said to serve the finest food in the world. In fact "the finest food in Switzerland"—a more easily won accolade—would probably be nearer the truth. But Fredy Girardet's amazing success has brought many imitators and devotees and he has to be included in any short list of world-famous chefs.

Girolles. Because this mushroom is considered the finest flavored by so many chefs it merits a separate entry, but it is seldom distinguished in reference books. I am not an expert in the identification of mushrooms, but the delicious variety that the French call girolle would seem to be the *cantharellus cibarius*. This can be identified by its firm texture and solid stem. The more widely found, and somewhat similar, mushroom sold under the name of chanterelle is the *cantharellus infundibuliformis*, which is floppy in texture with hollow stems. (*See also* **champignon,** page 55.)

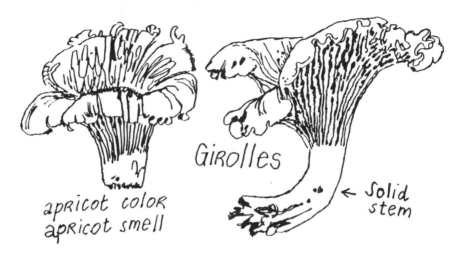

Girolles

apricot color
apricot smell

← Solid
stem

Glaçage means glaze, in the sense of chilling or freezing, but also browning under heat. It means coating with sauce or sugar, or covering cold food with jelly. Is that confusing enough? If not, here is another way of glazing. Take 2 pounds of carrots and cut them to about the same shape and size. (The professional cook would make them into exactly the same shape and size.) Boil them in a pint or so of stock, to which has been added a scant tablespoonful of sugar and 4 scant tablespoonsful of butter. Leave the pot uncovered so that by the time the carrots are cooked the stock has boiled down to a brown sticky gunk. Roll the carrots in the gunk and serve. When I worked in a kitchen this was called **carottes Vichy,** but now Vichy water salesmen seem to have persuaded cookbook writers and chefs to use Vichy water instead. My delicious carottes are now relegated to **carottes glacées.** Try both. Don't be disappointed if you don't get it exactly right first time. In a kitchen the chefs get to know the right proportion of vegetable to stock. The same recipe can be applied to turnips or onions, and so on.

Gnocchi. Essentially Italian, or perhaps Austro-Hungarian, these heavy dumplings—some made from choux pastry, some from semolina and some from potato—are eaten in the region around Nice. They are not very flavorful so they need a generous sprinkling of freshly grated nutmeg. Usually the dumplings are laid out in a dish, covered with cheese and then baked or grilled. In my home they come with a good rich tomato sauce.

Goujon: gudgeon, a small freshwater fish fried whole in the way English whitebait are served. Other tiny fish cooked in this style—floured and deep-fried—are called **friture.** Larger fish cut into strips the size of gudgeons are served as **goujonnettes.** All such dishes are served as a pre-dinner snack with apértifs, but I think these fried fish are too assertive and too filling for that.

Gras double. In France, where tripe is highly esteemed, this fatty outer layer of ox stomach is sold separately from the rest. However, veal tripe is the finest and honeycomb tripe the best part. For poetic names the egged, breadcrumbed and fried section of tripe that is called **tablier de sapeur** (sapper's or fireman's apron) takes a lot of beating, but we tripe eaters are poets deep down.

Most tripe is prepared and pre-cooked before the butcher sells it, but dishes such as **tripes à la mode de Caen** (a rich combination of tripe and calf's foot with vegetables, cider and Calvados) will still need another 10 hours on the stove. If you are in a hurry, tripe from a can is not too bad.

Gratin. This word is related to the English word "grate" and can mean to scratch and scrape. It's used to describe those delicious final crusty mouthfuls that are scraped by the greedy from the sides of a dish of baked food. So on the menu a gratin means a grilled combination dish that has been cooked to form a crust. This is often obtained by a top layer of breadcrumbs or grated cheese. Some chefs sprinkle crumbs inside the greased dish too. This makes it more crusty. I was taught that any true gratin can be cooked in a pastry case to make a quiche.

Grenouille: the mess funds or the club money, so *manger là grenouille* means to run off with the cash. It also means to eat frogs. Frogs, or at least their legs, are considered good eating in France, as they are in many parts of the world, including America. They are said to taste like fishy chicken, and they do, which is why I don't care for them. Most frogs' legs eaten in France come from the Far East. Vietnam is a major supplier.

Grive: thrush. Until very recently, this little bird was widely eaten throughout France. It was a favorite ingredient of terrines. Now the trapping of thrushes has been made unlawful. And a good thing too. I've eaten thrushes from time to time but prefer them sitting in the trees and singing.

Groseille à maquereau is a sharp-tasting berry well suited to contrast with the oily taste of mackerel. In England it was found to be a good counter to the rich fatty taste of the goose. So we call it a gooseberry.

Gruyère is a beautiful village in Fribourg, Switzerland. I know because when I swapped houses with some old friends, we found ourselves living close by and enjoying the local Swiss cheeses including Swiss Emmental, which comes from the Emme valley near Berne. But Gruyère is a word used to describe three French cheeses too (as agreed by the Stresa Convention in 1951). These include **Comté** (pale yellow with holes), the **Beaufort** (softer and virtually without holes) and the **Emmental** (darker yellow color with larger holes). These cheeses became famous hundreds of years ago because they kept for very long periods without deterioration; but to achieve this they used a great deal of milk. Nowadays although I find their nutty taste is delicious with nothing more than a piece of bread and a glass of wine, these cheeses are often used for cooking. Elizabeth David says, "All types of genuine Gruyère cheese should be cut into little pieces for cooking, never on any account grated, a procedure which causes it to form sticky masses rather than the long creamy threads."[14]

Guérard, Michel (1933–) says he set out wanting to be a priest or at least an actor. Nowadays he is well known for his practical jokes and his wife says he should have been a comic. But he has become one of the most famous chefs in the world. He acknowledges a debt to Escoffier and is one of the few modern chefs who has worked in great hotels and restaurants (*Maxim's, Lucas-Carton,* the *Meurice* and the *Crillon*) and for a private family too.

When he began his own restaurant in Paris he soon got two stars. But a road was built through the restaurant and his next job was cooking at a "hydro" (a place offering sulfurous baths and mineral water health cures) at Eugénie-les-Bains in south-west France. It was a challenge for any chef but he met that challenge. He transformed the hydro, married the owner's daughter and found enough time to invent cuisine minceur, in which fat and flour is replaced with skill and imagination so that the gourmet can eat, bathe and diet too. Now at his hotel *Les Prés et les Sources d'Eugénie* the diner is faced with two menus: *"La Carte Gourmande"* with its local foie gras and **la Marquise au chocolat,** and the menu headed *"La Dinette d'Eugénie,"* with its dietetic food about which I know nothing.

Guide. The most famous guide to eating in France's restaurants is the *Guide Michelin* published by the rubber tire company. It is a miracle of quantity. Well over a thousand thin pages provide detailed descriptions of hotels and restaurants, and use symbols to help the non-French-speaking traveler. As a way of discovering which hotels on your route have a lock-up garage, direct dial phones, love dogs and take your favorite plastic in payment, the Michelin is incomparable. It is their system of awarding stars for the quality of food and cooking that attracts criticism. One star for very good cooking, two if it's worth a detour and three stars for places worth a journey. (Their words; not mine.)

Certainly far too many stars are awarded. Some three-star establishments are mediocre in every way but keep their top rating year after year. Many of the one-star restaurants are amateurishly run places, open only for dinner on certain days of the week, and closed for months in winter. Waverley Root, the scholar gourmet whose book *The Food of France* required him to journey the length and breadth of the country, said, "The only two completely inedible meals I have ever had in France were both in restaurants to which Michelin had given a star."

At one time the *Guide Kléber*—sponsored by the Kléber tire company—was my preferred choice, but Michelin bought Kléber and killed the rival guidebook. Since then the editor has started another rival, *Bottin gourmand*. The alternative is Gault and Millau's annual *Guide Gourmand de la France*, which concentrates on food rather than sleeping accommodations. Gault and Millau invented the notion of nouvelle cuisine and their inspectors are unswervingly dedicated to chefs who serve it, which lessens the guide's value to me, since I don't want all my food arranged on plates by someone in the kitchen who doesn't care if I like gravy. On the other hand the Gault-Millau guide explains in simple French what they like and don't like about each place.

Relais & Châteaux is a full-color annual guide to the best hotels and restaurants. Primarily French establishments, but recently it has become worldwide. Get one from Relais & Châteaux, Hôtel de Crillon, 10 place de la Concorde, 75008, Paris, France.

Logis and Auberges of France is available free from your nearest French Government Tourist Office. It lists over four thousand family-run country hotels.

Guide des Relais Routiers is a listing of the favorite eating places of truck drivers. Such places display the blue and red *routiers* sign. You seldom go far wrong at such a place—French truck drivers are discriminating—and the portions are man-sized. Sometimes you'll get a meal that is truly memorable by any standards. And there's always somewhere to park your car!

Haeberlin, Paul (1923–), working with his son Marc, is the chef at the famous *L'Auberge de L'Ill* at Illhaeusern, Alsace. Together with his younger brother, Jean-Pierre Haeberlin, he owns this three-star riverside restaurant very near the German frontier. It is a mecca for German visitors, many of whom book weeks in advance and then come racing hundreds of miles down the *Autobahnen* to squeeze into the crowded dining-room and hurriedly consume just one meal here. For a German who wants to taste French haute cuisine this restaurant provides a perfect opportunity to eat well in a beautiful setting. But anyone who takes the trouble to explore this fascinating region of France, where so many restaurants offer cooking that is superb, hearty and authentically regional, might find food that is more robust and exciting.

Haricots: beans. These are seeds. They range from the green **fèves** (favas in America)—my earliest crop and particularly good if eaten when tiny—to small white haricots and **soissons.** Freshly picked they are sometimes served uncooked as **crudités** along with such things as raw carrots, cucumbers and spring onions.

The bean has often proved one of the peasant's last bulwarks against starvation. In India and Japan at times when rice was a luxury, the growers of rice sold it and themselves had to make do with millet or beans. In European winters, the potato—not easy to store even today—was a delicious escape from the eternal bean. In bleak regions such as Brittany, where wheat does not prosper, the bean is widely found. (Brittany's best-known dish is not one made from oysters, lobster, shrimps or cod but the **gigot aux haricots à la bretonne,** braised mutton with beans.) Little wonder then that the man who had absolutely nothing at all "didn't have a bean."

Incomparably best when used fresh, beans can be dried for storage. They are best kept hung up in their pods in a dry place. Some gardeners prefer to spread them out to dry, but in damp air they readily turn moldy unless artificial heat is used. Stored, they get harder month by month. In France the cook is likely to ask how old the beans are before buying them. In any case dried beans need soaking before use. Escoffier pointed out that beans should never be soaked for longer than three hours because after that there was a risk that germination would spoil the flavor.

Beans are used in winter dishes traditionally cooked with fatty meats such as pork and goose. They are found in regions where pork lard is the favored cooking fat (rather than butter or oil); for instance, Alsace, Lorraine and the cold Massif Central, where solid winter meals are needed. In these combination dishes, the beans make up the final top layer. During the cooking process the liquid level should be constantly added to keep it at the same level as the beans. In this way you can ensure that the beans absorb the layer of fat that rises to the surface. Other dishes in other lands use sliced potato to absorb the fat in the same way. It is this layer of fatty vegetable that browns during the final part of the cooking time. Since scorched beans are not to everyone's taste, it is usual to cover the top of such bean dishes with a layer of breadcrumbs.

Haricots verts: French beans, string beans, snap beans. A green bean grown to be eaten together with its edible pod. For that reason this is the vegetable the French mean when they say **mange tout.** Although these lovely little vegetables are the same species as the huge green beans that have to be "strung" and sliced up to be eaten, there is really no comparison. The real haricots verts must be picked while still small and thin, and must be cooked lightly. In France they are usually cooked in fast boiling water until they are almost done. Then they are drained, rinsed and plunged into enough ice and water to cool them instantly. When cooled they are drained and put aside until needed. For serving they are warmed quickly in a little butter.

Homard: lobster. The meat of the clawed lobster is sweeter than that of the **langouste** (clawless lobster), but the meat content is less than that in the equivalent weight of *langouste* because of the heavy shell of the lobster's claws. Enthusiasts for **langouste** say the meat is softer and more easily digested. I agree. All shellfish may seem expensive but one must take into account the time they take to grow. A lobster can take anything up to five years to reach a length of five inches. A really big lobster might be forty or fifty years old.

Unlike the langouste and crab, the homard is really good to eat only if it's cooked soon after being killed. My friend who runs the *vivier* in Mougins near Grasse,[15] a remarkable expert on shellfish, says the lobster "drains" after it is killed and the flavor and texture deteriorate quickly. He says a freshly killed lobster is best split in half and grilled, but not overcooked, and served with melted butter. He cooks them over the gray ashes of an olive tree wood barbecue, having dotted them with butter and tarragon. Eating there is a memorable experience.

A **demoiselle** is a small species of lobster found on France's northern coast, particularly the region of the Cherbourg peninsula.

Hors d'oeuvres: a selection of small appetizing dishes. A fine example in my notebook was one served to me at the noted *Auberge Jeanne de Laval* at Les Rosiers-sur-Loire: **les champignons à la grecque; la salade de champignons frais; la salade russe; la terrine aux foies blonds de volaille avec pistaches; les rillettes de la maison; les**

crevettes; les filets de sole farcis avec mousseline (sole fillets stuffed, sliced and served cold in vinaigrette), and **les petits oignons à l'Escoffier.** *See also* **Amuse-gueules,** page 9.

Huile: oil. If you usually go into a shop and buy any bottle of oil that takes your eye, perhaps it's time to change. There are dozens of different types of oil, and then hundreds of brands of each. Once you decide what you want, it will be much cheaper to buy a gallon can of it. If you want high-quality oil it will be worthwhile to seek out a specialist shop. For low cholesterol diets, oils such as sunflower, safflower, soybean, cottonseed, corn or sesame are all recommended.

Butter and other animal fats are bad for people who should have low cholesterol diets. For such diets olive oil and peanut (**arachide**) oil and most nut oils (with the notable exception of coconut oil) are in the medium category.

Olive oils come in a wide range of prices and flavors. Walnut oil is sometimes said to be the most delicious. It is very expensive—use it just for salads—and it turns rancid even more quickly than olive oil. All oil is best kept in a cool dark place. Walnut and hazelnut oil contain no wax and should always be kept in the refrigerator.

Huître: oyster. Cultivated oysters are conveniently divided into two basic kinds: the true oyster (**plate** or flat) and the craggy-looking Portuguese oyster (**creuse** or hollow), which are hardier, grow more quickly and are considered marginally inferior in flavor. For some visitors to France confusion comes from the way that both types are frequently named from the place where they are fattened. The ideal fattening beds provide slightly brackish water at a river mouth where a mixture of fresh water and sea water fattens the oyster's liver and makes it desirable to the gourmet. It is its liver which swells to make the oyster bigger and more flavorful, and this final finishing process that decides the flavor and quality of the oyster.

Take, for instance, **Arcachonnaises**, which are Portuguese (**Portugaises**) in type, and might have originated anywhere, but have been finished in the Arcachon Bay near Bordeaux in south-west France where, the story goes, a ship loaded with live oysters foundered and started the beds. **Bélons** are usually "flats" and are widely regarded as the finest oysters France produces. Finished in the River Bélon in Finistère on the Atlantic coast of Brittany, they become pink in color. But go to the Riac sur Bélon, a tiny place on the Bélon River, and eat *Chez Jacky,* one of the wonderful little places where they haul your lunch from the oyster tanks, and you'll find that Bélon oysters can be **Huîtres creuses de Bélon** or **Huîtres plates de Bélon** at three or four times the price. **Cancale,** on Brittany's plankton-rich Channel coast, provides one of the most famous names in the history of France's oyster beds. When you buy flats in Cancale they are labeled **plein mer** and get their taste from the open sea.

Oysters called **Marennes** come from the Vendée near Rochefort and are sometimes green and sometimes gray. **Vertes** (greens) are cherished because they are fattened in algae-rich ditches called **claires** and this provides their green color. **Bouziques** are a Portuguese type finished in Sète in the south. The warmer climate makes a difference but there is no agreement about whether the colder water improves flavor. My taste is for oysters (and crabs and lobsters too) taken from the colder waters.

In Brittany the flats are like English oysters *(Ostrea edullis)* in the way that they turn milky in appearance during the breeding season (May until early August) and are less good to eat, although I don't notice any lessening in the rate at which the French devour them. Portuguese—like American oysters—can be eaten all year round but vary in quality season by season. Oysters are graded by weight from number 11, the largest (100 weigh a little over 24 pounds), to number 4 (100 weigh almost 9 pounds).

Oysters need no cooking, no vinaigrette dressing, no lemon juice and certainly no Tabasco. They can be eaten directly from the sea and represent no hazard unless the water is polluted. Unfortunately almost all Europe's coastal waters are polluted, so it's advisable to get your oysters from a reputable dealer who will have ensured that they have been fed clean water. Oysters are vulnerable to diseases which spread quickly so that the beds sometimes have to be relaid with new ones. French beds have used English "natives" and English beds in Essex and Cornwall have been restocked with Bretons. In 1970 a parasitic disease killed every oyster in the Arcachon basin, and Pacific oysters *(crassotrea gigas)* were crossed with oysters from Charente and Brittany to restock the beds. But the new environment soon changed the texture and flavor of the visitors.

Hygiène: hygiene. The cook's responsibility for the well-being of the diner must be taken seriously both in restaurant and home. Clean hands, short nails, no rings or wristwatches, hair tucked into hat; all this should be routine in any kitchen. Hands should be washed, so should most food, although I don't rinse fresh fish unless it's to be eaten raw. Poultry must be rinsed inside and out. Vegetables and fruit often bear traces of chemical sprays if not rinsed under the tap.

Nowadays all wooden chopping surfaces and even wooden knife handles are being phased out in favor of plastics, which do not harbor bacteria.

Ile de France: the region round Paris. It is associated with the court and therefore with haute cuisine. Many regional dishes were only discovered when taken to Paris and this is echoed in the names they were given.

Île flottante: floating island. A dessert, a large "dumpling" of beaten egg white lightly cooked. It is floated on a sea of **crème à l'anglaise,** a rather rich, vanilla-flavored egg custard. The île flottante is usually garnished with a topping of toasted almonds and dribbled threads of caramel toffee. If the egg white is made into separate "islands," one per person, the same combination is called **oeufs à la neige** (eggs in snow). It is well suited to being made in individual portions. Tumblers or brandy glasses make suitable containers for each. In any case this is a dish that must be consumed soon after being made. A few hours to cool is enough. But make it the day before and your "islands" will have become dry and rubbery.

Until the 1930s, the name île flottante was given to a different dish. It was a sort of sponge cake filled with apricot jam, almonds and currants. Around this "island" a sea of egg custard or sometimes freshly crushed strawberries or raspberries was poured immediately before serving or at table-side.

Jambon: ham. In general it is fair to say that French hams are not outstanding when compared to the fine hams from Britain, Italy, Belgium, Germany and Spain. And anyone who has seen the mad scramble for such products when a bus load of French trippers are leaving Belgium knows that the French agree. The best French hams are the **Bayonne,** from Orthez near Bayonne. These hams are lightly smoked and served raw. The **Toulouse** hams are unsmoked. They can be eaten raw or cooked. They are often used in cooking. In France the word **York** is applied to anything they think might be somewhat in the English style. Don't expect too much of it; it will be good enough for a **croque monsieur.**

Jarret: knuckle, the lower section of the rear leg of pig or calf.

Juliennes are vegetable sticks of certain fixed dimensions. Unfortunately no one knows what those dimensions are. Challenged with this conundrum, a smooth-talking old chef I worked under said that it didn't matter very much as long as they were all consistent in size. He was right, of course. The important thing is that such prepared vegetables all cook evenly. In a professional kitchen the vegetables will be cut on a mandoline, a slicing machine that can cut sticks or slices (or fingers!).

julienne

Jus: juice. If meat or poultry produces in the cooking pan a wonderful brown flavorful juice, it means your roast is left dry and tasteless. So cook to retain the juices inside the meat. Make gravy separately using stock or, better still, **glace de viande.**

Kir: an apéritif made from dry white wine with enough **crème de cassis** (a sweet alcoholic blackcurrant liquor) in it to color it light pink. It originated in Dijon where most cassis is made, and took its name from a former mayor of the town. The best kir I ever had was undoubtedly the one served at the *Tour de Roy,* Vervins. We arrived for lunch on July 14 (Bastille Day) without having booked a table. The dining-room was packed, but we were greeted with smiles, a table was found. The menus arrived promptly and when we ordered a kir the waiter brought a chilled half bottle of white wine and mixed the drink at the table. In all the fancy restaurants and hotels I've been in before and since I've never seen a kir served with such style. The meal was perfect too. It included a specialty of the chef (Madame Desvignes— for here works one of France's best-known woman chefs)—**pêches rôties liqueur de cassis;** peaches cooked in cassis.

Kromeskies, also spelled **cromesquis,** can be any kind of cooked vegetable, poultry or meat, dipped into batter and deep-fried. Leftover vegetables can be used up like this, but one of the most dramatic examples must be the **cromesquis de foie gras en serviette** served as a first course at Marc Meneau's *Espérance* restaurant at Vézelay. Kromeskies are made of the same sort of things that go into **croquettes,** but the latter are usually coated in egg and breadcrumbs before frying. The filling for kromeskies and croquettes is called **salpicon.**

Lait: milk. In the final decades of the nineteenth century cooling and refrigeration made fresh, clean, wholesome, flavorful milk available to the whole population of the Western world except France. Many visitors to France celebrate their return home by pouring themselves a glass of good milk. Unless you live on a farm, good milk is virtually unobtainable in France; the French dairy industry is interested in cheese and butter. Many Frenchmen put no milk in tea or coffee and France has never been noted for its desserts. Milk in France is poor thin stuff that goes sour soon after purchase (perhaps because it's not properly chilled in transit), which is why French housewives buy tasteless UHT milk or sterilized milk, **lait sterilisé** (which is probably the best stuff in the circumstances). This low-quality milk is reflected in the lack of variety on the dessert menus of France's restaurants and explains the immediate success that commercial yogurt sales have shown in France.

Lamproie: lamprey. This name covers many species of freshwater and migratory fish-like vertebrates. These eel-like fishes have been a delicacy for many years. They have far less fat than eels (12 per cent compared with 26 per cent) and when they swim up the Gironde in spring they are enthusiastically caught by local people who make them into **lamproie à la bordelaise,** which restaurants have on their menus from April to September. The description à la bordelaise means just about anything any chef chooses it to mean.

Langouste is a clawless lobster. (Also called spiny lobster, rock lobster or crawfish.) This crustacean is found in the warmer coastal waters of the Pacific and Caribbean as well as the Mediterranean. It is much esteemed in France, where it is more easily obtained than the **homard** (lobster), which flourishes in colder northern waters. But the most notable biological difference between the two creatures is that the langouste is a migratory creature that moves vast distances over the ocean floor. This is why the langouste cannot be farmed in the way the homard is farmed.

Most of the langoustes served in French restaurants are the "Cape langouste," a South African species, but the finest flavored is the **langouste royale,** which is identified by two rows of white spots along the tail. If given the choice take a female with coral; the meat is sweeter. Allow at least a 2 pound langouste for two people. The meat of the langouste comes only from the tail.

Langoustine (a salt-water crayfish sometimes called a Dublin Bay prawn or scampi) is found in the Mediterranean and the eastern part of the Atlantic. It is long and slender and pale pink in color. Many of those served in restaurants are from frozen packs which have little flavor unless it comes from the sauce poured over them.

Languedoc. A region where the cooking is hearty and delicious, its history and folklore long and colorful. Unfortunately no one seems to know exactly where it is.

Lapin: rabbit. Rabbit should never be hung or the meat turns blue and looks awful. It has always been food for the poor man (while hare has often been rich man's fare). Because poor French peasants never had ovens, the rabbit dishes are mostly stews, but rabbit is tender enough to roast. Too many recipes are designed to make it taste like chicken. Better that rabbit is allowed its own fine flavor. (Less than a week after writing that entry in my notebook I found myself eating M. Maximin's cuisine at the *Chantecler* restaurant in Nice. I had boned, rolled rabbit stuffed with kidney and wild mushrooms. It was excellent.)

Lard: bacon. In France this is limited in variety but of good quality. **Lard maîgre** is bacon-like slices of pork belly (**poitrine**), chunks of which are used for flavoring soups and stews. What we call lard (refined pork fat) is called **saindoux** in France. Larding is the process of inserting strips of pork loin fat into meat that would otherwise become too dry when cooking. This loin fat is taken from near the skin of the pig; fat from the lean meat side is called "melting fat."

Lentilles: lentils, small legumes. These have a very high protein content (perhaps higher than any other vegetable). The tiny green whole lentils—**lentilles vertes du Puy**—are especially good. They are not suited for making into a purée; they are served whole as a vegetable, sometimes in elaborate sauces.

Liebig, Baron Justus von (1803–73). A German chemist whose experiments and discoveries made fundamental contributions to Victorian progress. Unfortunately his book *Researches on the Chemistry of Food* (English trans., 1847) started myths and errors that burden and hinder most present-day chefs. For instance, Liebig told his readers that juices (and therefore flavor) could be sealed inside pieces of meat by cooking the outside, as it "forms a crust or shell." Most cooks, and cookbook writers, from Eliza Acton to Fannie Farmer and even Escoffier in *Guide Culinaire* (1902), kept repeating this nonsense. The truth is that careful modern experiments have shown that meat cooked unseared loses less juice and flavor. Brown the outer surface if you want to. It will caramelize the sugars, and give an attractive color, but it won't seal juices or anything else into meat.

Lièvre: hare. During the Second World War Britain's housewives could get rabbit and hare without ration coupons. But after the war there was a reaction and these foods never became popular again. Even jugged hare—previously a delicacy—was shunned. In America such items are not regarded as food at all. But the hare remains a favorite in France and Germany. The saddle—**râble de lièvre**—and hind legs are the choicest parts. They can be marinated in red wine and/or cooked with blood to make a rich sauce. From the inquiries I made for the benefit of this book I found that many chefs who liked hare advised cooking it while it was still fresh. It is strong-tasting meat, they said; don't hang it. Those who voted in favor of hanging said it improved the flavor and it was necessary to collect the blood. Either way this rather tough animal is best used in stews or in terrines. If you want to eat it roasted you are better advised to get a young hare—**levraut**—which is one year old and weighs about 5 pounds.

Limousine: a style of cooking from Limousin in Central France. This former province, with Limoges as its capital, marked the northern edge of the langue d'oc speaking region. This is a mysterious place of windswept rocky plateaux and deep gloomy gorges. Expect food suited to such chilly places. Special favorites include red cabbage and chestnuts and, if you're there at the right time, wild mushrooms.

Lyonnaise, à la: in the manner of Lyon. On a menu this might simply mean with onions, but when you go there, expect the heavy winter food with pork products predominating. **Saucisson de Lyons** is a large salted pork sausage that is sold ready cooked. It is served (after simmering in water for about twenty minutes) with **lentilles vertes.**

Other local specialties include (flour-based) **quenelles,** such pork products as the rather chewy **oreille de porc** (pig's ear egged, breadcrumbed and grilled), **pied de porc** often with **beurre blanc,** which is far too rich in my opinion to accompany the fatty pig foot, or **tête de veau ravigote, andouillette à la moutarde** and **boudin noir aux pommes.** Tripe dishes, such as **gras-double eminc**é and **tablier de sapeur** (literally, "fireman's apron," but with other meanings too) are marinated, then egged, breadcrumbed and grilled. They are found in many parts of France but Lyons claims them as a local delicacy and they are readily available in the town's restaurants.

Macédoine: a mixture of fruits or vegetables hot or cold. Typically a large bowl of peeled sliced peaches and pears, or a mixture of red fruit—raspberries, strawberries, blackberries and red currants—to which just enough **sirop** (sugar dissolved in water) has been added. Put **kirsch** or some other such **eau de vie** in at the last moment. Serve chilled.

A proper vegetable **macédoine** is always made from small flavorful spring vegetables. Typically it would include small steamed new potatoes, steamed baby carrots and a handful of garden peas. Generous butter and chopped parsley are stirred in before serving.

If it's to be served cold, don't use butter; put oil and vinegar on the hot vegetables. Let it cool to room temperature (don't chill it). Cream or mayonnaise can also be used for the cold version.

When a mixture of such vegetables is used to decorate a meat or poultry dish the result is called **à la jardinière.**

Mâche is also called **doucette,** lamb's lettuce, lamb's tongue or corn salad according to where it grows. It is a small dark-leaf salad green that has long been popular in France and Switzerland and is now becoming more and more grown and used in Britain and America. It is useful for those of us who live in northern climates because it provides a winter salad. I've even pulled it out from under the snow at Christmas.

It was the new generation of chefs, looking for fresh, natural, local ingredients, who brought this homely salad into use for three-

Mâche

star meals. *Maxim's* in Paris made a specialty of a salad of mâche with beets. At his restaurant *Pic* in Valence, Jacques Pic makes his **salade de pêcheurs** from a bed of mâche upon which are heaped pieces of lobster, crayfish, shrimp, scallops and truffles.

Maître d'hôtel (sometimes shortened to **maître d'**) was originally a major-domo, a man in charge of the running of a big household. The term is still used in this way about the steward of grand establishments, but of course there are not many of them still in existence, so nowadays this word describes a head waiter (but it can mean proprietor too). **Maître de chai** is the man in charge of the vineyards. It is also the name given to the waiter who opens the wines and pours them. The man in charge of the restaurant cellars is called the **caviste. Beurre maître d'hôtel** is one of the least interesting **beurres composés** (*see* page 24), but an **entrecôte maître d'hôtel** is a steak served in a rich red-wine sauce.

Manche de gigot. A manche is a handle, and this is the bone used as a handle when carving a leg of lamb. **Manche à gigot** is a real handle which is fixed to the bone of a leg of lamb or mutton so that the carver can keep a firm grip on the meat. The ones I've seen have all been antique and most of them were made of silver. It is a useful device but can only be fixed to shank bone which has been bared, as is the style in French butchery. Since for my family the meat from the shank is everyone's favorite tidbit, the manche à gigot would not be welcomed in my home.

Mandoline: a slicing machine found in the kitchen of virtually every restaurant in France. I have never really mastered the technique of using the mandoline. I have purchased several of them, each time believing that some variation on the design will make a difference. I even bought a vast stainless steel affair at great expense, but the only one I use regularly is a small German one made of tin and plastic.

If you want to buy a mandoline, ask to see a demonstration before you make up your mind. And buy one that's easy to clean and—unless you are a trained chef—buy one with a finger guard and use it.

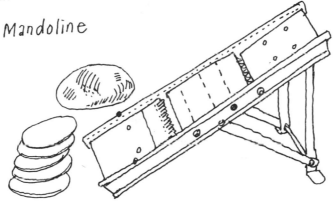

Mandoline

Marc: the residue of skins, seeds and pulp that is left over from the wine press. Distilled, this marc is made into a lovely drink also called marc. I was lucky enough to be invited to a tasting of **alcool blancs** and marc was included (although strictly speaking it probably shouldn't have been). I was interested to notice that all the professionals who work with these spirits preferred the marc to any of the other fruit schnapps such as the fragrant **mirabelle** and **poire.** Not long ago the Burgundy marc was the only one I ever encountered, but now marcs from other wine-producing areas—Champagne and Alsace—are widely sold. The enthusiastic PR men say that because of the way they are made, the better quality marcs are all free of the congerics that cause hangovers. A good try, chaps!

Marcassin. Wild boar less than six months old is a favorite winter dish. (Wild boar under three months old must not be hunted.) Its strongly flavored meat is usually prepared with red wine, and sweet fruits such as apples, pears and quinces and dried fruit too. *Chez Denis,* Paris, which Egon Ronay and I both remember as a gourmet mecca of the 1960s, made a reputation from such wonderful dishes. My neighbors in France resolutely hunt adult boars, **sanglier,** but I don't remember eating any. Could I have discovered a creature the French regard as inedible? Surely not?

Marché: a market, which in France is likely to be a real open-air market, rather than an air-conditioned supermarket. It is a myth that the chefs of great restaurants go each morning to the markets to choose their fish, meat, fruit and vegetables. Claude Terrail, proprietor of *La Tour d'Argent*—the most famous restaurant in Paris—said he personally prefers specialized suppliers to the hurly-burly of the street market, where there is a danger of getting carried away by a passing whim or the sales patter of the stallholders. The idea was also given short shrift by Nico Ladenis, restaurateur extraordinary and proprietor chef of *Simply Nico,* London, when he said:

> I am also asked repeatedly whether I grow my own herbs and vegetables. Unfortunately, the stories and the photographs of great chefs in cloth caps and heavy jackets braving the cold weather of winter mornings is more a practice set up for the camera and for the cookbook than an everyday reality. I do not go to the markets in the early hours of the morning and I do not grow my own herbs and vegetables. If I did, I would have very little time to run my kitchen and my restaurant. I would rather leave the task to my greengrocer and to the various growers. Just as my greengrocer doesn't presume to break into my world of cooking, I do not intend to spend my time buying ingredients in the early hours and tilling the land to grow herbs.[16]

But perhaps I should point out that Mr. Ladenis is also on record as saying that if he had a market like Paris's Rungis market within easy reach, he might be tempted to go more often. In practice the great restaurants and hotels have agents. Such agents have permanent offices in the fruit, vegetable, meat and fish markets and are expected to check the quality of the produce day by day. As well as this, hotels, which buy in bulk, often have longer-term contracts with wholesalers and sometimes with specialized suppliers of such things as smoked products, poultry, farmed fish or luxury foods such as caviar and foie gras. Big restaurants have more than one supplier of each commodity. One chef I know has deliveries of fish from five different suppliers every day. In this way the price and quality of the food is constantly compared and monitored.

In most well-run restaurants the footstuffs are weighed and checked for quality as they are delivered to the kitchen. Items not good enough, or not fresh enough, are rejected. A restaurant needs careful monitoring of purchases if it's to serve high-quality food without costly waste. So when you are buying food, be as fusssy as the great chefs. You do have time to go to the market, buy only the best and freshest items, and buy only enough for your immediate needs.

Margarine. In the nineteenth century the use of lubricants by Europe's expanding industries, to say nothing of the wider use of soap, created a shortage of fats and oils. Napoleon III offered a prize for the invention of a synthetic edible fat. Nowadays—when margarine is eaten because it is a healthy vegetable food—it is surprising to find that the prize-winning result was made from animal fat (suet) and milk.

Modern margarine is made from vegetable oils such as corn and soy. Some brands are labeled "high in polyunsaturates," which is recommended for lowering cholesterol levels, and virtually all have vitamins A and D added to them. But that doesn't mean to say that margarine is good for you or even safe to eat. Margarine is constructed in a laboratory and considerable doubts still exist about some of those "antioxidants," and "emulsifiers." If you have a slice of fresh home-made whole-grain bread, do you want margarine on it? If butter is too fattening for you, then so is bread. Anyway what's wrong with eating it dry? For cooking, use olive oil or butter whenever possible because margarine has poor flavor, especially when heated. (Warm some in a pan and sniff at it, if you don't believe me.) Margarine, like pasteurization and homogenization, is a French invention.

Marjolaine: the herb that we call sweet marjoram (*see* **origan,** page 146). But a marjolaine is also one of France's most famous cakes. It was invented by Fernand Point at his *Restaurant de la Pyramide* at Vienne. It is a very rich layer cake composed of different "butter creams." One layer is made from compounded butter, vanilla and cream. A second layer is made from chocolate. A third layer is praline cream. The three layers are separated by four layers of "cake," which are made from finely ground almonds and hazelnuts mixed with egg white and cooked.

Point's apprentice chefs took this recipe and adapted it to their own ideas, so that now the marjolaine is found in many restaurants. Outhier at his *L'Oasis* used to prepare a **marjolaine à l'orange.** The late François Bise spent three years with Point and his version even outdid the original by adding eau de vie to the vanilla, by making it richer and including a very bitter chocolate. I have tasted them all but I have a special affection for the Bise marjolaine because back in the 1950s I was in Talloires and could not afford a meal in the great *Auberge du Père Bise* restaurant. I went there in the afternoon and had tea and a slice of the famous marjolaine. It was a good compromise.

Matelote. Fish stews are usually delicate and have to be lightly cooked, but some fish, eel and pike, for example, can be cooked in wine. Such a fish stew using wine is called a matelote. It seems it was first used with river fish in the Île de France region, but the catch of the northern coast, and a surfeit of cider and cream, brought a **matelote à la normande**, which is a sea-fish version.

Maximin, Jacques (1949–). Maximin was born in the Pas de Calais, where his parents had a café tabac restaurant in Rang-du-Flier. He started his apprenticeship at the age of fourteen and moved on to Monte Carlo and to Paris. He worked with Roger Vergé at the famous *Moulin de Mougins* restaurant at a time when Vergé was at the height of his career, when the Moulin was serving food as good as any in France. From there in 1975 Maximin went to the old *Bonne Auberge* nearby in Antibes. And that restaurant too was to peak about that time (whether due to Maximin or other factors I could not say).

In 1978 this young chef went to the grand old *Hotel Negresco* on the front at Nice and made its *Chantecler* restaurant one of the best places to eat at along the whole Riviera. Always innovative, he was, as far as my experience goes, the first of the top chefs to offer a completely vegetarian menu. Now he has opened his own restaurant in Nice.

Mayonnaise: an egg and oil emulsion flavored with vinegar. To make it, the ingredients and the utensils must be at room temperature or even warmer. Two cups of oil might require 4 egg yolks for the emulsification to work, so don't stint on the yolks. Professional chefs seem to need less egg yolk; I don't know why. Olive oil is rather strong tasting for mayonnaise. Most people—including the Roux brothers—prefer it made with a mixture of olive oil and flavorless vegetable oil. It is often said that mayonnaise shouldn't be put into the refrigerator. Ideally that is so, but if it must go into the cold just be careful not to stir it or disturb it until it is again at room temperature. Then it will be stable again.

A mayonnaise is also the name of a dish bound by the sauce: **mayonnaise de homard** or **mayonnaise de volaille,** and so on. But vegetables bound with mayonnaise are usually called **macédoine.**

Mediterranean. The fish for **bouillabaisse** come from the Mediterranean and nowhere else. Some are included just for flavoring the broth. The finest ones to eat are **rouget de roche, chapon** and **loup de mer.** Reference books say loup from the Mediterranean is the **bar** that lives in the Atlantic, but chefs do not agree. Certainly the name rouget is used for different fish on different coasts of France. Loup is often cooked over an open fire using herbs as tinder. Rouget is more likely to be cooked in a pan with olive oil. Chapon (*see* page 60) is the most difficult to find. It's baked in the oven as befits its superior status.

Melon: the word used to describe many examples of a fruit that is usually reserved for use as a first course. In France, as in other European countries, many imported melons are sold, but melons from Cavaillon near Avignon are as good as any others. The **charentais,** a small cantaloupe with orange flesh that comes from the region where Cognac is made, is particularly fragrant and sweet.

Menu: a set meal for a fixed price. Usually the price will include wine, tax and service. Sometimes a limited choice is permitted, but in the cheaper restaurants the food has been purchased and the meal planned for very, very narrow profit margins. Don't expect the restaurant to permit you to change things unless you are a very long-standing client. **Menu dégustation:** a tasting menu. It is a fixed menu, usually consisting of tiny courses, designed to show the skills of the chef. It was probably that most genial man Jacques Pic at Valence who started it with his "menu Rabelais," which provides eight main courses and ends with a tableful of desserts. Anyone who has met M. Pic knows his spontaneous and amazing generosity (I did some drawings in his restaurant and he wouldn't let me leave without a gift of a bottle of wine) and I'm sure his "tasting menu" was motivated by those feelings. But now such menus have become a feature of almost all the most expensive restaurants and they are not all motivated by generosity. By observation I'd say that three out of four customers eating in three-star establishments order such a meal. But not me. I don't like eating lots of small conflicting pieces of food in rapid succession; it's like a cocktail party without the wooden sticks. And what wine can one drink to accompany such a confusion of tastes? All the chefs I've spoken with agree that it's better to choose two or three dishes you want to eat and eat them **à la carte.** The chef will be cooking them just for you, rather than by the batch.

  At home, too, most chefs urge restraint. Barrier and Vergé both said that meals at home should center upon one dish of the highest possible quality.

Merguez. Considering the number of Algerians living in France, especially its southernmost part, it is surprising that their presence has had comparatively little effect upon the cuisine. One of the exceptions is the presence of merguez: lamb and/or goat-meat sausages made bright red with **harissa** (cayenne pepper with cumin seeds), which are to be seen in almost every butcher's shop, although I doubt if many of them are still made exclusively from lamb or goat.

MeRGUeZ

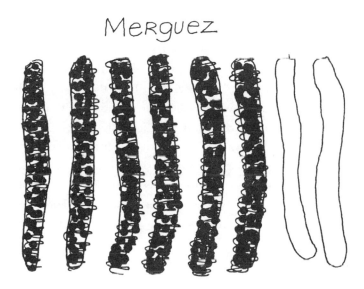

Mesclun is a Provençal word for a salad consisting of mixed local greens. **Mâche** and dandelion (**pissenlit**) are typical, but endive and chicory might be in it too. Some chefs like to include as many as ten different items varying in taste and colors. Herbs such as basil, parsley, arugula and savory are sometimes added.

Metric system. The various measuring systems influence our eating. In France your "quarter-pounder" will weigh 3½ ounces.

The best way for a cook to measure ingredients is by the use of proper scales (with weights, or a sliding weight) for, unlike machines using springs, they don't go wrong. Separate weights are best because you can have a set of metric weights as well as imperial. I find the American system of measuring by volume (cups, etc.) to be very convenient, but such recipes are not easily converted to measures by weight.

A la meunière is one of the most popular descriptions on French menus. It means food (for example, fish) lightly dusted with flour, fried in butter and finished by pouring over it more butter and chopped parsley. It's finished with a squeeze of fresh lemon juice and must be served sizzling hot.

Miel: honey. Real Provençal honey, from bees nourished on wild thyme and other hardy herbs of this region, is distinctive in taste. I agree with those who say it's incomparably better than any other honey. Although most people seem to prefer the lavender honey, Glynn Christian—who knows a great deal about such things—says that his favorites are orange blossom and lime blossom honeys. He also says that excellent honeys are produced in central London from bees that feed on the lime trees of Hyde Park. Certainly the smell of California orange blossom is one of the most beautiful smells that I know. Chefs prefer the delicate flavors of flower honey. Nowadays most honey on sale is inferior stuff and not worth getting fat for; some of them are made from beet sugar.

Mijoter: to simmer so that the surface of the liquid shows just a bubble now and again. **Frémir** is to poach so that the liquid "shivers" but there are no bubbles or movement.

Mirabelle. The warmer climate of France makes plums grown there a delicacy which plums grown in colder places cannot match. The mirabelle is a very small yellow plum that needs plenty of sun (so it's not grown in England). It is more often seen in fruit tarts or **confitures** than in a fruit bowl. Another such plum is the **quetsche.** Like the mirabelle it makes a particularly fine eau de vie. A special favorite dessert plum is the **Reine Claude.** (This one was brought from France to England by Sir Thomas Gage in the mid-nineteenth century and is called the greengage.)

Mirepoix: So many recipes begin with a mirepoix that some cooks start on the mirepoix even before properly considering exactly what they are going to cook. Sauces, stews and stuffings are likely to start this way. Every chef has his own style of making this basic preparation, but a typical one would be made by lightly frying diced carrot, onion, celery and small pieces of that belly bacon that the French call **lardons.** (The choice of butter, olive oil, goose fat or pork fat would depend upon the type of dish.) Ideally some fresh herbs would be added and these ingredients cooked until softened.

Mise en place is the kitchen work that takes place before the meal service begins. This is the time and place the real quality of a restaurant is decided.

Mise en bouteille au château means bottled within the precincts of a vineyard, domaine or estate. (A château doesn't mean a grand house; sometimes it's no more than a field or a factory yard.) You might expect this to be a guarantee of quality, since you would not expect inferior Australian or South African wines to be blended into bottles with such labeling. You would in that case be wrong. The wine producers are permitted to use any other wines for "blending." There are many instances where a tanker-truck full of Australian wine has been driven into a château and put straight into bottles that would eventually bear French wine labels saying *"mise en bouteille au château."*

Monastère: monastery. In the Middle Ages the traditions of cooking, and the developments and innovations of agriculture, and even the use of water power that led to the Industrial Revolution, were mostly due to the monastic orders. Cheeses such as **Maroilles, Muenster, Pont l'Evêque** were made in monasteries. Still today **Port Salut** cheese is produced by Trappist monks according to what is claimed to be a secret formula, but because the monks sold the name, their own cheese is now sold under the name of the abbey: **Entramme.**

The word "**Trappiste**" or "**Abbaye**" on a cheese label indicates a cheese made in a monastery by traditional methods using unpasteurized milk. (Pasteurized milk is convenient and cheap for the manufacturer but results in bland and uninteresting cheese.) **Chartreuse**—a sweet digestif—was originated by Carthusian monks in southern France. **Bénédictine** made by the Benedictine order since the sixteenth century—with a brief interruption due to the Revolution—is perhaps the oldest of such sweet liqueurs. It is a Cognac base, flavored with "seventy-five herbs, spices and flowers."

Montagné, Prosper (1865–1948). A native of Languedoc, Montagné was a chef and, in his day, was considered to be Escoffier's greatest rival. In the early 1930s Montagné wrote the amazing *Larousse Gastronomique.* This astonishing book has no equal. It contains well over a million words and ranges from history to chemistry in a way that makes it difficult to believe that one man could have researched it all in a lifetime. In fact he wrote it in three years! It was first published in an English translation in 1961 and has been revised and republished since.

Moules: mussels. When I was a student a plate of steamed mussels provided the cheapest protein food available. They are easy to prepare. For **moules marinière** put clean, scrubbed, closed mussels into a tightly closed pot, together with a glass of white wine, a finely chopped shallot and garlic, if you like it, and chopped parsley. After a few minutes on a very high heat the steam will have opened the shells. Discard any that are still closed and the mussels are ready to eat. But mussels grow fat in polluted water. Buy them from a reliable source.

Mouli-légume: a vegetable mill, a metal sieve through which food is forced by revolving blades. This excellent device strains out seeds, skins and other unwanted rubbish while forcing pulp through the strainer. The food processor's action of pulping food without straining out unwanted material is quite different.

Mousse: can be translated as foam, froth, lather, the head on a glass of beer or sometimes cream. In French cooking it is usually a sieved and pounded preparation (raw or cooked) that has been bound with a thickened sauce or with cream. A small mousse, bound with cream, is called a **mousseline.** Fish protein—and the egg that binds the mixture—curdles and separates readily, so it's best to cook a mousse in a water-bath (bain-marie) so that it doesn't get too hot. Frozen fish will lack albumin and should be avoided. My wife has tried using

Moulin Legumes

whole egg, egg white and egg yolk in these mixtures and found no difference in anything except color (the mousse containing yolk was yellow.) When spoonsful of mousse mixture are poached in simmering liquids the result is **quenelles.** Mousse mixtures are usually light in color and delicate in flavor. Choose a delicious sauce that provides a good color and will not overwhelm the flavor of the mousse. Mushroom, parsley or tomato might be good.

Moutarde: mustard. Dijon mustard (*see* page 86) is usually regarded as the best mustard in France and is the one used in the kitchen. Surely there is nothing simpler, yet more effective, than boiling up some cream with mustard to taste. Good with your **tournedos** or hamburger (sorry, I mean **bifteck haché)** even if, according to that intrepid gastronomic voyager Patricia Wells, the mustard grain is mostly from Kansas!

Nage: swimming; but in culinary French it also means a type of broth. Just as a **court bouillon** is flavored water in which food is cooked, so a nage is flavored water in which food is served. Usually, but not always, the food is fish or shellfish and the nage is the broth in which it was cooked.

Navarin: a stew of mutton or lamb with vegetables added. In spring it would include a selection of new young vegetables and be called **navarin printanier.** No wine is used in preparing a navarin.

Navet: turnip. With the exception of the Japanese, the French are the only nation on earth to have discovered the wonders of the turnip, perhaps because they concentrate on the small varieties. Turnip is the classic accompaniment to fatty meat such as pork or duck. They are good in stews (but don't overcook them). But best of all young turnips are delicious raw—better than radishes. Use them in salads, grate them as a vegetable or serve them with apéritifs.

Niçoise. The food of Nice on France's Mediterranean coast includes many fish dishes, some of them unique to this region. The local food is also rich in garlic, olives, olive oil and tomatoes. Anchovies and tuna (nowadays mostly canned) are favored too, and in summer the emphasis is on vegetables: eggplant, zucchini and artichoke are prominent.

　　Salade niçoise. Like **bouillabaisse** and **cassoulet,** the constituents of a salade niçoise are a popular subject for food writers who need something to write about. Some years ago I remember an animated correspondence on this subject in *Le Monde* newspaper. It went on for weeks and weeks. Waverley Root, the American gourmet, said it should have no lettuce. Quartered tomatoes, he said, with green peppers, black olives, raw fava beans, radishes and perhaps some hard-boiled egg. He added that **pissala** (anchovies pounded to a paste) and good olive oil are the only dressing.

　　Yes, that's fine. But most places in the Nice area would nowadays include tuna fish. For myself I like a few extra things in my salade niçoise; for example, some whole anchovy fillets and some **haricots verts** cooked but still crisp. And I'll take a garlicky oil and vinegar dressing (not too much vinegar). What about you?

Noël: Christmas, than which no feast is more important or more traditional. The Christmas Eve supper, served usually on return from Midnight Mass, is the most important meal of the year and yet it is deliberately *maigre.* Such meals are often local in character. In Provence— records the gourmet Richard Olney—such a meal would consist of salt cod with **raito** (a tomato sauce with red wine and anchovy) and winter vegetables such as cabbage or **blette** (chard). To contrast with such a simple main course, he tells us, there are always thirteen desserts, however simple each may be. Almonds, hazelnuts, raisins and dried figs are included because their colors are those respectively of the Augustinians, Carmelites, Dominicans and Franciscans.

Boudins black and white are usually considered essential fare. On Christmas Day richer dishes are served and such things as truffled chicken might be on the table.

Noix: nuts. Confusingly this is also the word the French use for walnut. At one time the walnut was so widely grown and harvested that in the Dordogne its oil was used for lamps. That is hard to believe now that walnut oil has become a fashionable and expensive luxury for salad dressings. The Dordogne is still the center for walnut production. They are shaken from the trees in autumn, which is a good time to visit this part of France, which has both scorching hot summers and bitterly cold winters.

James Bentley, in his fascinating book *Life and Food in the Dordogne,* says, "Most people in the Dordogne would prefer to use walnut oil rather than butter in almost any recipe. In fact, walnuts turn up everywhere." He also provides a tip for anyone who grinds walnuts in an electric grinder. If the machine gets too hot the oil will separate from the ground kernels. Jacques Pépin warned me of this same thing and put sugar with the nuts to absorb the oil. Flour will also do. When buying any sort of nuts, look for shrink-wrapped ones: oxidation makes the nut oil rancid. Keep them in the refrigerator.

Normandie: Normandy. For many people, all over the world, the name of this region is synonymous with memories of the fierce and bloody battles of the summer of 1944. For Normandy is the region of France that lies between the English Channel and the Paris basin. Here were the lands of William, the Norman Duke who became King of England by means of an invasion force going the other way.

France's paramount position as a land of good food is largely accounted for by a unique geographical position, which provides the markets of Paris with Mediterranean fish, and the wine, fruit and vegetables of the south, together with the fine meat and dairy products of the north. Normandy is rich farmland noted for cheese and butter, for cereals, sugar, meat, beer and cider and Calvados. On this coastline are landed fish of every kind including the fish which even French chefs call Dover sole. The crabs, lobsters, and shrimp are famous and so are the oysters and mussels.

But Normandy is not just a provider of good food: its cuisine is noteworthy. (Unlike Brittany, where an unparalleled abundance of seafood has produced no great dishes.) Devotees of **tripes à la mode de Caen, andouillettes,** pigs' feet and **boudins** will already know that Rouen, Vire and Caen are noted for these delicacies, and these three towns compete for the title of Normandy's gastronomic center. Rabbit dishes abound and hereabouts you'll also find **sole à la normande, sole à la dieppoise** and **moules à la marinière** as well as **canard à la rouennaise.** As in Brittany local people think of fish in terms of their livelihoods and prefer to eat meat. The products of the pig, so easily fed on scraps of any kind, can be seen everywhere. Sheep grazed on the coast of the Cotentin peninsula are said to acquire a distinctive salty flavor and this meat fetches high prices. Chilly winters provide the Normans with prodigious appetites. My friend Adrian Bailey—who is no mean trencherman himself—tells of entering a dining-room in Domfront for a mid-morning coffee and seeing men eating their tripes à la mode as a snack between breakfast and lunch!

The cheeses created here include **Camembert, Pont-l'Évêque, Livarot** and **Neufchâtel** and, oddly enough, the **petit suisse.** Many locals will advise you to eat them along with cider instead of red wine. This advice should be resisted.

Not all the apples are made into cider and Calvados; the local chefs use them in everything: pork, game and even salads contain apples. Throughout the world the menu term **normande** denotes a dish with apples or Calvados (although a **sauce normande** is quite different: a fish fumet flavored with mushrooms and thickened with egg yolk and cream). Apple desserts, and pastries, are many and varied: fritters, custards and open tarts often accompanied by the excellent local cream. **Crème fraîche,** fermented cream, is also a constituent in many Normandy recipes and, because the fermentation process causes cream to vary in taste and texture from place to place, produces a distinctive flavor.

Nouilles: noodles. In France noodles are found principally in Alsace-Lorraine and in Provence. In the region around Nice there are many such dishes that are indisputably Italian. But in Lorraine they are called **totelots** and have a special vinaigrette dressing to which cream and chopped parsley and garlic are added. This dish is eaten at Easter.

Nouvelle cuisine was identified and named by a food writer in 1973. Some of the tenets were undeniably good ones; for example, the emphasis on fresh, high-quality ingredients and minimal cooking times. There was a new emphasis on light sauces made by reduction and a movement away from thickening agents such as butter, egg and flour. But these ideas were not really new. Neither was the name: Jacques Pépin has in his library a book called *Nouvelle cuisine française*; it was published in the eighteenth century!

The worst excesses of the new fashionable cooking arise from the emphasis upon "art" and "creativity." For some chefs, cooking has given place to endless experimentation. I am reminded of Oscar Wilde's remark, "Fashion is a form of ugliness so intolerable that we have to alter it every six months." Recently a well-known food writer in a national magazine recommended restaurants where "highly individualistic . . . young chefs" were regularly preparing such dishes as: *Veal with ginger and lime, Red mullet in an orange and Pernod sauce, Breast of duck with ginger and rhubarb, Pigeon and mango salad, Calves' liver in citrus sauce.* I will not go on; either you like it or you shudder.

The traditionalists—and I happily declare myself one of them—are not opposed to experiment but do not wish to be experimented upon! We prefer the chef to keep his experiments to himself until they are perfected. Even then . . . we urge the creative chef to apply his knowledge, skills and invention to the classic dishes of French cuisine, cooking them to ever-better result from carefully selected ingredients. Dishes usually regarded as "classic" ones have become so because they have been favorites for so long, but every chef brings an individuality to even the most well-established recipes. Many customers like to watch skilled and knowledgeable waiters playing a part in serving the meal according to the customer's preferences: "Sauce on the chicken, sir, or alongside it?"

However, cost-conscious restaurant executives all over the world love *nouvelle cuisine,* and cling tenaciously to it, for it is in effect portion control plus hype. Chef-patrons face a conflict of interest.

Oasis: a famous three-star eating place at Napoule, near Cannes. Although Michelin gives it a top award, it was quite unlike the truly great restaurants such as *Taillevent, Bise, Bocuse* or *Troisgros.* These rather cramped premises in a side street used to be a *pension,* and it's something of a miracle that the remarkable Louis Outhier was able to make such an unpromising place so famous. It got its exotic name because of a palm tree struggling for space in the tiny yard, where in summer the tables are arranged. During the film and TV festivals in Cannes, it had to struggle even more fiercely, for personalities of big screens and small ones were fighting for tables here. But in winter one sat inside and was reminded very forcibly of the very modest little pension it once was. Louis Outhier, the patron-chef, worked as a commis for eighteen months under Fernand Point and he used and adapted some of Point's ideas. He serves **loup en croûte Fernand Point** (sea bass cooked in a decorative arrangement of pastry) and **brioche de foie gras frais** (foie gras baked inside brioche). At the time of writing M. Outhier has decided to shut his restaurant at Napoule to concentrate on his interests in America.

Ouefs: eggs. Where do you start to talk about eggs? There are so many kinds. But just as I believe the domestic fowl (**volaille**) is far more delectable than snipe, golden plover, pheasant, wild duck, teal, wigeon and so on, so I believe that the hen's egg is incomparably more delicious than any other egg I have tasted. That both the chicken and its egg are more versatile is indisputable. As Escoffier wrote, "Not one is so fruitful of variety, so universally liked, and so complete in itself as the egg. There are very few culinary recipes that do not include eggs, either as a principal constituent or as an ingredient."[17]

The egg is not easy to cook: the white becomes hard as plastic when heated to 178°F. Fernand Point sometimes asked applicants for jobs in his kitchen to fry an egg. He'd expect the examinee to use lots of butter and keep the temperature low so the egg white didn't harden and the butter didn't brown.

I am not sure that we exploit the egg's versatility in the way that French cooks do. We fry, we poach, we boil in the shell, we scramble and make omelettes. But we are less ready to cook the eggs in combination dishes such as **oeufs en cocotte, oeufs moulés, oeufs en gelée** or **oeufs sur le plat,** which offer the cook a thousand different ways of cooking eggs with other foods. *Larousse Gastronomique* devotes 27 pages to egg recipes, and my favorite cookbook, *L'Art culinaire français (see* Bibliography, page 228), devotes 25 pages to the egg. So why not try something new? **Oeufs pochés en gelée**, anyone?

Oignon: onion. The onion is possibly the oldest and most widely used vegetable on this planet, although perhaps some of the onion varieties that grow wild would not be easy to identify as a member of the family. Even the common European onion *(Allium cepa)* varies so much from place to place that some will make you cry as you pick them while others are mild enough to be eaten like an apple. For this reason it's worth trying the local onions wherever you go.

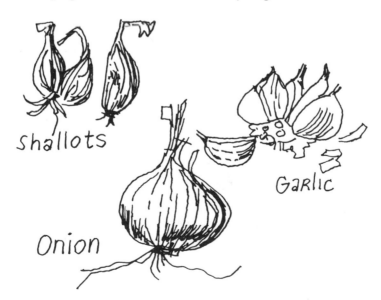

Onions are not easy to store and a partly spoiled one is best discarded as the nasty taste spreads quickly.

This vital ingredient of so many dishes is the botanical relative of the lily. In 1943 the Wine and Food Society published a booklet called *The Lilies of the Kitchen,* which dealt with onions, shallots, chives, garlic and leeks in such a way as to stress their family likeness. The daffodil is an inedible relative.

Olive: olive. Although the tomato found favor in France only recently, that other fundamental ingredient of Provençal cooking—the olive—has been grown and eaten in southern France since the ancient Greeks took it there. Olive trees live so long while continuing to bear fruit that some say it is possible that olives eaten today come from trees that were planted at the time the ancient Greeks arrived! Many experts say that the best Provençal olive oil is the world's best. Others would make the same claim for the best Italian oils, specifically those from Lucca in Tuscany. A great deal depends upon how much you like the flavor of olives and upon how well the oil has been stored. I like the olive flavor, so I buy the freshest oil I can find; even carefully stored oil loses its flavor as it gets older. And I seek out strongly flavored oils such as the Greek or Spanish ones. I like to have these in addition to high-quality olive oil and flavorless vegetable oils too. But then I am an oil freak.

The flavor of French oil is cleaner, clearer and less complex than Italian oil. The label "douce" means a light thin taste; "*fruité*" marks an oil pressed from unripe olives. It will be stronger and darker.

In the chilly mountainside village where we lived in Tuscany—not far from Lucca—I helped shake the olives from the trees, groaned under the weight of the sacks and watched the thin trickle of oil coming from the press. My neighbor's trees yielded about 1 liter per tree. One liter per tree, for all that care and attention and all that work. Remember that next time olive oil seems expensive. My friend Joe Tilson, the painter, another oil freak, who spends much time in Italy, compares his local oil with local wine and says price for price the oil must be the better value. He's right, of course.

So what about the storing? I would say that most bottled oil sold in Britain and America is rancid. Rancid oil tastes awful and is unhealthy. Light and heat are bad for oil. It turns rancid at room temperature in clear glass bottles. Buy good oil in tins. It's worth taking some trouble to find a shop where they understand about oil. Once opened keep it in a cool dark place. Bring it out in small measures as you need it. Don't worry about it going cloudy in the cold: that makes no difference. If you put it in the refrigerator watch for condensation. Water forming inside the container and dripping into the oil will eventually make it go bad.

What to buy? The best oil is labeled "extra virgin." It is cold

pressed and no chemical solvents, steam or other gimmicks are used to extract the oil from the olives. It has minimum acidity (about 1 percent). Oil marked "virgin" has 3 to 4 percent acidity. (For oil used in frying *see* **Friture,** page 104.)

Omble chevalier: *Salvetinus alpinus* or arctic char is a close relative of the trout. The American brook trout and the Dolly Varden trout come from the same family. It resembles the salmon trout but the omble comes only from deep, cold lakes. It is found in England's Lake Windermere and Switzerland's Lac Léman. In France only Lake Bouget and Lake Annecy have it. It is a delicacy served in local restaurants, and when I first went to Talloires on Lake Annecy back in the 1950s it was cheap and available everywhere. Over the years it has become more and more scarce. Nowadays it no longer appears on the menu at *L'Auberge du Père Bise* and the waiter whispers of its arrival. It is simply prepared; cooked in water or more often in butter, and served without a sauce of any kind. Such delicacies as the omble chevalier—with clean, clear flavor—demonstrate the difference between lake fish and sometimes earthy-tasting river fish, which are often categorized together as freshwater fish.

Origan (oregano). In Britain it's called "wild marjoram," a tough little herb that grows wild all over southern Europe and Latin America but varies in flavor from place to place. It is far more powerful than sweet marjoram and is not much used in authentic French cooking. (It is found in pizzas, but otherwise more in the south of Italy; also in the dishes of Greece, North Africa and Mexico.)

    Marjolaine, on the other hand, is what we call sweet marjoram. It is more fragrant and subtle and, yes, sweet. It is used in French cooking, with tomatoes and with lamb, but sparingly. There is also a famous cake called marjolaine (*see* page 130).

Oseille: sorrel. An herb with large leaves, which looks rather like spinach. It is used in African cooking, is popular in Poland and well known in Jewish cooking (where it is called *schav*). Several cooking experts say it tastes like spinach too, but I find little resemblance. Sorrel has a very powerful flavor that reminds me of fresh lemon juice. Used as a vegetable it usually has other things mixed with it to modify the flavor (for example, in Poland, sour cream and sugar). You have to search to find it on sale in England but in many European countries it is sold widely. I believe that the many "green" sauces found in northern Europe accompanying oily fish and eels were originally sorrel sauces and should be made as such.

Plant it in a pot and it will grow like a weed, which it is. A little of it finely chopped livens up a salad. It is the basis of a famous French dish (**potage de santé** or healthy soup) although I notice that Escoffier's recipe for it uses 3 puréed potatoes, 3 cups white consommé with only 2 tablespoonsful of sorrel (cooked in butter). Maybe he didn't like the taste of it.

My wife's favorite sorrel soup is a variation on this called **potage Germiny,** for which she finely chops "three big handfuls" of sorrel, softens it over a low heat in 2 tablespoons butter and puts it through the mouli. She then mixes ¾ cup cream with 1 tablespoonful of flour and boils it until the flour has cooked and thickened the cream. She then slowly pours 1 quart hot chicken stock onto the cream and adds the sorrel. Serve with garlic bread. Wonderful!

But the real reason we started to grow sorrel is because we decided it went so well with all the fresh salmon local fishermen bring to our door. Our favorite salmon dish is based on a *Troisgros* recipe, **escalopes de saumon à l'oseille Troisgros,**[18] and you must have 2 cups **fumet de poisson** (*see* page 106). Add half a glass of white wine and a quarter of a glass of vermouth to the fumet and reduce it by half. Strain and add heavy cream (**crème fraîche** if possible) and reduce again. Before serving, add shredded sorrel leaves and cook for half a minute to soften. The Troisgros brothers of Roanne were probably the first chefs to put a sauce on a plate, and arrange food on the sauce. When the food looks as good as a lightly cooked escalope of salmon, this is an attractive way to serve it. (A cautionary note: taking escalopes from salmon is very difficult. One of these days I'm going to watch them doing it at Roanne.)

Oursin: a sea urchin, a spherical spiky little sea creature which might have gone unmolested except that some adventurous gourmet discovered the soft orange inside is delicious. It doesn't need cooking. Sometimes its strong iodine flavor persuades even the French to mix it with other foods. When they do they treat it like truffle: they put it in omelettes or in scrambled egg or with potato. But don't go to a lot of trouble for me; I like it just the way it is.

Sea Urchin

Pain: bread. The bread supply dominates French towns and villages as once it dominated all Europe. Revolutions started outside the bakers' shops. Because the long thin **baguette** and **flûte** are stale by next morning the French go shopping every day. This means that they shop each day for fish and meat too. Upon this need to go to the baker the quality of French food depends.

Frenchmen who live in the remote country and have no local baker get their bread weekly. Not so long ago travelers saw huge cartwheels of bread sitting by the roadside waiting to be collected by local householders, for in those days few farmers had ovens to cook their own bread. These loaves were made to keep fresh longer.

The French who live in towns like the baguette, a long crusty loaf, and especially they like the crusty end. This is considered a treat that may be snapped off and eaten by whoever goes out to buy the bread. To cater to this preference a special type of baguette—the **épi** or wheat ear—is made with many crusty ends. The baguette used for sandwiches is split along the middle. At the table it is broken or cut into long pieces rather than cut into thin slices that I sometimes see the English slicing. Thinner baguettes are called **flûtes** and ones even thinner **ficelles** (strings) and fat ones **opéras** or **restaurants. Pain Viennois** looks like a baguette, but is sweet, white and fluffy inside. **Pain complet** is a whole-wheat loaf and **pain de seigle** is a crusty version of a different shape made from rye.

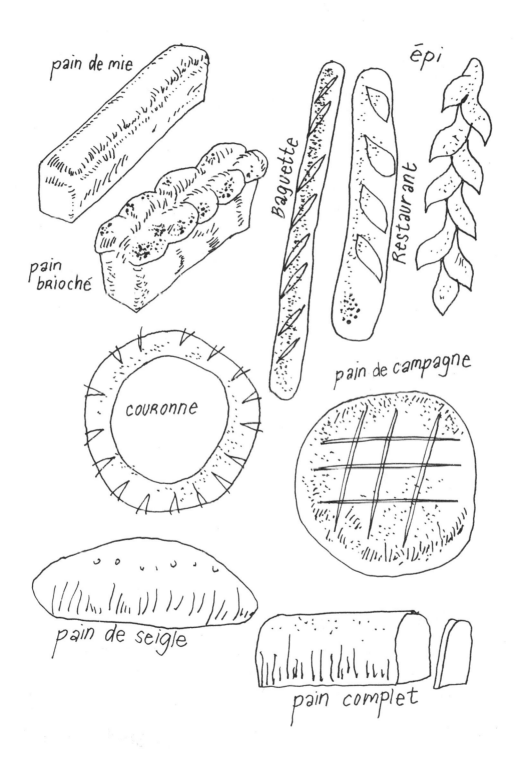

pain de mie

épi

pain brioché

Baguette

Restaurant

couronne

pain de campagne

pain de seigle

pain complet

Bread marked **pain au levain** (yeast bread) will be made with coarse flavorful "gray" flour (**farine gris**) and possibly from sourdough (the word "levain" means both sourdough and yeast). **Pain de campagne** will also be made from coarse flour. Such loaves are big and round in shape so that they will not go stale as quickly as a **baguette.** A **couronne** is a baguette with the ends joined to make a circle.

The "cottage" shaped loaves that the English and Americans eat are less popular in France. For sandwiches, making croûtons and for making breadcrumbs you buy **pain de mie**, but the French are inclined to regard it as something eaten only by those who are old or sick or both.

Palourde: France's best and most flavorful type of clam, a bivalve usually hardier and tougher to eat than the oyster. There are many varieties of clam (Tom Stobart, who is something of a specialist, guesses about eighty), but this name is vaguely applied to other mollusks of a similar sort. America has some magnificent varieties; the British export theirs.

In France the **praire** and the **clovisse** make up, with the palourde, the three best-liked clams. The praire is rather like the American cherrystone clam. All three are found on all coasts of France, but the clovisse comes mostly from the Mediterranean. Like other bivalves the clam is a filter, taking nourishment from the water that passes through it. It can be a dangerous harborer of poisons and pollution. Hurrah for farming: the palourde has been farmed in the estuary of the Loire for many years and other clams are usually treated in tanks before being sold. Beware of ones you find on the seashore.

Pan bagna: also **pan bagnat,** a Provençal way of saying **pain baigné** or bathed bread. There are as many arguments about what this sandwich contains as about how it got its name. Leaving the latter dispute aside, this is a summer snack of the south. Just about everyone would agree that good strong-tasting olive oil and ripe garlicky tomatoes must be pressed between bread (and left for anything from 30 minutes to 24 hours) so that the bread becomes soaked in oil and tomato juice. In this respect pan bagna resembles the Spanish snack *pan con tomate* (sometimes called *pan catalan*) virtually essential to life in Catalonia.

I insist that the tomatoes be red, ripe, skinned and seeded. Canned tomatoes are quite suitable. Typically the pan bagna would also contain canned anchovies, in which case the anchovy oil can be used to spread over the bread, this "bathing in oil" always being the first stage, and has perhaps given the snack its name. Capers, pitted black olives, gherkins and mushrooms are also popular additions; so are artichoke hearts and very fine slices of mild raw onion or, better still, shallot. Canned sardines, lettuce and hard-boiled egg can be used but purists would say that the result is not really pan bagna (although more than one expert in the Nice region said that pan bagna is a **salade niçoise** made into a sandwich).

Some like to use a whole baguette, splitting it right down the length. Others prefer a large round loaf which has been split into two layers. In either case the soft inside of the loaf is removed and some of it can be mixed with the other ingredients; for example, mixed with the pulp of the seeded tomatoes. For individual portions bread rolls can be used, and the ingredients can then be varied according to family preference and prejudice. The result must not be crusty but soft, if not to say soggy. To make sure of this, some cooks moisten the bread, or even dip it in water.

In any case, wrap the reassembled loaf tightly in plastic wrap or foil and put a weight on top. A large firm loaf will need a heavy weight, a soft roll little or none. Leave it for anything up to 24 hours. Slice it just before it's served. But be warned: a pan bagna that tasted wonderful with a bottle of chilled wine in the Provençal sunshine will never be quite the same when made elsewhere.

Paner: to coat with breadcrumbs. The breadcrumbs may be fresh and soft or crisp and toasted.

Panure à l'anglaise: an egg and breadcrumb coating for fried food. Typically a fish fillet is dried carefully, very lightly coated with flour and the excess flour shaken off. (This is very important because that excess flour will otherwise undermine the coating and it will come off during the frying process.) The fillet is then coated in beaten egg and drained for a minute before being buried in breadcrumbs. The breadcrumbs are pressed onto the fish with the flat of the hand and they are left for a few minutes to dry. Then the fillet is deep-fried. Why do I remember it so clearly? This was the first kitchen job I did without supervision. But before he departed the chef made sure I knew exactly how he wanted it done.

Papillote means cocoon. This is a folded envelope of heavy paper (foil is also used) inside which food and flavorings are cooked. The envelope is opened at the table. Fish, and any items that need short cooking, are best suited for this method. For family cooking it is fun to let everyone assemble his own choice of flavorings.

Restaurants de Paris are quite different from those found in the countryside, where highly publicized patron-chefs endlessly try new ideas. Paris is a stronghold of culinary conservatism. New ideas, new dishes, new restaurants and chefs come but inevitably they go. It was the food critic Christian Millau who told *Time* magazine[19] that the chefs of nouvelle cuisine had "turned down the capital." Adding, "It's impossible to have the really great cuisine in Paris now." (But of course Millau's idea of really great cuisine is nouvelle cuisine.) The most famous establishments in Paris are the oldest and most traditional ones: *Lasserre, Grand Vefour, Tour d'Argent* and of course the mighty *Taillevent*, that all restaurants look upon with admiration and envy.

However, many experts—including Egon Ronay—would put Robuchon's *Jamin* at the top in Paris, and the *Lucas-Carton* (where Alain Senderens is at the stove) would come a very close second.

Pâté: the word used to describe hot and cold pies and various meat, fish or game mixtures, some of them enclosed in pastry, and some not. I've heard many explanations for this apparent misnomer, the most convincing one being that the mixtures were always in a—sometimes inedible—crust when sold in medieval pie shops. When forcemeat mixtures are cooked in a pot they take the name of that pot—a **terrine.** Nowadays the word terrine implies a coarsely cut, strongly flavored garlicky mixture that often contains pork and pork liver and a high proportion of fat. The fat adds flavor and makes it soft and easy to spread. **Pâté maison** and **pâté de campagne** are grandiose names for coarsely ground pork and liver mixtures that would be more accurately described as terrines.

When the word pâté is used for mixtures without pastry, it should be reserved for finely chopped mixtures of delicate expensive ingredients. The most famous mixture is **pâté de foie gras,** specially fattened goose liver. This too is sometimes prepared in a virtually inedible crust.

Pâte: a different word. It is used to cover a range of doughs and pastry mixtures and even includes yeast doughs and batters.

There are many different doughs in regular use in the French professional kitchen. All pastry chefs seem to have their own methods, their own recipes and, confusingly, their own names for the results.

However, **pâte à choux** is a hot-water pastry. Warm water, butter and flour are mixed to make a soft warm dough **(panade),** which is stirred over heat to partly cook the flour. While it's still hot, beaten egg is stirred into it. This pastry is used for éclairs and such items as the small cheese-filled amuse-gueules called **petits choux au fromage.** At the wonderful, cheerful *Chalet Bel Air* restaurant at Mouchard, Jura—and you need something cheering if you're in the Jura in winter—I had delicious fresh escargots cooked inside choux pastry puffs to start my Sunday lunch. The menu name seemed to be making a pun on snails on cabbage, but perhaps that was just my inadequate French.

Pâte brioche is a wet sticky bread dough, yellow with egg yolk. It is not very difficult to make. My twelve-year-old son got perfect results the first time and every time. It is used to make breakfast breads among other things.

Pâte brisée is the chef's all-purpose pastry. It is used for such things as quiche, tart and pie and is served hot or cold.

Jacques Pépin[20]—one-time chef to three French Presidents— offers a typically French recipe for pâte brisée. He rubs 5 ounces (very cold) butter into 2 cups flour, moistens it with 1/3 cup of cold water and adds a mere half teaspoonful of sugar. This results in the sort of rather hard result that the French like. But it will withstand long cooking in hot ovens. So when it's used for Pépin's apple tart, which has a raw apple filling and is cooked for 1¼ hours, the pastry survives and is delicious. Pépin uses butter for pastry for sweet dishes and a mixture of butter and lard for savory ones, or dishes served warm. And next time you hear yourself saying you've no time to make pastry, remember that a novice student at La Varenne cooking school[21] in Paris takes no more than 5 minutes to do this. The instructor takes 30 seconds!

A useful variation on this pastry is **pâte sucrée** (often called **pâte sablée,** or "sand pastry," on account of its sandy brown color). The proportions are 8 ounces flour, 3½ ounces superfine sugar, 4 egg yolks and 4½ ounces butter. It is not easy to handle and is chilled before cooking.

Pâte feuilletée is flaky pastry. Usually it is interpreted to mean pastry of a thousand leaves (mille-feuilles), but some historians say this sort of pastry got its name from Feuillet, chef to the house of Condé. Whatever the truth of it, the cooked pastry should rise in layers that separate like leaves.

The first day I was assigned to assist the pastry chef I was determined to be as helpful and as knowledgeable as possible. So when he arranged his utensils to make flaky pastry I asked him if he would like me to cut the butter up into small cubes. He thought this was very funny. He was a big blond Polish refugee, gloomy beyond compare, so his howl of laughter was shattering. I learned that day that professional chefs don't dab little cubes of butter over the dough, and fold it in three, the way you are told to do it in ladies' glossy magazines.

The professional way of making pâte feuilletée is to wrap the (flour and water) dough around the butter, like brown paper around a parcel. Then you roll it flat. Turn it and roll it out again for a total of six times. It's not easy to manage—the butter pops out; the secret is to get the texture of the fat softer than the texture of the dough. You do that by "kneading" the butter before you start. So how much flour and how much butter? Henri-Paul Pellaprat has a precise answer to the question. He mixes the flour and water dough (**détrempe**) and when he is satisfied with it, he weighs it. He then measures out butter equal to exactly half the weight of the dough.

Carême liked this sort of flaky pastry. He advised that it should go into the oven within eight minutes of the final rolling. It is a good tip. It shows why even hastily put together home-made pastry is usually superior to shop-bought or frozen pastry.

Magazine writers are likely to tell us that the cube and dab recipe is "flaky pastry" and the other is "puff pastry." In French cooking no such distinction exists. There is, however, a pastry called **demi-feuilletée.** This is made from the off-cuts left over from the feuilletée. These trimmings (**rognures**) are rolled again and used for dishes in which the evenness of rising and texture are less important. Always the pastry chef will use his finest pastry for dishes that will be served cold. Demi-feuilletée is used for individual hot pies and pastry cases.

To appreciate the pastry's chef's art, go into a pâtisserie and see the amazing display of **croissants, brioches, éclairs, gâteaux, petits fours, friandises,** wedding cakes and birthday cakes, **palmiers,** fruit tarts and sometimes hand-made chocolates too.

Pétillant: a sparkling bubbly taste experienced on the tongue rather than bubbles seen in the glass.

Petit déjeuner: breakfast. Fashions in eating change constantly. The traditional French breakfast is a bowl of coffee with milk in it and a piece of dry bread. In my youth I remember being with workers who regarded a measure of eau de vie as an essential part of their breakfast. In Brittany coffee might come with a crêpe. The great French hotels and restaurants cater to a high proportion of foreigners. Breakfast there includes all kinds of exotic ingredients: croissants, brioches and fresh fruit. For the British, toast, butter, honey and jam; cheese for the Dutch and Germans; cereals and freshly squeezed orange juice for the Americans.

Petits légumes: likely to be a side plate containing a selection of small lightly cooked vegetables. It is one of the best of recent restaurant fashions.

Petits pâtés chauds. These little pies are always round in shape and served one per person. They contain various mixtures—usually pork or veal and pork—and ideally the filling is marinated in wine or brandy overnight. French chefs delight in double meanings and these little pies, served hot, are likely to be peppery. At *Père Bise* they add truffle to the filling of their **pâté chaud poivrade**, and when the waiter serves it he slices the top from the pie and pours some of the **sauce poivrade** into it before replacing it. The sauce is then left on the table for those who like their pâté chaud very poivrade. The sauce is made from a reduction of red wine and veal stock with shallots. To this ground black pepper is added.

At *Chapel's* restaurant I had a superb eel pie, **pâté chaud d'anguille,** served with two different butter sauces.

Pic, Jacques (1932–   ). Chef-patron of *Pic* at Valence, he is widely considered the most hard-working, dedicated and generous of the top-rank chefs in France. He is never to be seen on the publicity junkets that so many of his colleagues indulge in. But his skills and determination are undoubted. Pic was probably the first of the top chefs to change to electric ranges. When the Troisgros brothers thought of doing the same they went and consulted him. When he created his "menu Rabelais," with eight main courses and at least as many desserts, it was a sensation. Every ambitious chef wanted a menu dégustation to display his wide-ranging creativity and ingenuity.

His father, André Pic (1893–1984), was one of France's most successful chefs and restaurateurs of the 1930s. When André's health declined after the Second World War, and his restaurant lost its reputation, his old friends Point and Dumaine would not take young Jacques into apprenticeship. He went elsewhere—to Paris and to the famous *La Réserve* at Beaulieu-sur-Mer—and then came back to his father's restaurant at Valence, and regained the coveted three-star Michelin rating that his father had won and lost. Pic is probably the only top chef willing to take completely untrained apprentices into his kitchen. He gives jobs to young people from his town to ease the problem of youth unemployment.

Pied de porc: pig's foot. Is this the most unfashionable dish in French cuisine? I only know that mention of it guarantees shudders of disapproval. The Royal Doulton porcelain company once asked me what dish I would most like to see photographed on one of their plates; I unhesitatingly said **pied de porc farci** and they refused to believe it. The PR department suggested other meals more suited to their reputation and mine. I told them to go the way of the pig's foot.

In France I delight in the way that cooked and ready to eat pig's feet are on sale at the charcuterie. I relish a visit to any restaurant (such as *Tante Claire* in London) where pied de porc is served boned and stuffed and flavored with truffle. I've tried preparing this at home (the pig's foot must be cooked for at least five hours and de-boned while warm), but I can never get it to look so neat and tidy, so I put it in a terrine, or some other small pot, for the final cooking period. Sainte Menehould in the Champagne district is famous for this dish and many other pork specialties. One way of treating the cooked and cooled foot is to paint it with melted butter and roll it in soft breadcrumbs before grilling it. This is **pied de porc pané.** I prefer it with light, mustard-flavored sauce.

There are stories of Fernand Point serving a meal to the President of France in 1938.[22] On the menu was **délices de St. Antoine en feuilleté**—pig's foot in flaky pastry. Legend says President Lebrun shed a tear at the consideration and care that had put such a wonderful dish before him.

Pieds et paquets: feet and packets. Nowadays, alas, no feet are anywhere in evidence in this very popular **daube,** which consists mostly of sheep's tripe with a little salt pork in rich white-wine sauce with generous garlic. It often comes with tomato too. It seems almost certain that the original recipe used sheep's feet to get the heavy gelatinous sauce, but modern recipes suggest calf's foot. The canned version of this dish will give a rough idea of what it tastes like, which is useful if only one member of the family relishes the idea of trying it.

Pigeonneau is a pigeon or what in America is called a squab. It's not an ordinary pigeon, the tough old bird who ruins the vegetable garden and makes an unpopular regular appearance on the dinner tables of many of England's grand country houses. These birds are 3–5 weeks old, their meat is dark but lacks a gamy taste, they're of a breed reared specially for the table. Often they are corn-fed and having never flown they are tender enough to be roasted.

Pintade is a guinea fowl. The French name comes from the word for "painted" because of its speckled plumage. Waverley Root, the American gourmet, was once a guinea-fowl farmer. He calls it "the most flavorful bird of the barnyard." The French seem to agree with him, for this bird is widely reared despite the great difficulty that comes with farming it. For the chef it remains a luxury dish and it's typically served with wild mushrooms and a wine sauce. My local traiteur even prepares pintade in a curry sauce! But not for me.

Pipérade originated as a Basque dish. Now it varies from region to region but it is a homely dish, usually a pan of **ratatouille** (a mixture of well-cooked summer vegetables) into which raw eggs have been dropped so that they poach in the vegetable mixture. For something more like the original version let red peppers predominate and use tomatoes, onions and mushrooms.

Pissaladière is widely described as an "onion and anchovy pizza tart," and in many places that's what you'll be served. It is a dish from Provence and originally the topping was made from **pissala** which is a purée of young anchovies and sardines. Nowadays, the topping is almost always made from canned anchovies with a fondue of chopped onions (onions sweated to a lumpy purée) and pitted black olives. This is cheap street food and so the base is often just bread dough like a pizza, but some chefs insist that an authentic pissaladière uses a brioche dough made with eggs and (despite its southern birthplace) butter.

My own recipe uses 3 beaten eggs with 2 ounces butter and 12 ounces flour and is mixed with tepid milk to which the yeast has been added. This makes one pissaladière, and after the dough has risen and proofed, it is topped with a fondue made from 5 onions. Add anchovy (whole or mashed) and black olives according to taste. Cook in a medium oven for 30 minutes.

Pistou: a Provence dialect word meaning a crush and a mash, and pistou is a pounded mixture of freshly gathered basil, cheese, olive oil and garlic. (It is very like the Italian *pesto alla genovese* which also has toasted pine nuts in it.) It is found mostly in that part of southern France where Italian dishes have infiltrated French menus. Here the basil flourishes in the sun and humidity and will fill a kitchen with its aroma. There is probably no other dish that so depends upon the high quality of the ingredients. Although in Italy a really fine quality cheese of the Parmesan type is considered vital, in France various cheeses are used. The French put their pistou into a vegetable soup—**la soupe au pistou**—it is a celebration of spring and an abundance of fresh young vegetables. In it you'll find peas, tomatoes, onions, haricots verts, fresh soft white beans like flageolets, zucchini, potatoes and sometimes pasta too. A minestrone, you say? The French think it's la soupe au pistou. Don't let's spoil their meal.

Pocher: to poach. To cook gently in water or flavored liquid.

Poêle: a stove. When a French chef speaks of **poêlage** he probably means cooking in a closed pot (either over direct heat or in the oven) using fat and little or no liquid. A poêle is also a type of frying pan with very shallow sides. A **sautoir** is a pan with higher, straight sides. Food fried in it is well spaced to encourage the steam to escape, and this will help the food to crisp and brown.

The other sort of frying pan is a **sauteuse**; it has sloping sides. The sauteuse is shaken in use, to make the food jump (**sauté**) violently or turn over. The amount of fat used is absolutely minimal so there will be no splashing.

It's worth remembering when ordering your meal that in a good restaurant the dishes called sauté on the menu will not be started until your order comes to the kitchen. So your **poulet sauté** will be cooked expressly for you. So will such things as chops, liver slices, steaks, fish and so on.

As for the materials from which such pans are ideally made, that is something for personal decision and individual pockets. In a domestic kitchen, we are probably looking for a solid, durable pan without hot spots, one with the ability to hold heat after coming off the stove.

Aluminum is an excellent conductor, but it will affect the flavor and color of any acid foods. Stainless steel is convenient to clean, but for some inexplicable reason it is expensive despite a glut of steel so vast that taxpayers finance much of the European manufacture. It is a very poor conductor. Iron is cheap and quite a good conductor, but it rusts easily, discolors some foods and needs a lot of care and attention. Iron with enamel or other surfaces is probably a good compromise, but it can chip. At the very top of the price scale, Georg Jensen of Fifth Avenue, NYC, sells a pan of layered copper, stainless steel and silver. *C'est magnifique, mais ce n'est pas la cuisine.*

Most chefs continue to prefer traditional pans made of copper. But the chef probably doesn't have to re-surface them with tin periodically (although the old-time chef did exactly that). Professional chefs, it must be emphasized, like copper because they want a pan which will cool rapidly when taken off the heat. Chefs need control. That continuity of cooking, that keeps the food hot and gives you a chance to switch on the TV news and lay the table, is not wanted in a restaurant kitchen. As one piece of food is cooked, another one is started. Speed and control are everything.

Point, Fernand (1897–1955). Point was one of five men who took the ideas of Escoffier (without abandoning them) and created some of the better elements of present-day French cuisine. To take them in chronological order, I would start with **Edouard Nignon** (1865–1935), of whom it is said, "He spent half his life in white and the other half in black," for at the age of forty he abandoned the kitchen and became a maître d'hôtel. Nignon was an immense influence on the way restaurants were managed and menus created, but he was essentially a Parisian in spirit. The other four men were provincial and three of them had the good fortune to be on the main route between Paris and the Riviera at a time when wealthy people were discovering the pleasures of motoring.

Alexandre Dumaine (1895–1964) made the *Côte d'Or* at Saulieu a favorite place at which a gourmet would break a journey. Chef-patron **André Pic** (1893–1984), father of Jacques Pic, did the same thing at his restaurant at Valence. Together with **Marius "Père"**

Bise, with his restaurant on Lake Annecy, these two men made the role of the chef important in a way it hadn't been since Escoffier. So did their contemporary, the astounding Fernand Point, proprietor of the restaurant *La Pyramide* at Vienne (which was also on the route south). This was the man who influenced the restaurant trade more than any other man before or since.

Point was a "character," a bon viveur who believed that restaurant proprietors should be in the dining-room, not the kitchen. He employed a fine chef, Paul Mercier, and let him get on with the cooking while Point made sure his clients were content. So dedicated was Point that he refused to leave his restaurant even when he was invited for the maiden voyage of France's superb new ocean liner, the *Normandie*. He was brusque with people who smoked during their meal or arrived late, but—although his restaurant soon became a fashionable place for the international set of London and Paris—he made no distinction between his famous clients and his unknown clients, and I would say that is the finest policy for a great restaurant.

Everyone wanted to know Point's secrets. Proprietors of other restaurants sent their sons to work for him and he was a great teacher. Thuilier, both Troisgros brothers, Outhier, Chapel, young Bise and Bocuse worked at *La Pyramide*. Pierre Troisgros said that it was a revelation to find a kitchen where Escoffier's strict rules could sometimes be broken. Bocuse was with him for six years. Even though some of those people stayed only briefly and others had very lowly positions, it is a staggering list and all those "stars" acknowledge their great debt to Point. Remember too that their tuition came at a time when chefs were obsessively secretive about their craft; Point fought against that secretiveness. We should also note that Point attracted these disciples in his role as maître d'hôtel, not chef, although he had worked as a chef. (He was a poissonnier and a saucier in such top kitchens as the *Hotel Majestic* in Paris.)

And lastly we should note the things that those disciples *failed* to learn from their mentor. Point knew that a really good restaurant is run from the dining-room, not from the kitchen. He mixed with his clients and listened to their praise and their complaints. In his role of proprietor he made sure the dining-room service was always excellent, and he told the kitchen how to please the clients.

Compare this to today's chef-patron, so many of whom spend most of their time in the kitchen inventing unusual "combinations of flavor" and arranging food on plates. Or jetting round the world to the restaurants for which they are "consultants." They are not in touch with the wishes of their clients. And when they do parade through their dining-rooms the clients find it difficult to criticize the cooking of a chef-patron. This role change more than anything else has caused the sharp decline in standards of both service and food. Waiters, relegated to the role of plate-carrying, are demoralized; chefs are self-indulgent. The next generation of patrons might look afresh at the careers of the mighty Edouard Nignon and Fernand Point.

Poire: pear. Pears need more sun than apples and they flourish on dry stony soil. Because France has both those things in abundance, French

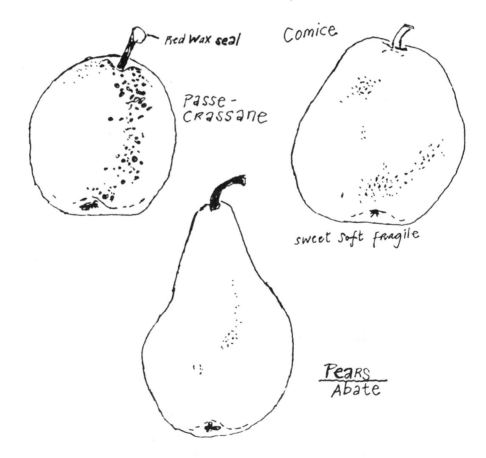

pears are arguably the best in the world. When choosing them, don't pay too much attention to appearance: some superb ones are unattractive. The William and the Comice are usually considered the best dessert pears. **Poire William,** a very fine **alcool blanc,** is of course made from the William pear.

Poireau: leek. One of the oldest foods known. The men building Egypt's pyramids were fed on it and the Israelites in the desert remembered it with longing. It's a hardy plant that survives the cruelest winter to provide food for Lent. It is revered in France as an ingredient for soups and stews and cherished as a vegetable fondue or as a gratin. In some regions of France a leek fondue is mixed with beaten egg and put into a pastry case and topped with more pastry to make what is called a **flamiche.** The affinity that leeks and onions have with sugar is marked by the way that a flamiche might be sweetened and flavored with alcohol and served as a dessert. You flinch? That's how the French feel when they hear that a real English Christmas pudding contains beef suet, or that Americans put pineapple and cherries on their baked ham.

Poisson: fish. Surely the best thing that has happened to the gourmet in recent years is the development of fish farming. Although I live on the sea and have grown blasé about having fresh salmon and salmon trout arrive at the door straight from the water, I would not take on any cash wager that depended upon my recognizing farmed salmon from what is now being called "wild." For people living far away from the sea there are great treats in store. Americans—once notoriously indifferent to fish, as I have found when serving it at dinner parties— are eating more and more of it. In America farmed fish is mostly trout, salmon and catfish but others are sure to come.

A fish chef I once worked with frequently said that a meal wasn't "serious" if it didn't include a fish course, and went on to say that a real fish course provided a whole fish to each diner. Remembering him I'm always pleased if I can find a suitable fish with which to do that. The appearance of the **rouget** makes it particularly attractive as a fish course.

Almost any fish is delicious served tepid with a dressing of flavored olive oil. I first had this sort of dressing at *Baumanière*. M. Thuilier told me that he put finely chopped tomato (no seeds or juice), basil and shallot into the oil for two days before straining it and serving it. He used this on his **rouget au basilic,** which was poached in a **court bouillon** strongly flavored with orange and lemon juice.

No one knows more about cooking fish than the Sordello brothers who run *Restaurant de Bacon*, a luxury fish restaurant in Boulevard Bacon, Cap d'Antibes. They say that fish must never touch ice or the flavor will drain from it. (In effect, of course, the ice freezes the fish at the point of contact and there is little sense in paying fresh fish prices for frozen fish.) At Bacon the fish are kept from the ice by a layer of heavy plastic. At this virtually unique restaurant customers choose their fish and specify the way they would prefer it cooked. The menu lists **Loup, Daurade royale, Chapon, Sar, Corb, St. Pierre, Marbre, Pageot, Merlan de palangre** and **Denti** and suggests the following ways of cooking them: **au basilic** (with basil), **à la nage de legumes** (poached with vegetables), **au cerfeuil** (with chervil), **grillé au fenouil** (grilled over burning fennel), **à la vapeur** (steamed) and **huile d'olive, citron, cerfeuil** (baked inside a paper bag with oil, lemon juice, chopped tomato flesh and chervil). Some customers prefer their fish raw. For them there is a **Salade de poissons crus** which is dressed with herbs and lemon juice.

Chefs disagree about serving fish with red-wine sauces. Some say only hard-fleshed fish and eels can withstand the red wine. Alain Senderens, a respected Paris chef now at the *Lucas-Carton,* served sea bass in red-wine sauce at his restaurant, *L'Archestrate,* and said, "Fresh fish can take red wine—old fish, perhaps not," and chose Pommard to accompany it.

Freshwater fish vary as greatly in flavor as they do in appearance. Fish from deep mountain lakes are particularly good and the same goes for fish from fast-running streams. River fish vary a great deal and those from slow-moving water sometimes taste muddy.

Poissonnerie: a fishmonger, and in France this is a very serious business. My local man offers a wonderful range of fish and shellfish. He is skilled and knowledgeable and good at preparing and filleting. So are the people in many fish shops in other parts of the world. But does your local man cook exquisite fish soup and sell it by the liter? Does he have beautifully prepared fresh escargots?

The fishmonger in Mouans-Sartoux near Grasse makes the best fish soup I've ever tasted. It varies from season to season according to the availability of the fish. He says the superb flavor is from the use of tiny crabs and **fiele** or **congre** (conger eel). He stresses that there is no need to use the expensive fleshy part of the eel; the tail is just as good. Without these two ingredients a fish soup will be bland, he says, no matter how much fish you use to make it. For background flavor the other essential is fish heads: as many as you can get.

Poisson d'Avril is nothing you should find on a menu. It's a joke or trick on the first day of April.

Poitrine fumée: smoked (pork) belly. Used in chunks (**lardons**) these are fried for a **mirepoix** or used warm in salads.

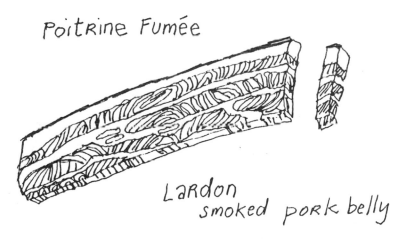

Poitrine Fumée

Lardon
smoked pork belly

Pommes. *Pomum,* the Latin word for fruit, eventually became the word for apple. Apple. What would life be like without this most delicious and versatile of garden fruit? It flourishes best in northern climates and has become a part of our heritage. Would history have recorded the event had Mr. Tell's son had a potato shot from his head? Would Isaac Newton's first thought have been of gravity had he suffered the impact of a ripe plum? I say no. And would Adam have given a second glance to an offered orange? An apple is the symbol of so many things:

sex, Halloween, marriage. Typically found in the English countryside, as well as in Austrian strudel, there is nothing more American than apple pie.

There are so many varieties of apple—tens of thousands, they say—that no one has counted or classified them. The Royal Horticultural Society's garden at Wisley, England, has over 700 varieties. The fruit specialist here eats a different one every day for breakfast and so comes round to the same kind of apple every couple of years. Comparison of British with French varieties invariably produces bitter argument. Merchants say that no one will buy a marked, bruised, specked or discolored apple and so they stock varieties that endure a bit of rough handling. Not surprisingly this leads to the growers producing apples with this as the prime characteristic. By the time the grower takes into account color and general attractiveness, disease resistance and storage life, flavor comes rather low on the list. Lucky people with ground enough to start an apple tree (you need a sapling; seeds are not reliable) should go for the most flavorful variety. Never use so-called cooking apples. I prefer to cook with sweet, flavorful

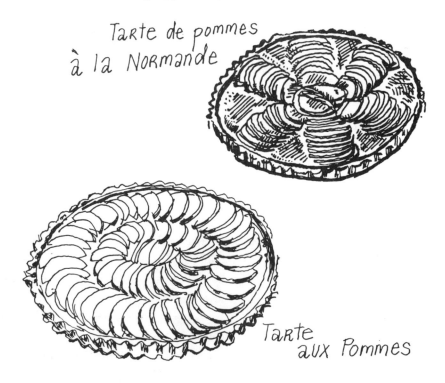

Tarte de pommes à la Normande

Tarte aux Pommes

dessert apples which, if a little undercooked, taste just as good if not better.

To my mind the most spectacular apple dish is the simple, but carefully prepared, apple tart (**tarte aux pommes**), its apple slices arrayed in patterns and glazed with home-made apricot jam to give it a sparkle. A close second comes the wonderfully chaotic **tarte Tatin** (*see* page 194). The **tarte de pommes à la Normande** is another dish that is both spectacular and delicious. Thinly sliced apple is laid into a pastry shell like the spokes of a wheel. The spokes are half-buried under a **frangipane** (an almond pastry cream with a touch of alcohol in it), although some cooks prefer a lighter custard.

Pommes de terre: (literally apples of the earth) potatoes. Confusingly this is often abbreviated to *pommes,* so your purée of apple might turn up as mashed potato. Michel Marucco—the maître d'hôtel at *Père Bise* for countless years—denied any possibility of confusion. He said that in French kitchen parlance mashed potato is always **pommes mousseline.** But last year at *Bise* the menu included a new dish: **tatin de pommes de terre au foie gras et truffe.** It was in the style of the traditional upside-down apple tart (**tarte Tatin**) using potato, truffle and foie gras. In another such double entendre Georges Blanc, who became the youngest three-star chef-patron in France, serves a **tarte aux pommes de terre.** It is an open potato tart which is designed to look exactly like a tarte aux pommes. Deighton's rule of thumb for distinguishing apple from potato is that when pomme comes first (**pommes Anna**) it's potato, but when pomme comes last (**purée de pommes**) it's apple. The French cook's versatility with the potato is delightfully described by James Bentley, an English resident in the Dordogne.[23]

> Speaking for myself, **pommes sarladaises** is the most refined way of cooking a potato known to mankind. Others might prefer the little balls of potato known as **pommes beynaçoises,** cooked at nearby Beynac-et-Cazenac. Still others prefer **pommes segonzac,** from Périgord blanc, where the potato is enhanced with chicken liver, sausage meat and truffles. Equally acceptable

is the traditional Dordogne stew made from potatoes and small **champignons,** the purée of potatoes that customarily accompanies **entrecôte,** or potato croquettes with chopped walnuts.

The pommes sarladaises—or **pommes de terre sautées à la sarladaise**—are potatoes fried in goose fat with lots of sliced truffles added half-way through the cooking process.

But the classic potato dish is probably **pommes de terre dauphinoise.** This starts with 2 pounds thinly sliced (yellow fleshed) potato half-cooked in milk. Anne Willan[24] says that the acidity of the potato presents a problem with this dish unless this first lot of milk is discarded, and fresh milk added. In any case you need to have about 3 cups milk intact by the time it goes into the oven. The milk and sliced potato are put in a basin with seasoning, a trace of garlic, grated nutmeg, a beaten egg, and 4 ounces finely chopped Gruyère cheese. Stir it to mix. Then lay it in a shallow oven dish and dab the top with more butter and Gruyère. Cook in a moderate oven for about 40 minutes, although some chefs leave it very much longer. Escoffier's recipe is very like this. Lyn Hall prefers to put 1 pound sliced potatoes into 1¼ cups whipping cream. Grated cheese goes on top. No chance of curdling. During the Second World War Fernand Point was brought before the magistrates for using black-market cream. His defense was that "no one has the right to betray a **gratin dauphinois.**" More recently there has appeared the **pommes de terre savoyardes.** For this the problem of the curdled milk is solved by the Procrustean solution of omitting the milk and substituting chicken stock.

The naming of these dishes as from Savoy and Dauphiné is particularly happy because the inhabitants of these eastern regions (rich in milk, butter and Gruyère-style cheeses) were the first French people to eat the potato, which they did in about 1650. (It wasn't until the mid-eighteenth century that Parmentier, a prisoner in the Seven Years' War, brought his enthusiasm for potatoes back from Prussia.)

Pommes (de terres) frites are French fries. They are fried twice: once to cook the inside by means of steam generated by the immersion in hot fat; a second time (in hotter fat) to crisp and color them. Usually they measure ⅜ inch square in section because that's one of the settings between the blades of the mandoline slicing machine.

Thinner sticks—³⁄₁₆ inch square—are fried only once and are called **pommes de terre paille** (straws) if fried pale in color, or **allumettes** (matchsticks) if browned and made very crisp.

Porc: pork. It is a joke amongst chefs that if you eat a fine steak, or a fine piece of lamb, you congratulate the chef, but if you eat a fine dish of pork you should congratulate the supplier. It is difficult to make tough pork into a delicious dish. Even fine pork has to be cooked with great care and attention. It is often said that any part of the pig can be fried if sliced finely enough. It is also true that any part of the pig can be tough.

Porchetta. A specialty of the Nice area. This is a whole baby pig boned and stuffed with breadcrumbs plus every edible part of the pig from tongue to tail. The breadcrumb stuffing contains herbs and a great deal of garlic, peppercorns, cumin and coriander. The stuffed pig is re-formed into a gigantic sausage before being cooked. It is sliced and served cold. Porchetta is sold cooked and ready to eat in local shops; it is not normally made at home.

slice of Porchetta

Port. Although the British believe that they are the only people who drink this fruity fortified wine from Portugal, the French are the largest importers of it. But in France it isn't passed round the table with the walnuts; it's served as an apéritif. It is not, to my knowledge, used in cooking.

Pot-au-feu: the "pot that is always on the fire." From it, with its varying ingredients, the peasant took broth and meat and vegetable according to the season and good fortune. In modern times such pot luck has been made into a specific dish of which a French cook is very proud. There is even a cut of beef called **macreuse à pot-au-feu.** Typically the beef (not salted beef, mark you) is cooked in water, vegetables (onions, leeks, carrots and cabbage) being added towards the end of the cooking period.

Brillat-Savarin said that the meat of a pot-au-feu is cooked in water "to extract its soluble parts."[25] This is a valuable definition. A modern scientist, Harold McGee,[26] talks of "maximizing the conversion of tough collagen in the connective tissue to water-soluble gelatin." That is the real magic of the chef's trade: the only successful answer to the alchemist's quest comes when the otherwise useless tough collagen is made into flavorful, sticky meat gravy. In the pot-au-feu the process is taken to extremes: all the best of the meat goes into the broth.

When a pot-au-feu is served, the meat and vegetables are served together and the broth separately. To return to the words of Brillat-Savarin, "The meat despoiled of its soluble parts is called **bouilli.**" The meat thus despoiled has little flavor left in it, so on the table with it you'll find mustard, pickled gherkins and perhaps some freshly grated horseradish. There are countless variations on this dish, some very grand. **Pot-au-feu albigeois** resembles a cassoulet with beans, raw ham, veal knuckle, goose and sausage. For some, a pot-au-feu must have veal; others prefer a tough old fowl, which might be filled with a delicious breadcrumb, chicken liver and salt pork stuffing. A **potée** is a simpler but comparable dish based on pork, cabbage and potatoes. All such dishes have a long cooking time to produce flavorful broth and tender meat.

Pots, glazed and unglazed. Lately I have seen cookbook writers advocating the use of unglazed pots. One suggestion was that the pot should be soaked in water before use. The fact that such porous materials absorb water means they'll absorb juices and flavors and harbor bacteria. Don't use them. The same applies to the unglazed clay pots sold for baking chickens. They provide nothing that can't be obtained with pots made of other materials, and are a potential danger to health.

Poularde, poulet, poussin, chapon and **poule.** A poulet is a young chicken of the sort you'll find on the supermarket shelf. There are many varieties: free-range, corn-fed and so on.

A poussin is a baby chicken, perhaps so small you'll need one per person. They are bony and lacking in flavor so they need a good sauce or accompaniment. Grilling them provides an appetizing color while retaining the juice and flavor. The way to do this is by making **poussin à la crapaudine,** which literally means a chicken like a toad. A poussin or a small chicken (or sometimes a pigeon) is hammered flat, breast upwards, the backbone having been removed with a heavy knife or shears. The bird is then flat enough to grill. The resulting shape of the bird makes it look somewhat like a toad.

A chapon is a capon, a castrated cock about 6 months old. Sometimes expensive but very good for roasting.

A poule is an old boiling fowl that no longer lays eggs. It is too tough for many recipes but excellent as **poule au pot,** sometimes called **poule au pot Henri IV,** which is prepared in the manner of a pot-au-feu (*see* page 170). But I notice that Escoffier's recipe for poule au pot says choose a tender hen. In other words don't make it with a poule!

Perhaps he would have used a poularde, a specially fattened 5-month-old "roaster," a flavorful juicy chicken if correctly cooked. (But poulardes don't exist outside France.) Of all the recipes for this bird **poularde en demi-deuil** is the most famous simply because of its memorable name. This "chicken in half-mourning" is so called because of the black slices of truffle that are inserted under the breast skin before the chicken is cooked in **bouillon.** This dish was made famous by a lady known as Mère Brazier,[27] who in a small restaurant in Lyon's rue Royale served to endless happy customers the same meal every day. It consisted of **quenelles de brochet, poularde demi-deuil** and **fonds d'artichauds au foie gras** with a young Beaujolais to drink. No wonder her restaurant has kept going ever since, still serving the same meal.

When I am lucky enough to get some wild mushrooms I like to make a dish I first encountered at *Père Bise,* where it is poetically called **Volaille d'automne.** Take a chicken whole or in pieces. (As with all such chicken dishes served "wet," the skin of the chicken must be removed, or the chicken must be fried for long enough to get the fat out of the skin. Discard this fat.) Heat a cupful of good stock in a heavy pot and put the chicken into it. Now add as many wild mushrooms as you can spare. Ideally there should be the same bulk of mushrooms as there is chicken. The pot should have a well-fitting lid (in the original version the lid is sealed with a flour and water paste). Cook in the oven at about 350°F. It will take an hour or 90 minutes according to the size of the chicken and how closely packed are the contents of the pot. Dried mushrooms are not at all bad for this dish.

Provence: a region of south-east France that was a province until the Revolution divided the land into départements. For the purposes of this book I've used it to refer to the area where the Provençal dialect is spoken, which is the coastal area from the mouth of the Rhône all the way to the Italian border.

Prune: plum. The French grow many delicious varieties of all shapes, sizes and colors. **Quetsche,** made into a liqueur of the same name, is famous. **Pruneaux** are prunes. Those dried plums that are so widely regarded as geriatric food are a delicacy in France, where varieties of plum are selected for drying because they do not ferment at the pit. These are soaked and gently cooked in sirop to make a compote regularly offered on the dessert chariots of France's great restaurants. To make a **compote de pruneaux** soak prunes overnight and drain them. Then cover with a half-and-half mixture of water and sweet white wine. Add lemon peel, cinnamon or other aromatics if you like. Poach for one hour. Cool. Serve. Look also for filled prunes, for example, **pruneaux d'Agen fourrés**, which are prepared and sold in boxes like luxury chocolates.

Quenelle. One of my friends, explaining to his father what a quenelle is, described it as a dumpling made from fish forcemeat. His father looked unhappy at the prospect of fish-flavored ones. The description is correct only if you forget any comparison with dumplings made from dough, as dumplings usually are. The sort of fish mixtures used for quenelles consist of very finely minced fish with egg whites and varying amounts of heavy cream. This rich mixture is called **quenelle mousseline.** Put into small molds the results are called **mousselines.** In theory light meats such as chicken and veal can be used instead of fish, but I have never seen such quenelles. At one time the pike quenelles (**quenelles de brochet**) were almost the only ones ever seen on menus. How much pike went into them is anyone's guess.

These mixtures—with variations of seasoning and fish—can go into larger molds or be used to stuff baked fish. For quenelles, spoonfuls of the mixture are dropped into simmering water so that they cook and become firm. Over the last few years quenelles, fish mousses and mousselines have become an essential part of the repertoire of dinner-party hostesses. It is of course the popularity of electric "food processors" that has made what, back in 1960, Elizabeth David called "a lengthy and tedious business, involving much pounding and sieving"[28] into a relatively quick job. This is fine by me, for I like these mixtures very much, especially when they are accompanied by the sort of carefully made sauce that their rather bland flavor demands. And Mrs. David makes a valid point about them when she complains that ready-made quenelles sold in Lyon's shops—and those in restaurants too—are likely to contain a substantial amount of flour. These heavier mixtures are in fact **quenelles lyonnaises.** They have a **panade** (a cooked preparation of seasoned flour, butter and milk) added to the fish and egg mixture. They are heavier and different from the quenelles mousselines and they need to be poached for about 45 minutes before being served.

My wife, who must have made a thousand mousses, regularly uses a recipe of Nico Ladenis[29] which employs only the whites of the eggs. So it was a surprise to be shown at *L'Auberge du Père Bise* that François Bise made his fish mousse using only the yolks of the eggs. Our experiments revealed that there was no difference in the compared results except for the yellow color that the yolks provided.

Quetsche: a type of plum that being less than wonderful to eat is dried to make prunes or a very fine **alcool blanc.** In Alsace the **tarte aux quetsches,** made like a **tarte aux pommes,** is deservedly famous.

Quiche. A quiche is a gratin baked in a pastry case instead of in a gratin dish. Any gratin can be a quiche and vice versa. The most famous is **quiche lorraine.** The pastry case is dotted with **lardons,** small pieces of smoked pork belly (sliced bacon being virtually unknown in France) or pieces of ham. Beaten egg with cream is then poured into the case, and it is baked gently so that the egg is cooked but soft. Sometimes cheese is put into the egg. It's delicious, but cheese is not an ingredient of an authentic quiche lorraine.

Ragoût. Do vague words come into wide use because they are vague; or do words become vaguer in meaning as their use spreads? Certainly the only thing you can be sure about if a ragoût comes to the table is that it won't be a roast. Even then . . . !

Raie: ray, skate, a large white flat fish of which the "wings" are eaten. In France it is almost invariably cooked as **raie au beurre noir** for which it is steamed or poached. Browned butter to which a trace of vinegar has been added is poured over the cooked fish.

Rascasse noir. This unattractive fish (with sharp poisonous spines) is variously called "scorpion fish," "toad fish" (**crapaud**) and the "sea devil" (**diable de mer**). It is said to be the only fish essential to a "real **bouillabaisse**," which represents a triumph of salesmanship; for this brown rascasse is less than delicious. It is used mostly to flavor soups. (Compare **rascasse rouge,** page 60.)

Ratatouille: a mix-up. This Provençal dish of well-cooked mixed summer vegetables usually includes zucchini, eggplant, onions, **poivrons** (bell peppers or capsicums) with tomatoes predominating and it has a garlicky flavor. This mixture is cooked to the consistency of a **fondue** using good olive oil. Herbs are used according to personal taste. It is served hot or cold as a vegetable.

The best ones I ever ate are made by Freda, my mother-in-law, who has lived many, many years in France. She uses lots of eggplant and lots of onion, little or no tomato. Her recipe is as follows: very gently fry chopped onion, **aubergine, poivron vert, poivron rouge** and **courgette.** These must all be fried separately, straining and using the same oil. Don't overcook and don't let anything go brown: the secret is to retain the juices in the vegetables. When all are done and set aside, gently fry a small piece of hot chili pepper and garlic to add a flavor to the oil, which is by now very flavorful. Mix all ingredients together and simmer for 20 to 30 minutes so the flavors blend. Discard the hot pepper and garlic. Serve.

Ravioli. Although obviously an Italian pasta dish—found in the region near Nice—the opportunities for putting bizarre fillings into these pasta envelopes have been exploited by France's nouvelle cuisine chefs. Would you believe oysters?

Repertoire. As far as a chef is concerned, this is likely to be a pocket-sized book. It lists, and very briefly describes, every dish he is likely to be asked to cook. This is a vital reference book if suddenly an old customer (or the boss) wants something not on the menu. (The kitchens of expensive restaurants are frequently faced with orders from customers who never give the menu a glance.)

Taking a typical repertoire,[30] looking up **ris de veau** and choosing an entry at random we read under the sub-heading *Maintenon*: *"Le ris de veau étant glacé, le dresser sur croûtons et le garnir de purée soubise et de lames de truffes. Sauce Suprême autour."*

For a professional chef that description is enough. Is it enough for you? A fuller description in English is provided on page 232.[31]

Reposé: rested. It is said of roast meat and poultry which is given anything from 15 to 45 minutes in a warm place after being cooked. This "resting time" will let the meat settle. Now it will be easier to carve, and lose less juice than meat carved immediately from the oven. Also that resting time gives you a chance to sharpen the knife and deglaze the pan.

Restaurant. Restaurants are a comparatively recent innovation. Until the eighteenth century there were inns for coach travelers (most of them dirty and squalid), and specialized cook-shops, **traiteurs,** where town dwellers could go for take-away dishes. For those with nowhere to take their food, the cook-shops provided a table where they could sit and eat it; it was called a **table d'hôte.**

All such places were tightly controlled by bureaucratic rules and regulations. In 1765 a soup shop named one of its special dishes a "restaurant" because of its restorative qualities. The cook-shops (traiteurs) were licensed to sell sauces and ragoûts, and their owners tried to get the offending establishment closed down. They pointed out that this "restaurant" wasn't a soup; it was a sheep's foot in white sauce. It was unfair competition, they said. But they lost their case.

Other establishments advertised restaurants in signs so prominent that the customers called these eating places "restaurants." The owners were soon officially classified as "restaurateurs." There was a choice of dishes and plenty of places to sit down. They were expensive but quieter, more comfortable and more formal than inns. There were no set meal times; customers could have what they wanted at any time. When, a generation later, the Revolution came, the guillotine put many of the chefs from grand houses out of work, while enriching many "radicals" who knew how to manipulate the Revolution to their own advantage. The old rules and regulations, about who could sell what, were annulled. The Revolution spawned bureaucrats by the hundred; and they had to eat. Napoleon's ruthless conquests made France powerful and Frenchmen rich. Paris was full of men who wanted to meet and entertain others for business or pleasure.

Restaurants met this need. They provided fine food and wine, and *chambres séparées* where both business gentlemen and ladies could practice their respective professions. But there was no place in these new establishments for the ostentations of the grand banquet, with its architectural set-pieces (**pièces montées**). A new sort of cuisine began. It was a "restaurant cuisine" that has dominated our world ever since.

Nowadays restaurant distinguishes an eating place more grand than a bistro and quieter than a brasserie, a place to eat a formal meal at a table you've reserved in advance. What does one want of a modern retaurant? For myself my needs are simple. First, there must be an emphasis upon food. I don't want a big menu and I am happy to eat the same dishes again and again, as indeed I do. I prefer traditional dishes perfected by skilled chefs; I distrust experiments or "exciting" flavor combinations. There must be proper regard to the seasons and the market. I want fresh food when it's in season. For that reason I like to see a menu—printed or hand-written or typed on a word processor—that is newly compiled every day. And dated. And why not expendable menus that can be on the table throughout the meal? Simple paper menus that you can look at as soon as you sit down; that you can take away with you or scribble upon if you so wish?

The next priority is that the staff should take a long-term interest in the success of the restaurant. I don't want high-pressure salesmanship, but neither do I want neglect, rudeness or even long faces. Now and again even a smile. In fact this means I incline towards the family-owned restaurant. I wish more guidebooks helped me to find them.

Third, I want space and daylight. I don't enjoy dark subterranean eating places no matter how good the lighting and ventilation. I like to be able to move my chair back an inch or two without knocking some poor devil into his soup. I want room all round the table for the waiter to serve the meal without putting his shirt cuff in my mouth. I'd like to eat a meal without a handful of cutlery being thrown into the center of the table with a resonant clang, and a happy cry of "Who's having the fish?"

Why is it that some restaurants can't evolve a system of ordering that denotes which customer ordered what? It is not difficult.

I like cloth napkins (and cloth table covers if possible). I like water on the table without having to ask for it. Iced water even. And I want butter that hasn't been recycled. Do I ask too much?

Reveillon: a meal eaten after Midnight Mass, especially one eaten in the early hours of Christmas Day or New Year's Day. For most Frenchmen these are the two most important festival meals of the year.

Rhum: rum. The British drink rum from Jamaica and Barbados or Demerara rum from British Guiana. Americans buy Puerto Rican rum or Jamaican. But French rum drinkers say the rums from Martinique (birthplace of Napoleon's Josephine) are best.

Rillettes: a fatty flavorful spread that can be made from roughly chopped fatty pork (for example, belly) left in a low oven overnight. Herbs and spices improve the flavor, and a small proportion of hare, rabbit, goose or duck may be added. Next morning the cubes of meat are shredded (using two forks) and left to cool. It is spread upon bread or toast. Make it in a pot that will look good on the table. Serve it as a first course, an appetizer or a snack. It doesn't keep well; the fat tastes rancid after two or three days. But meanwhile it's delicious.

Riz: rice. It is grown in the Camargue, the southernmost part of France, but this is the extreme edge of the rice-growing region and the climate makes it a difficult crop. A lot of the rice eaten in France is imported from Spain or Italy. Spanish rice can be as good as any, but it is often poorly sorted and packaged, and chefs say it is unreliable. Italian rice—mostly from the Po Valley—is preferred, the poorer quality being used for soup and the best for the **pilau.** Short-grain Piémont rice is used when the aim is to serve rice which has absorbed flavored liquid, for example for **risotto à l'Italienne** or **risotto aux truffes,** which is the same recipe with truffle sliced over it. Longer-grain Patna rice is used for the drier sort of presentation mound built high on the plate and called a **pilaf** or pilau.

There's far too much fuss made about cooking rice. In fact it's very easy. There is no accurate time to cook rice; neither is there an accurate amount of water that rice should absorb. Rice will go on absorbing water until it swells to the bursting point. It is simply a matter of deciding how much water you like in the rice you usually buy. Measure the water: try one and a half times the volume of the rice for your first experiment. Cook it; lid on or lid off, boiling or simmering; stir it whenever you like, start with hot water or with cold but cook it until the water is gone (making sure the rice doesn't burn). Taste it now and again as it cooks and swells, and decide how you like it best. Serve it.

If you like rice with separate grains (in many parts of the world, where chopsticks are used, they do not like separate grains), wash the rice under the tap before cooking it. Or buy washed or pre-cooked rice.

Brown rice is rice that is unpolished. It has more flavor, more protein, more oil and vitamin B too. It is easier to digest than polished rice. The only thing I don't understand about it is why anyone eats any other sort.

Rognonnade. This dish has no translation; it is uniquely French. A veal loin is boned, trimmed and rolled, so that a whole veal kidney—all its fat removed—forms a pink slightly underdone center filling for the meat. Most French butchers will prepare it so that the exterior is barded with strips of pork fat and the whole thing neatly tied into a roll, and ready for the pot. A rognonnade is cooked inside a closed pot, with a **mirepoix** to give extra flavor, and some white wine to keep the meat steamy. Although Jacques Pépin cooks it as a roast, giving it 30–45 minutes at 400°F.

Selle d'agneau, a saddle of lamb (a double loin cut), can be carefully boned and kept in one piece. This too is sometimes rolled and stuffed. Lamb kidney mixtures are often used for this.

A leg of lamb is sometimes prepared in a similar manner. It is boned and its center filled with kidney. In this case the kidney is chopped and lightly cooked and mixed with fried onion and breadcrumbs. Otherwise the kidney might be too underdone.

Roquefort: one of France's great cheeses, or perhaps we should say one of the world's great cheeses, for some enthusiasts would place it at the very top of any such list. Eat it between March and September.

Blue-veined, soft, yellow and summery (it's not good in winter), it should be made solely from ewes' milk and matured for a year to get its yellow color.

One visit to the town of Roquefort shows that this bleak spot does not produce the tons of cheese that bear its name. But all genuine roqueforts are put into the dank but naturally ventilated caves here to pick up the drifting spores of *penicillium roqueforti* from which the veining comes as the cheese ripens.

Roquette: rocket, arugula. One of my favorite salad vegetables. Easy to grow in almost any climate, it tastes like peppery walnuts. Use it alone or in mixed salads.

Rosé: pink, and **vin rosé,** a pink wine. Such wines, especially the pink champagnes, are held in contempt by some people who associate them with chorus girls in 1930s nightclubs. But the better examples of these pink wines are the delicious produce of great expertise. One wine expert told me that he'd never had a poor quality pink champagne: it was a guarantee of reliability. Poor quality vin rosé is bright red; look for a light brownish color.

Rouille: rust. This is also a very strong garlic mayonnaise given its red rusty color by cayenne and paprika pepper. Madame Prunier (with famous fish restaurants in London and Paris) started serving rouille with **bouillabaisse** instead of the more traditional **aïoli.** It caught on.

But rouille is usually served with fish soup. Stir it into the soup or spread it on toast or bread and eat it. In France indigent students order fish soup, knowing that they will be able to fill their stomachs on the big pile of bread and bowl of rouille that is put on the table first. Writers do the same thing.

Sabayon: wine and egg yolks, when beaten over a very low heat with sugar and white wine (or Madeira or marsala), thickens. It is served as a warm dessert. Back in the good old days, it was often made by the waiter at the table-side. In Italian cooking it is called *zabaglione*. Nowadays the word sabayon is used by nouvelle cuisine chefs when they thicken cooking liquids with beaten egg yolks to make a (flourless) frothy sauce.

Saignant: bloody, pink, the most common order for steaks, chops, liver and the like. While cooking, tiny red spots appear on the surface. If served immediately this is said to be saignant. Even less cooked is **bleu** (blue), while **à point** will bring a steak slightly more cooked than saignant but not **bien cuit** (well done). Tenderizers, which are plant enzymes, don't start to work until a temperature of 140°F is reached, so they will be no use for a steak cooked saignant.

Salade means salad as well as meaning a jumble or muddle. Elaborate mixed salads, California style, are rare in France. It will usually be just lettuce, **mâche,** or something similar, a refreshing mouthful that comes after the main course and before the cheese. Salad spinners make drying washed lettuce quick and simple. Before serving keep salad in the refrigerator using an absorbent cloth bag for it so it dries still more. It is tossed with a vinaigrette dressing immediately before serving. When dressed it should be "fatigued" and slightly limp. Wine is not served with a salad course to avoid the conflicting taste of the vinegar.

Salamandre: a salamander, a lizard, also a mythical fire-breathing monster and thus the name of an iron implement which can be made red hot in the coals of an open fire. It's then held very close to foods which have to be browned; for example, sausages, fish slices. Nowadays the absence of coal and wood-burning stoves has resulted in a new sort of salamandre. These gas—or even electric—grills produce an intense heat. It is a device which most chefs regard as virtually essential in a restaurant kitchen.

Salmis is a very old way of preparing game birds, used in Italian cooking since the Middle Ages. The birds are partly cooked, then cut up and the cooking process is finished at the table. The famous **caneton Tour d'Argent** is a salmis. Nouvelle cuisine, which consists almost entirely of filled plates brought from kitchen to table, has virtually eliminated many dishes that required such skills of dining-room staff.

Salpicon: food diced and bound in a warm sauce. It is the filling for **kromeskies** (*see* page 121).

Sardine. All over the world small oily fish of this sort are landed and sold as "sardines." But strictly speaking the sardine is a young pilchard (*sardina pilchardus*). Being an oily fish it is good for grilling, and in many parts of the Third World grilled sardines provide cheap protein for the poor. The oil content means that sardines (like herring and salmon) turn rancid quickly so they must be soon eaten or refrigerated. For this same reason this is a favorite fish for putting into cans with oil, olive oil or tomato sauce. Such canned sardines are highly regarded by the French and some expensive brands are stored in the belief that they improve with time. Such "vintage" sardines are now sold in the top Paris food shops such as Fauchon and Hédiard. (Both shops are in the Place de la Madeleine, Paris 8.) The sardines canned by Rödel of Bordeaux are often chosen as the world's best. Serve them with bread and butter, lemon and black pepper.

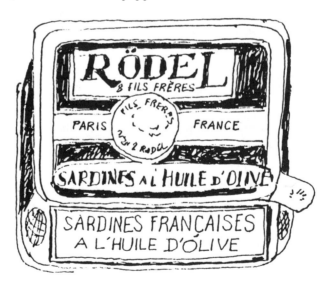

Sarriette: savory; a bitter herb that is used in France when cooking beans. Small goat cheeses are sometimes smothered in it. It should be used sparingly, for it is quite powerful. Summer savory is considered better than the winter variety.

Sauce. Of all the categorical demands of those converted to nouvelle cuisine the elimination of flour from sauces is the most far-reaching. Most converts want sauces based upon reduced cooking liquid or fat in which the food was cooked. Sometimes alcohol, butter or cream is added, or egg is beaten into the liquid to make a **sabayon.** Sometimes vegetable purées are used to thicken a sauce.

That remarkable food journalist Paul Levy, writing in the *Observer* newspaper in 1980 (having been told the same thing by "God knows how many chefs and their wives or maîtres d'hôtel"), reported, "The liaison is *never* made with flour, which is universally considered indigestible when combined with animal fats. Thus all classical sauces based on a flour and butter **roux** have been flung out of the window." Levy went on to say that Julia Child seemed to be the one dissenting voice. She said that flour was the ideal thickener for some sauces. She was not an admirer of the new sauces.

Well, that was some years ago, and the dust has settled on the kiwi fruit. Nouvelle cuisine is not as universally admired by all those chefs and their wives and their maîtres d'hôtel. It never did really influence domestic cooking. And when one looked at it more closely, it was clear that those animal fats, butter, cream, eggs and alcohol that were being substituted for flour were far more fattening and unhealthy than that much-maligned substance that man has been eating for about 6,000 years.

Sauce tartare: made like mayonnaise, but you start with the yolks of hard-boiled eggs, stirring them hard while adding mustard and then adding the oil a little at a time, just as with a mayonnaise. When the emulsion is complete add chopped chives, parsley, chervil and gherkins. Some recipes add cream too.

Steak tartare is a preparation of raw beef. One excellent Parisian restaurant[32] served 9 ounces minced beef alongside which the following ingredients were arrayed to be mixed according to the customer's instructions: a raw egg yolk, finely chopped onion, tomato ketchup, lemon juice, olive oil, chopped parsley, Worcestershire sauce, fresh pepper and salt and Dijon mustard. The garnish was watercress.

Saucissons. These are the large sausages sold in the charcuterie to be sliced and eaten without cooking. Many of them contain raw meat that has been salted, smoked or dried. **Saucisse** is the smaller variety that needs cooking. The most common of these are the **saucisses de campagne** (country sausages), which are made of pork and dried for a week. They are intended for soups and stews and you should cook them in liquid, not fry them. Some like **saucisses de Francfort** need only warming. **Saucisses de Toulouse** are no more from Toulouse than frankfurters come from Frankfurt. They contain coarsely chopped meat and are the best choice for the **cassoulet. Saucisses de Périgord** contain pieces of truffle and are usually made with wine. **Saucisse d'Espagne** is the dried, smoked Spanish *chorizo* under another name, although the French ones are usually milder than the fiery ones from across the border. The most unusual sausage I found was the **saucisson aux légumes,** brightly colored by its chopped vegetable content. Don't be put off by its strange appearance; it was rather good to eat.

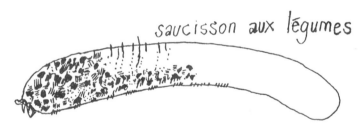

saucisson aux légumes

Saucisson fumé: smoked sausage, usually of salted pork. Some varieties are very hard like salami, and are thinly sliced and served cold; others need to be poached in water for 20 minutes or so before being served. Of the many varieties on sale in a local market I sketched the ones on the page opposite.

    Morteau or **Jesus de Morteau** is a large shiny-red salted and smoked pork sausage that takes its name from a town in the Jura. It is a favorite at Christmas. **Saucisson de Lyon** is another large sausage of coarsely ground pork and very salty in flavor. **Gendarme**—as well as being a member of the rural police force run by the French army—is jovially applied to salt smoked herrings

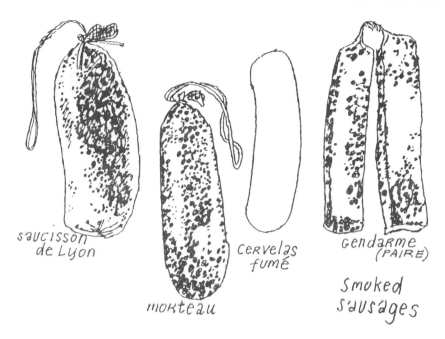

saucisson
de Lyon

cervelas
fumé

Gendarme
(PAIRE)

morteau

Smoked
Sausages

(hareng saur) and to a hard smoked sausage, rectangular in shape, resembling in flavor and texture the German Landjaeger wurst. They are sold in linked pairs. **Cervelas** is a pale pink smoked pork sausage of delicate texture and garlicky flavor. They vary greatly in quality but the good ones are delicious. This is a favorite sausage for wrapping in brioche. It is often served cold and sometimes as an ingredient in a salad dressed with vinaigrette. But it tastes better hot.

Saumonette: preposterous misnomer for the dogfish. In some parts of France it's called **roussette.** Its ugly head and rough skin are usually removed before it's put on display at the fish shop, revealing its pink flesh; hence the name. In Britain's fish and chip shops it's fried in batter and called "rock salmon."

Sauter: jump; to fry in a frying pan or skillet. A **sautoir** is a straight-sided pan in which the food jumps when a sudden jerk of the pan turns the food over. To avoid getting splashed with hot fat, minimal amounts are used. Sautéed food is often finished in liquid using the same pan.

Sel: salt. It is a common myth that salt "brings out flavor." If this were true wine tasters would put it into their wine and tea tasters put it into their tea and so on. The fact is that flesh foods contain salt (and so to a lesser extent do vegetables), and when these foods are cooked so that they reduce in volume (for example, stocks and broths), the taste of salt increases too. So salt is added to foods in an attempt to confuse the palate: to persuade you that the taste of the salt is the flavor of concentrated protein.

Salt does not add to flavor, it disguises flavor, and it is unhealthy too. The foods used in the kitchen already contain more than enough salt, but salt is addictive and people who use it want more and more of it. I haven't used salt in the kitchen for many years, although I put it on the table when we have guests. The manufacturers of processed foods like to feed and promote salt addiction (and sugar addiction too) and if you read the very tiny print you'll find lots of salt has been added to most prepared foods; for example, canned soups, ice cream, canned vegetables and even fruit pies.

Salt types vary according to whether they have been evaporated from the sea or dug out of mines. There are flavored salts too (garlic and celery) and ones with chemical additives to make it pour more easily. ("When it rains it pours.") But it is all sodium chloride and, unless you are hacking your way through a jungle and losing body salts through perspiration, it is bad for your health and destructive to your sense of taste. The same applies to MSG (monosodium glutamate), which is such a widespread cause of sudden nausea, headaches and giddy spells that such symptoms are called "Chinese restaurant syndrome."

Selle: saddle, a double loin cut—usually of lamb or mutton—from behind the ribs, rack or **carré.** A beef carcass comes to the butcher split in two, but a lamb carcass comes whole. This provides a chance for him to cut a saddle, which is two loins joined together. This can be boned and rolled to make a spectacular "boneless loin roll" and lamb kidney can be rolled inside it, like a stuffing.

If the word selle appears on your menu, you'll probably get a double loin chop or what is sometimes called an "English chop." Although I remember that when we were dining in *La Bonne Auberge* in

Antibes, my wife was served a famous specialty of the chef, Jo Rostang, **selle d'agneau en feuilletage,** a tiny saddle of lamb, boned and rolled, filled with spinach stuffing and cooked *en croûte.* Although such a dish is too large for one person, the order was taken without complaint or comment and the waiter insisted that I share some of it. That is what I call a real restaurant.

Selon grosseur, S.G., is a menu marking to show that a dish will be charged according to size or weight. A lobster dish or caviar is typically priced in this way, or rather left unpriced in this way.

Semoule: semolina. Originally this was durum wheat, but now it includes any coarsely ground flour including rice and corn. Its coarseness brings air, and thus lightness, into flour-based foods that would otherwise be too heavy; for example, gnocchi. It is used to make dried factory-made pasta. Fresh egg noodles should not be made from semolina; use household flour. The result will be far better. Semolina has an appetizing flavor and even Britain's much maligned semolina pudding—made with butter and cream—can be delicious. In France semolina is available in varying fineness. **Semoule de maïs** is sometimes labeled polenta and can be used for that dish.

Service. This is a supplementary charge made by the management and put on your restaurant bill. The implication is that the waiter gets his money, that it is in effect a tip. But you cannot be certain that your waiter will ever see it. **Service compris** marked on a bill means that the tax (called TVA in France) is included and the management does not expect you to pay the waiter anything above the total on the bill. They have taken it from you already. **Service en sus** means that the management expects you to give a tip to your waiter. So does the waiter. Which reminds me of a wonderful story about Alexander Korda, the film producer,[33] who was warmly and enthusiastically welcomed into any restaurant in London, even those establishments with which he'd run up gigantic unpaid bills. Asked how this could be, Korda said, "Always tip in cash." It is a good policy.

Sirop: a sugar and water mixture. The Roux brothers make their **sirop à sorbet** by boiling 2 pounds 3 ounces sugar and 6 ounces glucose in 5 cups water. Such syrups are widely used in France, where the compote (fruit poached in syrup) is the most popular type of dessert. When, at the end of the nineteenth century, canned fruit imported from America created such a sensation in Europe, the contents of the cans were compotes. The fruit cooked in syrup exactly suited the canning process.

Syrups or compotes are the basis for ice creams. A mashed or blended can of fruit is a convenient way to make either water ice or (with equal amount of cream added) a fruit ice cream. However, the compote is not good from a nutritional standpoint. All sugar is unhealthy and even the light cooking of the fruit destroys its vitamin content.

Sole: sole. The French are not a great fish-eating nation. Their per capita fish consumption is only a quarter that of the Danes and two-thirds of the Britons. Transport is of course a major problem, and sea fish is just not fresh enough by the time it reaches most French restaurants. True sole (*Solea solea*) is found in the Mediterranean but the best ones come from the North Sea.

Although sole has a fine clear flavor when newly caught, that is not why it has achieved a paramount position in the chef's repertoire. The sole is available all the year round. It is expensive. It can be fried, grilled, steamed and baked. Its fillet is solid: it can be rolled, twisted and shaped and even beaten flat and otherwise handled without falling to pieces. (Try such recipes with a plaice fillet to see the difference.)

Sorbet: water ice. I am tempted to leave it at that, for the science of ice-cream making is very complex. Water of course freezes hard, so to make edible frozen foods we use ingredients that will not freeze hard: fat and sugar mixtures.

The professional French chef starts with a **sirop à sorbet** (*see* recipe above). To make a **sorbet au champagne** mix 3 cups of this syrup with a bottle of champagne (plus one lightly beaten egg white and the juice of a lemon) and freeze it. Or put it in an ice-cream maker (**sorbetière**). So far so good.

But what about the sorbets made from fruit and fruit juices? This is more difficult because the professional chef wants a sorbet that comes straight from the freezer to the table and is soft enough to eat. (Is that possible? Yes, for in a professional kitchen there is no space or willingness to take ice cream from the freezer in advance and let it soften at room temperature.)

To make such sorbets the cooked fruit is mixed with sugar syrup in the exact proportions that produce the right frozen texture. The sweet flavor of such mixtures is not taken into account; the amount of sugar added is measured solely according to a hydrometer (which reads specific gravity in degrees Baumé). A syrup made with 6½ pounds sugar and 3½ cups hot water will measure about 30 Baumé. But the addition of fruit purée will of course change the specific gravity. And each fruit requires a different specific gravity reading to make the frozen texture right. Because, like sugar, acidity lowers

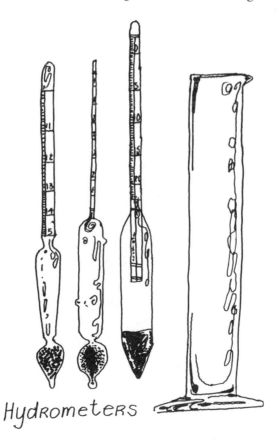

Hydrometers

the freezing point of such mixtures, acid fruits have less sugar added. Aim for 17 Baumé. Don't add any alcohol until you've got the hang of it, because alcohol reduces the temperature at which it will freeze. If you want the flavor of alcohol—a fruity **eau de vie** can do wonders for a fruit sorbet—pour it over each portion when serving it.

If you feel like experimenting with this fascinating subject you should buy the type of hydrometer that floats (not the syringe type). Or you can do as Helmut Loibl does when instructing at the renowned Culinary Institute of America. He uses a whole raw egg (in its shell) instead of a hydrometer. He adds sugar to the flavored water to make the egg float until a small circle "the size of a nickel" is exposed. This proportion of water to sugar is just right, he says. But he likes to whip a little egg white into the mixture "to make the sorbet smooth." If you are already an expert in this business I suggest you write a book about it, for even the professional ice-cream manufacturers need to know more. And many domestic cooks would like to make something from the fresh fruit crop.

Sot-l'y-laisse: "oyster," small juicy morsels on each side of a chicken's backbone. Literally it means "only fools leave it."

Soufflé means to inflate or puff up. The soufflé is one of the most effective weapons in the cook's armament. It's quick and easy and all you need are eggs, butter and flour. Make a **sauce béchamel** so that it's precisely as stiff or slack as your bowl of beaten egg whites. Beat egg yolks into the warm sauce, then pour the mixture onto the beaten egg white. If they are of the same texture they will mix (or fold as the recipe writers say) easily without smashing the bubbles too much.

Acidity helps the beating of the egg white, so some chefs add a pinch of cream of tartar to every egg white. But even more helpful is the addition of sugar. One or two teaspoonsful of powdered sugar per egg white added gradually while beating adds to the stability of the foam. This is very useful when making **omelette norvégienne** (baked Alaska). This is ice cream on sponge cake and covered all over with beaten egg white before being baked in a very hot oven. Note that the egg white becomes less stable when in contact with a cold surface.

To continue with your soufflé: add a filling if you have it; for instance, chopped fruit. Pour the whole mixture into a well-buttered dish (a straight-sided soufflé dish for the best results). Cook it in a hot oven.

A soufflé doesn't have to be made from a béchamel; you can beat the egg yolks into a purée of fish, fruit or the like and stir that into the beaten egg white. This is called a flourless soufflé. And soufflé mixtures do not have to be confined to making soufflés. At *Baumanière* they put a sweet mixture into a once-folded crêpe so that it opens in the oven. Recently I did the same thing using a boned trout instead of a crêpe and filling it with an herb and shrimp mixture.

The best soufflés set the protein with the bubbles at their largest. For a creamy texture with a slightly runny middle set the oven at 400°F. For one cooked right through, especially if it's a large one, 325°F will be better. Otherwise your big soufflé will be nicely crisp on the outside but collapse wetly in the middle. Some chefs cook them in a bain-marie to provide a moist steamy oven for a slow gentle set.

In restaurants chefs and waiters like a slightly over-cooked soufflé; undercooked ones can collapse before you get them to the table. Because of this, restaurants are likely to serve a sauce with the soufflé to moisten it.

Pommes soufflés are slices of yellow waxy potatoes (**pommes de terre Hollande**) fried twice in such a way that they become little inflated air cushions.

Soupe. Originally this was a mixture like oatmeal porridge and the English sop (bread dipped in soup) is from the same root; so is the word supper. This porridge was the peasant's main meal and eaten in the evening. His midday meal was bread or hard cheese eaten in the fields: luncheon means slice. Even today the French peasant might say soupe to mean his evening meal. For such historical reasons some chefs do not think a soup is suited to a luncheon menu.

Soupe de poisson is a soup made from fish, perhaps including shellfish. Often the soup is made thick by pounded flesh and colored by shell. **Soupe aux poissons** is a fish soup which contains pieces of fish, like a stew. Wine is not served with a soup course.

At *Lyon de Lyon* I was served a wonderful rabbit and lentil soup. I particularly liked the way in which lentils and pieces of rabbit were placed in a soup plate on the table and the soup was ladled over it. At the fish restaurant *Bacon* in Antibes, the various fish of the bouillabaisse are removed from the skin and bone and arranged with slices of potato on the plate before the soup is poured upon it. This attractive way of serving would suit many other soups; for example, crab, lobster or thick soup with sausage slices.

Sous vide: under vacuum. A recent method of food preservation. Fresh raw ingredients are sealed into a plastic wrapping from which all air is withdrawn. This "shrink-wrapped" pouch is then stored at about 32°F, which is a little cooler than the average domestic refrigerator.

This technique began sometime in the mid-1970s when French chefs found that the foie gras dealers were sending whole goose livers to them sealed in transparent plastic vacuum packs. They found that they could cook the livers without unwrapping them. Furthermore the juices and fat that are normally lost remained inside the sealed package and so there was no weight loss. This meant a considerable financial saving. Chefs, with labor costs always rising, found that it was worth installing a sealing machine in their kitchens. They could then have their staff preparing vegetables for use the following day, or long after. Now many restaurant kitchens keep the refrigerator drawers filled with small shrink-wrap packs of beautifully prepared raw vegetables for use as and when needed.

It was not long before the international food companies got into the act. Instead of raw meat or prepared vegetables being wrapped in this way, the sous vide idea was adapted to produce "gourmet meals" that could be heated in steam ovens for immediate use in restaurants that had no kitchens! These meals included such ambitious dishes as "rack of lamb" and what is audaciously called "poached salmon." French Railways installed the machinery and were the first to use the method extensively. The director of food research for *Hilton Hotels*—who use it in their hotels—said it is the way of the future.

Sabim, a catering company, built a Paris factory to mass-produce sous vide meals.

The famous restaurateurs, the Roux brothers, brought it to Britain. Some who have tasted the results say it works well for long-cooked stews and things that are easy to heat up but is less good for quickly cooked things such as fish. Another user says it is good only for complex sauces. Lyn Hall—an authority on the science and skills of food preparation—says, "The volatile oils which we savor when eating are completely drawn out by this process." *Business Weekly* says a kitchen payroll can be expected to drop by 20 percent and that sous vide "helped cut food preparation from 42 percent to 33 percent of costs," adding, "But those savings have not been passed on to customers. They have gone directly to the restaurant's bottom line."[34]

Sucre: sugar. Perhaps it is enough to quote a historian who has a specialized knowledge of sugar's history. Leaving aside the miseries of the slave trade, toothaches and obesity, says Henry Hobhouse, author of *Seeds of Change,* "after the acknowledged drugs sugar is probably the most damaging of the commonly consumed addictive substances, and is known to be associated with at least one type of cancer."

Sugar is an unnecessary part of our diet. Eating sugar gives an immediate "fix" for the blood sugars and it is this elation which makes people of all ages crave sugar. The craving is chemical, not psychological, and becomes more and more frequent. And when the body becomes used to sucrose, it finds the digestion of starches and fiber more and more difficult. So the sugar addict avoids such foods as whole-grain bread, raw vegetables and fruit which are so necessary for good health. On the other hand, people who eat enough starch and fiber do not crave sugar. Readers who want to kick the sugar habit should note that the processed food industry, which makes virtually all its income from selling unhealthy foods, puts sugar into everything from sausages to soup, from cheese to cornflakes. Artfully it also makes sure there is plenty of sugar in the high-fiber foods it packages.

Table d'hôte. Originally this was a real table in one of the cooked food take-away shops that came hundreds of years before restaurants were invented in the eighteenth century. Here the take-away customer with nowhere else to go could sit down and eat. Often the chef-patron would eat at this table too.

My old friend Quentin Crewe[35] says, "In some sleepier provincial towns, in small commercial hotels, you may still find the real table d'hôte where for a modest sum you will eat whatever the family are eating." Nowadays this expression is used in Britain to mean a complete fixed price meal, which in France is called a "menu."

Taillevent, named for a fourteenth-century chef, is a restaurant just a short walk from the Arc de Triomphe. Formerly this old house was an embassy and the interior reflects that tenancy. The proprietor, M. Jean-Claude Vriant, chose for his chef Claud Deligne, and between them these two men created what most French experts regard as the finest restaurant in the world. Forget all the publicity-chasing chefs and their nouvelle cuisine; here is a discreet mixture of the old and the new.

Tarte: tart. A pastry liner into which the cook can put fruit, savory or cream custard fillings. Vegetable fillings such as onion are not unknown.

Tarte Tatin, or more exactly **la tarte des demoiselles Tatin,** was invented by the Tatin sisters, Caroline and Stéphanie, at their *Hotel Tatin* in Lamotte-Beuvron, Loir-et-Cher. It is still on the menu there. It is a dramatic variation of the sort known in America as an upside-down cake. Apple—sometimes in large pieces or even in halves—is caramelized with butter and sugar in a frying pan, a crust (**pâte brisée**) is put on top and it's cooked in the oven. Finally the whole thing is turned out and served apple side up.

A **tourte** is a covered tart or pie. A **flan** should be a custard tart, but usually turns out to be a caramel custard.

Tendron. For many a Frenchman this word is enough to conjure up visions of his favorite dish, **tendron de veau.** This middle cut of breast, which in America is called riblets, includes the crunchy cartilage which makes it so popular. These ½-inch slices, taken from the

195 • T H É

full width of breast meat, are braised with just a trace of stock to moisten them. The result is sticky gravy, and browned slices of veal with the edges crisp.

Terrine: a forcemeat, usually a rich and fatty preparation cooked inside an earthenware pot—terrine—from which the finished dish takes its name. Pork, pork liver, game or poultry—or combinations of them— are used and the mixtures often include strips of such meats arranged to effect a decoration when sliced. Terrines can be simple or elaborate. Lately fish and vegetable terrines have become fashionable.

Richard Olney[36] feels strongly about them. He doesn't like such mixtures put inside pastry. He chops the meat by hand; grinders massacre the meat, he says. Cognac for the marinade "lends a false, slightly rotten, gamy taste and renders the terrine indigestible." An eau de vie added just before cooking is far better, says Olney. No unnecessary liquid; no milk in which bread is soaked. Instead a "highly reduced gelatinous stock." I'd say he has got his priorities right. In short, don't embark on making a terrine unless you'll provide first-class ingredients and careful workmanship.

Thé: tea. It consists of tiny leaves, buds and sometimes flowers of one species of camellia. In China, where it was probably first used as a drink in the sixth century, the tea was boiled up to make a stimulating but coarse-tasting drink quite unlike the delicate ones that Europeans made when they discovered the delights of tea in the seventeenth century. Still today tea is boiled in North Africa, Turkey, Australia and by people who like that fierce flavor. Good coffee can be made from any reasonably fresh water, but tea will vary a great deal according to what the water is like. Some tea merchants will sell you tea suited to the water supply of the place where you live.

There can be little doubt that tea—like coffee—kept its place as one of the world's most popular drinks because only scalding hot water will bring out its true flavor. This meant that throughout all the times and places where the water supply was dangerously impure, boiled tea was a relatively safe drink. Nowadays, with safe water taken for granted, sweet carbonated drinks supported by billions of dollars of advertising are taking the place of tea and coffee.

But tea is a sophisticated drink that will not readily give way to fizzy colas. In China it is the staff of life; Russians thrive on it. In Japan it's the basis of their most elaborate ritual and for it the most exquisite porcelain was developed. The economy of the Indian sub-continent was drastically changed by it. Some British colonists grew rich on the crop, while other British colonists, resenting the restrictions and tax on tea imports, staged the Boston tea party and began the American Revolution. British demand for it led to the design of not one but two of the most efficient and beautiful ships that ever sailed: East Indiamen and clippers. Tea comes blended and unblended, smoked (lapsang souchong), fermented (black), half-fermented (oolong) and unfermented (green), and is consumed hot and icy cold. The names are pure poetry: Lapsang Souchong, Earl Grey, Darjeeling, Gunpowder, Twankey, Keemun and Ching Wo. Nowadays, says Jennifer Lang (author of *Tastings*), after water tea is the cheapest beverage in the world, costing about one-sixth of the equal amount of brewed coffee.

Tea was so precious and expensive that traders in China and Europe adulterated it with the leaves of other plants and herbs: jasmine, orange, lemon, bergamot, gardenia and many other plants were used. Some tea drinkers found the adulterated teas very much to their taste and some (jasmine and Earl Grey, for example) remain popular today.

In France brews (**infusions**) made from other plants are taken very seriously. During the Second World War, shortages prompted the French to rediscover all kinds of old herbal "teas." Most good French restaurants offer a selection of such drinks. These would possibly include chamomile, agrimony, bergamot, verbena (**verveine**) and lime flowers (**tilleul**). These herbal infusions (**tisanes**) are said to remedy everything from tiredness and constipation to impotence. They are useful for people allergic to tea and coffee, as many people are. Jacques Pépin uses them as flavorings.

Additionally there are ordinary teas to which added flavors have been given. Thus although, in some Arab countries, mint tea means boiling water poured upon mint leaves, in others mint leaves are added to the brew of tea. The most common such flavoring is a slice of lemon, although it should not be added to an expensive China tea, which is drunk without milk, sugar or anything else.

Although serious tea drinkers like to brew tea for at least three minutes, the caffeine in tea increases as the tea is brewed. To get a strong-flavored, low-caffeine cup of tea, brew plenty of tea for a short time. Small children should only be given tea that has brewed for no longer than one minute. Tea without milk sometimes forms a cloudy sheen on its surface—due to the chalk in the water; a slice of lemon or lime removes that sheen as well as adding flavor.

A **salon de thé** is usually a few tables and chairs in the rear part of a pâtisserie. Such places came back into fashion in France in the 1970s. They serve coffee, tea, cakes and sandwiches. Very often it can be a convenient place to get a light meal too. Lately chic salons de thé in Paris can be found in combination with shops selling books or antiques and the "muzak" will be Mozart and Haydn.

Thuilier, Raymond (1890–). The people in the restaurant business are an exclusive fraternity. The successful chefs take each other's sons into apprenticeships and instinctively join in the sort of mutual declarations of uncritical admiration that in other countries are the *modus operandi* of actors and physicians. So what of the chances of an insurance man who, aged fifty-one, finds an infinitely remote site on an inhospitable peak, and wants to start a restaurant there? And what if he did so at the depths of his country's greatest disaster: 1941?

It's true that Raymond Thuilier's widowed mother ran a hotel and passed to him a passion for cooking. And although Thuilier preferred kitchen whites to the dark suit of a patron, he did not appoint himself maître-cuisinier for his restaurant; he employed a first-class chef. And he went into partnership with a lady who was happy to devote her time and skills to the dining-room and the clients. It is also true that Thuilier had nursed this obsession for most of his life, and that he'd made friends with some of the great chefs and restaurateurs of France, including Fernand Point.

It was also his good luck that the local official from the tourist department, who encouraged Thuilier with his audacious project, was a man named Pompidou. He remained a faithful client after becoming President of France.

In 1946 the restaurant, *L'Oustaù de Baumanière,* opened at Les Baux, its site surmounting the Val d'Enfer (Valley of Hell). It took only a couple of years to get Michelin's attention and a star. By the time he'd been open for eight years he had the top award of three stars. He extended *Baumanière* to include many luxury bedrooms and opened another excellent hotel and restaurant nearby. He has vegetable gardens to provide him with fresh produce. Additionally M. Thuilier is the mayor of the village. In his spare time he is a dedicated amateur painter. But his restaurant is not neglected. In 1972 he served a meal to the Queen of England. His life provides inspiration for those middle-aged people who feel like changing vocation.

Raymond Thuilier is not interested in the new theories of some of his fellow chefs. Nothing is new in cooking, he insists. I shall never forget my first visit to the *Baumanière* kitchen. This was long before Barrier at Tours had built for himself a kitchen bigger than his dining-room, or the Troisgros brothers had created the amazing kitchen at Roanne. In those days most kitchens were the same dark cramped places that I remember from my days working in them. But Thuilier's kitchen was breathtaking: it was the smallest, darkest, most inconvenient and uncomfortable little place I'd ever seen. It was the first time I'd ever encountered an electric machine for rolling pastry—a device like a stainless steel mangle—and it took up so much space that you had to squeeze between it and the stove to get to the sink. I could not help wondering what kind of man Thuilier must be to go to so much trouble to start a restaurant and then consign himself to such a place. The question remains unanswered. Thuilier, a tough, outspoken, yet studiously polite perfectionist, was never the sort of man to reveal much of himself.

Tiède: tepid. The fashion for lukewarm foods began when chefs started to serve salads with hot croûtons and hot bacon pieces. Then the fat of the cooked bacon was mixed with a trace of vinegar to make a warm salad dressing. Then came warm foods served as part of a salad: slices of warm foie gras came first and then a salad with warmed goat cheeses. And the fashion is not confined to salads. Chefs have discovered what the housewife has always known, that pastry is more tasty warm than cold. Haeberlin at *L'Auberge de l'Ill* offers warm flaky pastry with his woodland strawberries to make **feuilleté tiède aux fraises des bois.** Refrigerated food tastes stale and flavorless. Cold lobster, cold chicken, cold duck, cold salmon and so on are much more delicious if freshly cooked and served at room temperature. Just about all cold foods are best served tiède.

Tomate: tomato. From Latin American *tomatl,* which was the Aztec name for tomato. The first varieties coming to Europe in the sixteenth century were yellow. The Italians called them *pomodoro* (golden apple) which the French wishfully made into *pomme d'amour* (love apple). It is astounding that it took hundreds of years for the tomato to become popular. In the early nineteenth century it was not widely eaten. Even by the 1890s few people dared to eat them raw. It is hard to envisage Provençal or indeed Italian cooking before the tomato took over.

The tomato was one of the earliest successes of the canning industry, and canned tomatoes—whole, chopped, paste, purée or sauce—provide a year-through standby for any cook. Canned tomatoes ripen on the vine and usually have more flavor than shop-bought ones. Read labels and avoid salt or sugar. Some chefs buy big cans of purée and freeze them as convenient cubes. Paste in a tube must be kept in a refrigerator after it's opened.

Nowadays the tomato is one of the world's most popular foods. It dominates European and American cuisine and its use in commercial food preparations is without equal. There are many varieties, and I grow at least four different ones in my garden: a large, ugly, flavorful brute, a tiny "cherry" variety, a less interesting commercial hybrid that crops generously and never fails, and one or two that I change from year to year for the sake of experiment.

In the kitchen the freshly picked tomato is a delicious ingredient of salads and sauces. For salads they should be skinned and the watery pulp and seeds discarded (for use in sauces). To remove the skin, use a fork to hold the tomato in fast boiling water, or in a gas flame, just long enough to break the skin. According to its ripeness this will require from 10 seconds to 1 minute. Immediately plunge the tomato into cold water so that the flesh doesn't cook. Now the skin should come away easily. Slice the tomato into halves, always through the equator, not pole to pole, and remove seeds and juice. Cut the flesh up, toss in a viniagrette made mostly with good olive oil and add a little freshly ground pepper, and fresh basil if you can get it. A salad of tomatoes that have been skinned and pulped is incomparably superior to a salad of sliced ones. Checking my text for errors, Lyn Hall remarked that she preferred to use a skimmer when skinning tomatoes. Forks pierce the flesh. She is, as always, entirely right.

Topinambour: Jerusalem artichoke. (*See* **Artichaut,** page 13.)

Tour d'Argent: a restaurant noted for its view of Notre Dame cathedral and its roasted ducks. It is arguably the most revered restaurant in the world, for its history can be traced back to 1582 when King Henri III went there. Its association with duck begins with the mysterious Frédéric, who bought the premises in the 1890s. A few years after Frédéric took over, the *Tour d'Argent* began serving a roast duckling served in a very original way (although the recipe was in essence a **salmis**).

Caneton Tour d'Argent was a lightly roasted duckling. Its raw liver was chopped and cooked rapidly at the table-side with port and Cognac. To this was added a little duck consommé and the juice and blood from the crushed carcass, which had been pressed in a silver duck press. This was poured upon the sliced breast meat of the roasted duckling. The legs were grilled to cook them a little more and served with salad as a second course. Nowadays there are usually more than a dozen duck dishes on the menu: **caneton aux figues, caneton aux huîtres** and the remarkable **caneton Marco Polo aux quatre poivres,** which has evolved through many changes.

I was a teenager when I first went to Paris. The Second World War was only just over. I sold a pound of coffee beans and that deal yielded about enough to eat at the *Tour d'Argent.* I had never been to a grand restaurant before. I asked for the duckling cooked in the classic style. The waiter mournfully told me that it was only served for two persons. I fingered my money and told him I'd have it for two. The waiter was determined to give me my money's worth; he went through the whole ritual and served me the duck as four courses.

Perhaps the *Tour d'Argent*'s duckling would not have become world famous had the originator not had the splendid idea of presenting to each customer who ate one a numbered certificate. King Edward VII—while still Prince of Wales—had number 328 and the present Queen, while Princess Elizabeth in 1948, had duckling number 183,397.

But with or without numbered certificates the *Tour d'Argent* remains one of France's great restaurants. Back in 1964 my old friend Vernon Jarratt, a remarkable restaurateur himself, wrote about Paris restaurants that had survived and remained great since 1903.[37] He named three. Of them the *Tour d'Argent* is now the only survivor. There is little doubt that the restaurant has maintained its position amongst France's top eating places because of the dedication of its proprietor, Claude Terrail. He has been described as a playboy and admits to "a host of other pursuits: hunting, the cinema, the theater, women . . . my philosophy is always to do everything I do seriously, but never to take myself seriously."

It seems to work.

Tourte: a closed-top tart, a pie, sweet or savory. The word for an open-top tart is **flan,** but this word often signifies a tart containing custard or cheese. Sometimes flan means a **crème caramel.**

Traiteur: a take-away cook-shop; a caterer. No tables and chairs but a skilled chef in a well-equipped kitchen and a counter where you can buy all manner of prepared dishes. Here you'll find aspics, vol-au-vents, cooked chickens, various hams and terrines as well as fruit tarts and cooked desserts. Most such shops prepare one special dish every day and provide a list of the month's schedule. Such lists can be interesting and instructive, as also can be a close inspection of the foods on sale.

Troisgros, Jean and Pierre. There was a universal sadness at the death of Jean Troisgros. It was not just because of the loss of a mighty talent, nor because it was the end of a partnership that had become nothing less than a legend. It was because *Les Frères Troisgros,* Roanne, Loire—one of the greatest restaurants in France—was such a happy place.

Anyone who worked there, as waiter, commis or chef, invariably tells you that of all the places they worked this was the one that they remembered with pleasure. And yet this was not because the discipline was lax or the proprietors easy-going. I stood in the kitchen one day and heard Pierre admonish one of his employees with force enough to lift the poor fellow's feet off the ground. Such scoldings are not uncommon. But there is never any lasting bad feeling and the Troisgros brothers always kept a sense of proportion about everything, including making money. On one visit I noticed that Troisgros's excellent own-label champagne was cheaper than the cheapest available sparkling rot-gut at the nearby autoroute sandwich counters. No wonder almost everyone in the dining-room was drinking it.

Generally speaking "three-star" restaurants, with their big staff-to-client ratios, give better value for money than fried chicken or hamburger chains. The competition is fierce and many proprietors willingly cut profits in order to win the coveted top award. But the Troisgros go further, for they always believed that it was vital to preserve their local custom. Their father, Jean-Baptiste Troisgros, was something of a local character and there are more stories about his eccentricities than about those of his sons. He moved into the premises, a rather unattractive building opposite Roanne railway station, and ran a simple commercial restaurant of the sort that can be found opposite the railway stations of most other towns in France. But with a prescience that is given only to loving parents he managed to get his two sons jobs in *La Pyramide* under the supervision of the mighty Fernand Point.

When they came back to Roanne and worked for their father they were ambitious, but it was their father who told them that the foundations of their business must remain local clientèle. They were convinced. So while most other three-star restaurants cater largely to Americans, British, Swiss and Germans, a glance around the *Troisgros* dining-room will always show a representative selection of local people. Asked about the success of the restaurant Jean said, "It is the family atmosphere. It is the Roannais, the people of the town, who make it. We created an ambience, children are welcome here. We are not sophisticated, opposite the station."[38] For this reason, as well as the low prices, it is especially difficult to get a booking at their restaurant.

Nowadays Pierre's son is to be seen at the stove. If experience is anything to go by, then Michel Troisgros will be the tops. He has worked with Chapel, Vergé and Guérard. He worked at the *Connaught* in London, with Giradet in Switzerland, at *Comme chez soi* in Brussels and at *Taillevent* in Paris. When his mother heard we lived in Ireland she said that he worked at the *Arbutus Lodge* in Cork. In the old days Jean was considered the sober traditional cook (a **saucier** by nature, said his brother) with Pierre the inventor. Now the roles have changed and it is Pierre who explains to his son that they must not go too fast into the realms of fantasy. Pierre says he doesn't want to embrace nouvelle cuisine, but rather than say he cooks the **cuisine traditionelle** he calls his own style **cuisine contemporaine.**

The relationship between Pierre and his late partner, and now his relationship with his dynamic son, provide a constant and curious ambivalence at Roanne. There is simplicity and ostentation. The overdecorated bedrooms provide an example of the latter, and so in a way does the (all electric) kitchen they designed and built in 1978. It is still bigger and grander, lighter and better equipped than any other I've seen. (And I've seen many.) The menu has examples of the simplicity, so that of their most imitated dishes one is the **mosaïque de légumes.** But the other most famous dish is the **escalope de saumon à l'oseille Troisgros** which requires great skill in cutting the escalope and expensive fresh salmon. A legacy of their father's cost-cutting was the way in which food had to be put on plates in the kitchen and carried to the tables (rather than served from trolleys in the grander manner of more expensive establishments). The brothers continued with this "plate service" in order to keep their prices down. Not surprisingly, perhaps, it is this cost-cutting "plate service" of Troisgros senior that is so enthusiastically imitated by the exponents of nouvelle cuisine.

Trou de milieu: a Cognac, Armagnac, quetsche, mirabelle, fraise, mûres des forêts, poire, marc, kirsch, or some other such drink served to revive the appetite before the main meat course. It was an ancient custom that such a drink was offered to diners on a silver tray by the daughter of the house. In Normandy Calvados was served and called **un trou Normand.** Alcohol-flavored sorbets are sometimes served at this stage of a big meal.

Truffe: truffle, small, hard, black, spherical parasitic fungus that grows on the roots of oak trees and hazelnut trees when limestone or calcium carbonate is present in the soil. Dogs and pigs root for them. The season begins some time before November and you may still find them in March. When Pope John XXII moved from the Dordogne to the palace in Avignon he planted oaks in the hope that truffles would grow on them. Many other hopefuls—including some Japanese food companies—have invested time and money to encourage the growth of these expensive delicacies. So far no one seems to have discovered the secret; or, if they have, they are keeping very quiet about it.

A century ago the French harvested 2,000 tons a year; now they are lucky to find 100 tons. James Bentley, who lives in the Dordogne, home of the finest truffles, says that lately thieves have been stealing truffles from well-known trees. It is difficult to catch the miscreants and some victims become so angry about it that they chop the trees down. Thus truffles get rarer and rarer.

Less high quality truffles are found in Spain. Some of this crop is taken to the Dordogne and sold as local produce. So are truffles from Provence. Truffles don't keep; they are sometimes dried (although deep-freezing is better) and are best rejuvenated by soaking in wine. Madeira is said to be ideal for this purpose. Bocuse stores his under lard or goose fat; others bury them in uncooked rice. Canned truffles are good. The grades, starting with the finest, are **extra, premier choix, deuxième choix, truffes en morceaux** and finally **pelures,** which are skins and tiny fragments. **Jus de truffes** is also sold in cans. If you are going to chop them anyway, it is worth trying some of the less expensive pieces.

Working on the principle of "Ask the man who drives one," I repeat Bentley's advice about an **omelette aux truffes.** He puts 3 ounces of diced truffles, a small tablespoonful of goose fat, a teaspoonful of Cognac and a small glass of Monbazillac into a saucepan and cooks it covered until the liquid has almost evaporated. (Yes, you'll have to look every now and again.) Separately prepare 8 lightly beaten eggs. When the omelette pan is hot and ready, put in a spot more goose fat. Then tip eggs and truffles into the pan to cook. Sounds good, eh?

Truffe sous les cendres literally means truffle cooked in hot ashes, but it really means cooked at a low temperature. Originally a truffle was wrapped in a slice of fatty raw pork, then in some pastry and cooked in a fire or oven. Some three-star chefs have revived this idea and they put the whole truffle or truffles into a small pot with brandy and stock (there are many variations). Sometimes the pots are specially designed for the purpose, for this is a dish ordered by people who want everyone to know that they are rich. Truffles are much better used to flavor other foods; for example, potato or chicken. Truffles are disappointing to eat on their own.

Tsuji, Shizuo. Described by many as Japan's foremost authority on Japanese cooking, he runs the Tsuji Professional Culinary Institute, Osaka, where about 2,500 students are enrolled. A staff of 220 teach the undergraduates as well as postgraduate courses in Chinese and French cooking. It was Tsuji—an authority on French literature and Bach—who brought Bocuse and other luminaries to teach in Osaka. This played a major part in the "Japanization" of French cooking.

Tuiles: roof tiles. Apart from their curved shape this makes a poor name for the lacy wafers made from egg white, butter, sugar, flour and almonds. Julia Child, with typical down-to-earth approach, calls them "almond cookies," but these delicate petits fours are unlike any cookie I've eaten.

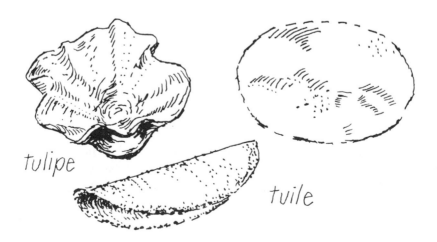

tulipe

tuile

Tulipes: tulips, are wafers from a similar batter mixture (without almonds) and formed while warm into brittle cups in which fruit and ice cream are served. You eat the cup too.

Turbot: turbot. A large white European sea-water flatfish highly esteemed by French chefs who regard it as the equal of salmon and sole. **Barbue** or brill is a scaly softer-fleshed sub-species of turbot and is also highly thought of, which is another way of saying expensive. The chef is most likely to prepare these fish in a very simple way—poaching in a **turbotière** or steaming—and accompany with an elaborate sauce. Point used vermouth, Chapel uses champagne, Guérard likes saffron and Senderens serves it with grapes and tea!

Val de Loire: the valley that follows the course of the Loire. The land through which this great river runs is marked by the towns of Orléans, Tours, Angers and Nantes. It has never received from foreigners the attention that it merits as a gastronomic center. Yet a wonderful variety of meat, poultry, eels and river fish comes from this region. Angling and shooting are the favorite local pastimes and in the season there is plenty of game for the cook. The market gardens are famous for fruit and vegetables, and although the Loire wines are not the great labels, they are light and fresh and many of superb quality. So is the local cider. The Trappist monks at Port-du-Salut near Le Mans created the famous cheese, although nowadays it is all made in factories. The charcuterie of the region is memorable. The skills of local pastry cooks have made various sorts of game pies famous, and Pithiviers has given its name to both a lark pâté and to the delicious **gâteau de Pithiviers,** an almond-cream tart that I put high on my list of top favorites.

This region at the heart of France is also at the heart of French cooking. A fact that has not been lost on restaurateurs, for although as I write this there are no three-star restaurants here (*Barrier* at Tours having been demoted), the Loire Valley provides a selection of fine restaurants not easily matched anywhere else in France.

Cuisine à la vapeur: cooking by steam. Cooking by steam is not always convenient for commercial kitchens—and it yields no cooking liquors from which sauces and so on can be made—but for domestic cooking it should be employed wherever possible. Steamed food loses fewer of its soluble salts, fewer vitamins, and more important, less flavor than is lost by boiling. So it's particularly suited to delicately flavored foods such as fish, scallops, clams and lobster. Simon Hopkinson, chef at the *Bibendum* restaurant in the newly refurbished Michelin building in London, told me that because of its high albumin content he prefers to steam fish and fish mixtures.

Paradoxically steam cooking takes place at a lower heat than boiling. (If you doubt that, try boiling and steaming potatoes and discover which is faster.) This is because the food in a steamer cooks when the extra heat of the steam is lost and it condenses. Steamed food is cooked by conduction.

Recently more and more kitchens are being equipped with "pressure steamers." The process is like pressure cooking, but they are quick and easy to use so that individual portions of vegetables can be cooked to order. One famous restaurant even cooks its foie gras in this machine.

For the cook the only important thing to know is that some food spoils at boiling temperature. Albumin, a protein found in milk, fish, meat and eggs, coagulates and hardens as it gets this hot. Ovalbumin, the sort of albumin in eggs, starts to coagulate at 140°F, so egg mixtures like mousses are particularly suited to steaming. Chinese cooks know this—only the wok is used more than the steamer in Chinese cooking—and their delicious egg custards, and their fish and vegetables, are steamed. (But in a steamer the resulting custard will set; if you want a custard sauce it's better made in a double boiler so that you can keep stirring it.) Another useful steaming tip from a Chinese chef: you can cook on the serving plate if you wrap a little paper over the food to stop water from the lid dripping on it. The paper also concentrates the steam for the cooking process. And food in a steamer is not buffeted around in the way that food is knocked about in boiling water. So steaming is excellent for fragile foods. I always steam asparagus, wrapping paper on stalks.

The London-based chef, Nico Ladenis—who prefers steaming to

poaching—dips fish into butter before it goes into the steamer. He says this retains flavor and moisture.

Experiments showed that boiled vegetables lost 43 percent of their protein, steamed vegetables 16 percent. These were vegetables cooked to the same extent; but the less cooking that vegetables are given the better.

Vapeur. Another aspect of steam is the steam that is inside the food. All edible food contains large proportions of water. When pieces of potato for pommes frites are plunged into boiling fat, the potato is cooked by steam! Egg custard, a loaf of bread, a potato and even a grilled steak are full of steam at the moment the cooking is finished. Freshly cooked food is light and fluffy. Eat it while it is warm. As the steam goes from it the texture and flavor of the food will change. Never again will it be so good to eat.

Veau: veal. The American cook is too ready to put veal into the frying pan, and perhaps the French cook is too ready to pop it into the pot. But say that to a Frenchman and he'll tell you about the **rognonnade** (*see* page 179) (veal loin rolled around a veal kidney and pot-roasted) and say it is one of the world's great dishes. And what can you say? He'll be right. And for many Frenchmen the sheer extravagance of roasted veal, **rôti de veau,** makes it a favorite celebratory meal.

Vergé, Roger (1931–). One of the most famous chefs in France. He trained in Paris at the *Tour d'Argent* and the *Plaza Athénée.* Then he traveled and worked around the world before opening *Le Moulin de Mougins* near Cannes on the Riviera. He is on record as saying that he avoids "the excessive provincial use of garlic or herbs."[39] My own reaction to a couple of days at the *Moulin* was reckless: I canceled all my appointments so we could stay for the rest of the week. On reflection it was the right thing to do. It was not long after that that the *Moulin* got its third Michelin star. Nowadays it has become a place to see film stars rather than gourmets.

Vessie: pig's bladder. The only times I've encountered this esoteric ingredient is when I've ordered the famous **poularde en vessie.** This dish is mentioned in *Le Cuisinier gascon* written by the Prince de Dombes in

1740, but the modern dish is said to be a creation of Fernand Point. He called his creation **poularde en vessie Marius Vettard** (Vettard was a fellow restaurateur who had the famous *Café Neuf* on the Place Bellecour in Lyon). Point's recipe used a poularde, a specially fattened foul weighing about 4 pounds 6 ounces from the famous breeding region of Bresse. The chicken was stuffed with chicken liver which had been pounded with truffles, foie gras and a dash of Cognac and bound with beaten egg. The trussed chicken was then put inside the prepared bladder together with a glass of Madeira, a glass of brandy and root vegetables. The vessie was sliced open at the table-side so that, as Fernand Point puts it, "A subtle aroma will waft out." Since then, this dish appeared regularly on the menu of Point's restaurant *La Pyramide* (although, perhaps signifying some change in the recipe, the name of Vettard was dropped and it was called **poularde de Bresse truffée en vessie).** Bocuse serves a version of this dish using half a chicken in vessie for two persons. He puts rice inside the chicken. The one I had at Chapel's restaurant was described on his elaborate menu as **poulette de Bresse en vessie les petits légumes nouveaux sauce albufera.** It was generously truffled and stuffed with foie gras. The vegetables were carrots, turnips, haricots verts and a julienne of celery.

At a time when the *Vivarois* in Paris had three stars in Michelin and poularde en vessie was offered as a specialty I took my in-laws there. To show them that I knew my way around I thought a spectacular vessie splitting, and aroma wafting, would be appropriate. So I was more than a little surprised when our poularde en vessie arrived from the kitchen as two slices of boiled chicken breast arranged with garnish on a plate. It was, explained the waiter apologetically as we looked upon this sad little platter, nouvelle cuisine.

Vin: wine. Even as late as the eighteenth century wine was just wine. The French considered any wine older than five or six years to be stale and not worth drinking. But by 1762 new attitudes were emerging. The *Dictionnaire de Commerce* was listing fine wines—champagne and burgundy at the top—and there were great variations in the prices paid for different wines.

Joseph Berkmann, gourmet, restaurateur and wine dealer, estimates having drunk at least a bottle of wine per day for thirty years. He attributes present-day high prices to three causes:

1. French wine consumption has dropped sharply (they drink only half of the amount they did in 1945) and so they buy better wines.

2. The northern hemisphere has discovered wine so there has been a switch from beers and spirits to wine.

3. Many wine merchants have become commodity brokers by offering wines **en primeur.** In this way neither grower nor wine merchant has to finance stocks such as first growths that require up to ten years to reach maturity. Originally this "first tranche" was sold to the trade which bought at a preferential price, giving the proprietor enough cash to pay for the vintage. Mature wines were released later, at a higher price, reflecting costs and market trends. During the last 15 years this investing role has gradually been taken over by wine drinkers, who sometimes reaped a substantial profit. This parallel market was made possible by Christie's and Sotheby's, who act as clearing houses for privately bought stocks. Thus the London auction houses have seen an amazing increase in the prices for mature wines.

Prices, says Joseph Berkmann, have now gone over the top and he believes that the next decade will see a return to a less speculative market. But meanwhile Château Pétrus 1961 fetches $10,000 a case; and 3,000 cases of Château Mouton Rothschild 1975, offered at $30 a bottle, were found to be imitation with forged labels.

White wine sales have been boosted by immense pressure from vested interests. This is especially true in America, where most wine drinkers have been persuaded that white is good for them, or at least less bad. Recent research in Switzerland (Joseph Berkmann tells me) has proven beyond doubt that regular drinking of white wine tends to make a person nervous and irritable and disturbs the normal sleeping pattern. In France I found that most wine producers and merchants agree (off the record) that white wine is a less healthy drink than red. Chefs too mostly prefer red wine. Many of them, including Pierre Troisgros, encourage their customers to drink red wine with fish. (A chilled Beaujolais or a very young Pinot Noir from the Côte d'Or goes well with fish. But tannic wines based on the Cabernet Sauvignon grape can taste metallic when served with fish.) I found even white wine producers preferred to drink red wine. There was good news for those who liked the taste of tannin—as found in Barolo and Rioja— for it is said to be good for you.

White wine is less likely to produce a hangover headache although this varies from person to person. Roughly speaking the more carefully a wine is made, the less likely it is to give you a headache. (This is even more true of brandies and spirits.)

Almost all champagne is carefully made, and it's a drink relatively free of headaches, but the carbonic acid can give you cramps. Without sulfur, wine would oxidize but sulfur affects some people. It is found in cheap wines and also in wines from vineyards, or vintages, that suffered a lack of sunshine. Most experts told me that white wine gave a stiffness of the finger-joints and knees. One (white wine) vineyard manager said he sometimes stopped drinking for a week until the stiffness went away. Acid wines cause a stiffness that comes from crystal deposits in the joints. It is a kind of gout. Champagnes and rosé wines which contained unfermented malic acid can cause this.

I asked Joseph Berkmann about his personal drinking preferences:

> In France—and other wine-producing countries such as Spain and Italy—emphasis is given to the drinking of red wines. Red wines containing tannin are considered beneficial to health. White wines are regarded as apéritifs and even fish is often accompanied by young red wine. I regard drinking a young undeveloped claret with **Coquilles St. Jacques meunières** as one of the most beautiful combinations I ever eat. I am growing less interested in old wine, and at home seldom drink twenty-year-old wine. This is because the old wines lose tannin and I like the tannin and believe that red wines with plenty of tannin are better for me. I avoid champagne except for celebrations as I find it gives me headaches and gout! In short, I like good clarets of medium age at any time and any place.

After all my research I was left with widespread personal opinions, different medical effects upon different people and no easy rules. But it seemed to me that wine should not be consumed on a regular basis. Drink it with food and choose what you enjoy best, but never forget that alcohol is, literally, a poison. The chefs I spoke with all disapproved of people drinking spirits—or cocktails containing spirits—prior to eating a meal (some added "or at any other time"). In line with most cooks I don't drink (or serve) wine with soup, with salad, artichokes or with egg dishes.

Vinaigre: literally *vin aigre* or sour wine; vinegar. There are many types of vinegars. They are made from cider and malt and other substances, but the finest one for the cook is wine vinegar. The cheapest vinegar is not much better than battery acid; the most expensive ones are flavored with fresh raspberries. There are many ways of making vinegar and the ones made with very poor wine make poor vinegar.

Good vinegar is as carefully made as good wine, so it's hardly surprising that my friend Joseph Berkmann, the restaurateur and wine merchant, makes his own vinegar and it's as delicious as any I've ever tasted. When I can't get a bottle from him I buy vinegar made by the lengthy and elaborate Orléans process, **vinaigre d'Orléans** (check the labels). Oddly enough I can't find any Orléans-style vinegar in California. Come on, American vinegar producers, there is plenty of wine on hand.

Lately we have seen raspberry vinegar hailed as one of the new natural aspects of nouvelle cuisine. Actually a recipe for it appeared in the original edition of Mrs. Beeton in 1861. I must say my heart sinks when I see raspberry vinegar mentioned on a menu, not because I dislike it, but because it is usually a warning that you are about to suffer some of the worst excesses of that terrible craze.

Aceto balsamico is red wine vinegar that has been aged in oak barrels, with the bung left open to allow limited contact with the air.

The wood "perspires" and about 10 per cent is lost each year by evaporation. It is stored for many years so that the bite of the vinegar is replaced by a strong mellow flavor and I'm told that the inhabitants of Modena, Italy (which is famous for the stuff), sip it from liqueur glasses as a digestif. The real thing is fashionable and very expensive but I'm told that most of it sold outside Italy is really no more than sweetened grape juice.

Vinaigrette is a salad dressing made from oil and vinegar plus anything else you feel in need of; for example, mustard, garlic, salt and pepper. Some people like strong-tasting olive oil in the dressing; some like less flavor of olive, and so mix flavorless oils in proportion. Use first-class vinegar, but use it in small proportions (as a martini drinker uses vermouth). One part vinegar to five parts oil is entirely enough to my taste.

Some people can't resist adding items to the vinaigrette: capers, finely chopped shallots, chives, parsley, tarragon and so on. The result is called **sauce ravigote,** and it's used with boiled foods such as beef, chicken, fish, pig's foot and anything so rich that it needs a sharp dressing.

Violet or **figue de mer.** I have eaten many strange things, but none looked less edible than this soft-shelled, dark brown, somewhat oyster-like sea creature. Cut through its shell with a sharp knife and you'll find an egg-yolk-colored center that looks rather like an oyster. The flavor is quite strong and the texture chewy. In late autumn they are on sale in many shops and restaurants along the Mediterranean coast. Eat one or two; they are not usually eaten by the plateful.

Vive: weever fish. This fish, considered essential for **bouillabaisse** and **bourride,** grows to 1 foot in length but is usually smaller in the Mediterranean area. It likes to lie buried in the sand but its spines are venomous (and cause disabling pain if trodden upon)—hence its alternative name **vipère de mer**—and fishermen should handle it with care.

Vivier: literally fish tank. Here are tanks of aerated sea water (maybe fresh water too) in which lobsters, crayfish, crabs and fish are fattened. The breeding and raising take place elsewhere: a big lobster might be forty years old!

My local man at Mougins provides tables and chairs and a chilled bottle of local wine while you wait for him to barbecue one of his specimens over the ashes of an olive wood fire. Just as enjoyable is the conversation, for he knows a great deal about his tenants. He'll tell you how people used to eating shellfish from colder northern waters are often surprised to find the flesh of Provençal shellfish softer and different in color. He'll tell you about the ferocious crustaceans from the Cape of Good Hope, the delicious **langouste royale** and the **cigale de mer,** a lobster from the even warmer waters of Martinique, Morocco or Florida.

Volaille: poultry. Although even in France the supermarket shelves mostly feature one sort of bird—the **poulet**—a little searching will uncover a source of the ones that the restaurant chef demands: the **poussin** (a tiny bird for grilling), **coquelet** (very small cockerel under 2 pounds 3 ounces in weight, **poularde** (a specially reared plump bird not seen outside France), **poule** (usually an elderly egg-layer for boiling), **coq** (cockerel for stewing even if young) and the **chapon** (capon—the finest roasting bird). The chickens of Bresse and Le Mans are particularly favored and accordingly priced.

All chickens come from the shop tightly trussed. This is a legacy from the days when chickens were roasted on a spit. Unless you are going to use a spit, remove the strings so that the heat can get to the meat of the thigh. Don't put any forcemeat into a chicken that is to be roasted in the oven; better to let the heat get inside the carcass and cook it through. Of all the hundreds of recipes for chicken, one of the oldest and most dramatic is **poularde de Bresse truffée en vessie.** You can't do that without a pig's bladder. But another favorite, **poulet à l'estragon,** can be done by anyone who can hold a bunch of fresh tarragon. There are many variations of this old country recipe— which is now on the menus of many great restaurants. A poulet, or a poularde, is cooked in a pot together with a little wine and a handful of freshly picked tarragon. (A plastic "roasting bag" works rather well for this recipe.) Keep the chicken warm while straining off the juice and wine mixture. Add an equal amount of cream. Boil it up quickly and serve it with the chicken. Even simpler is the **volaille "truffée" au persil** that Michel Guérard serves at Eugénie-les-Bains as part of the cuisine minceur that he invented. And not a truffle in sight, for this is a dieter's version of the old demi-deuil recipe of Escoffier's time. Chop herbs—parsley, chives, tarragon—and shallots and mushrooms in whatever proportions you like. Stir this into a carton of **fromage blanc,** which is a bland, almost fatless cream cheese. Loosen the skin on the breast of the chicken and insert this stuffing between meat and skin. Roast the chicken lightly. Say about 50 minutes at 400°F.

Vol-au-vent: a cup made from puff pastry. Into it the chef puts various savory concoctions, usually with creamy sauce binders. It is a useful device for a first course and delicious if freshly made pastry is used.

Vouvray: light, low-alcohol white wines from the Touraine region. Some vouvrays are still wines and some are naturally sparkling. Sometimes even the merchant doesn't know which will be **pétillant.** If it says **mousseux** on the label it means the merchant didn't want to take any chances: the bubbles have been added. Personally I'd far rather have a still one than the mousseux, for it's a pleasant wine. If I drank wine at lunchtime, this might be the one.

Acknowledgments

Thank you to everyone whose brains I have so assiduously picked for this uneven, incomplete, lop-sided opinionated collection of matters that I found interesting.

Thank you to the management of the Univers Hotel at Arras who found my bag in the courtyard, and in it my notebooks containing the whole text ready for typing. Thank you to the hotel client—Mr. Anthony B. Instone—who with spontaneous kindness took the bag with him and restored the notes to me.

Thanks to my agent Jonathan Clowes, for whom this book provided more than the usual share of problems. Thanks to Anton Felton, who read the text and offered valuable advice and improvements. For the splendid map on page xv I must thank Rodney Paull. Thanks also to my fiction editor Rosemary Cheetham, who agreed to be my editor on this one too, and to Valerie Buckingham who nursed it at all stages, and also to everyone else at Century Hutchinson.

Thank you to the nice people at Bantam who produced this attractive edition.

For advice in the preparation of the text I must mention those expert friends Elisabeth Evans and Lyn Hall, who both waded through early notes and made many valuable suggestions. Jacques Pépin was the most knowledgeable teacher and I am indebted to him for his most generous Introduction. I am also grateful to my old friend Egon Ronay for the splendid Foreword and to both for encouragement during the preparation of this book.

As far as possible I have given the sources of the quotes used in the text and I am grateful to the illustrious chefs named there. Other friends who helped and encouraged me in my questions and my note-taking long before I knew I was writing a book include Joseph Berkmann, wine-merchant, gourmet and host extraordinary; Madame Bise, restaurateur, and Michel Marucco, her maître d'hôtel; Anthony Blake, that master food photographer; Anton Edelmann, maître-chef, Savoy Hotel; Anton Mosimann, chef-patron of Mosimann's Club. And many others who must forgive me for not including their names. Also unlisted are various friends, neighbors, merchants, chefs and restaurateurs in that region of Provence where my relatives live and which I can't help but think of as "home." I hope there is no need to add that I have no connection with any of the establishments or manufacturers mentioned here; neither have I accepted hospitality from anyone at all.

Never intending that my notebooks should be published, I did not take proper care to record the names, times, places and dates of the conversations. Some interesting facts cannot be given proper acknowledgment. I hope both my informants and my readers will forgive me.

The following list of books comes largely from my own shelves. As you will see from my comments, I have a very limited appetite for cookbooks, few of which are written by practical cooks. This book has been compiled from talks with experts rather than from books; readers requiring a more scholarly reading list are referred to the excellent bibliography in Elizabeth David's *French Provincial Cooking*.

Reading a French language recipe requires only marginally more French than reading a menu. Translators of books both fiction and non-fiction are notorious for arbitrarily chopping and changing things (as I know from personal experience), so you might be better off with French originals.

Bibliography

Bailey, Adrian, with photos by Phillip Dowell, *The Book of Ingredients* (Michael Joseph, London, 1980). Based upon work by Elisabeth Lambert Ortiz. A really superb reference book and great fun for browsing.

Barr, Ann, and Paul Levy, *The Official Foodie Handbook* (Timbre Books, New York, 1984). A fund of expert information buried under unrelenting jokiness. Essential reading and reference.

Beard, James, *Delights and Prejudices* (Atheneum, New York, 1964). Memoirs and recipes from a cook-gourmet whose memories of London and Paris reach back to the early 1920s. Of his many excellent books this remains a particular favorite of mine.

Beck, Simone, with Louisette Bertholle and Julia Child, *Mastering the Art of French Cooking*, Volume 1 (Knopf, New York, 1961). The work that transformed American and British attitudes to cooking. Directed primarily to the American housewife, it is a most comprehensive attempt to tackle French cooking from scratch and bring it to a wide audience. How amazing that Julia Child's excellent and amusing TV cooking lessons have never been broadcast on British TV.

Beck, Simone, and Julia Child, *Mastering the Art of French Cooking*, Volume 2 (Knopf, New York, 1970). Louisette (Bertholle) de Nalèche dropped out of the team that a decade later produced a fine follow-up to the previous volume.

Beck, Simone, *Simca's Cuisine* (Knopf, New York, 1980). Julia Child has produced some cookbooks working on her own. This is Simone (Simca) Beck's only volume of recipes. It is more of an interesting curiosity than a basic text-book. Despite the fact that Simca lives in a small village in Provence, these recipes are adapted to American shopping and tastes. Too much so, perhaps.

Bentley, James, *Life and Food in the Dordogne* (Weidenfeld & Nicolson, London, 1986). Not a cookbook by any means, but an entertaining account of an Englishman living in France.

Bertholle, Louisette, *Secrets of the Great French Restaurants* (Weidenfeld & Nicolson, London, 1973). Translation of *Les Recettes secrètes de meilleurs restaurants de France*. The knowledge of Mme. Bertholle makes this a particularly good book that overcomes this tired formula of collections of recipes from famous restaurants.

Bertholle, Louisette: see also Beck.

Bocuse, Paul, *La Cuisine du marché* (Flammarion, Paris, 1976). It was Haydn who said, "Never criticize the work of a royal composer; you never know who might have written it." The same thing could surely be said about the cookbooks that come from France's famous chefs.

Bocuse, Paul, *The New Cuisine* (Granada, London, 1978). A translation of *La Cuisine du marché.*

Braudel, Fernand, translated by S. Reynolds, *The Structures of Everyday Life,* Volume 1 of the three-volume classic, *Civilization and Capitalism, 15th–18th Century* (Harper & Row, New York, 1981). With the other two volumes, *The Wheels of Commerce* and *The Perspective of the World,* following soon after. Braudel, a Frenchman, is widely regarded as the greatest social historian of this century. This richly illustrated three-volume work, carefully translated into English, is the most wonderful source of information about the history of eating and drinking. Braudel writes of the whole world and tackles economics, but his comments about the food and drink of his own country are particularly accurate.

Brillat-Savarin, Jean-Anthelme, translated by Anne Drayton, *The Philosopher in the Kitchen* (Penguin Books, London, 1970). *La Physiologie du goût*—of which this is a curiously renamed translation—was published in 1825. It is arguably the most famous book ever written about food and cooking. It is an amusing and entertaining book and, you might be delighted to hear, doesn't have a recipe in sight.

Buishand, Tjerk, Harm P. Houwing and Kees Jansen, *The Complete Book of Vegetables* (Gallery Books [W. H. Smith, Inc.], New York, 1986). First published in Holland, a serious work that describes 400 species, with superb photos. Not much about tastes or flavor but still the finest book of its sort I've ever seen.

Campbell, Susan, *The Cook's Companion* (Macmillan, London, 1980). An inappropriate title for a very good and comprehensive guide to kitchen implements. Over 2,000 drawings.

Chantraine, Charles, *La Cuisine Chantraine* (Mueller, London, 1967). An interesting collection of recipes from Belgium's oldest restaurant.

Chelminski, Rudolph, *The French at Table* (William Morrow, New York, 1985). An amusing and idiosyncratic account of gastronomic France "from the Gauls to Paul Bocuse," written by an American resident there. Packed with serious information and well worth seeking out.

Child, Julia: *see* Beck.

Christian, Glynn, *Delicatessen Food Handbook* (Macdonald, London, 1982). An excellent reference to everything on the shelf.

Claiborne, Craig, *The New York Times Food Encyclopedia* (*New York Times,* 1985). Compiled by Joan Whitman from the writings of the *New York Times* food correspondent, it includes all sorts of mad and marvelous foodie facts. Some of it is rather tongue in cheek.

Claiborne, Craig, with Pierre S. Franey, *Classic French Cooking* (Time-Life International, 1970). A typical Time-Life production: a lavishly illustrated book that includes lots of recipes.

Clark, Linda, *Know Your Nutrition* (Keats Pub Inc., New Canaan, Connecticut, revised ed. 1981). Big best-seller, written in racy popular style, by author of many books on cooking, health and nutrition. Vitamins, minerals, and so on, are treated chapter by chapter in an exhaustive and well-referenced handbook.

Conil, Jean, *Haute Cuisine* (Faber & Faber, London, 1953). Well-established classic. Written by a skilled professional chef.

Courtine, Robert, *The Hundred Glories of French Cooking* (Farrar, Straus & Giroux, New York, 1973). A translation of *Cent Merveilles de la cuisine française,* recipes with anecdotes in flamboyant French style.

Crewe, Quentin, and Anthony Blake, *Great Chefs of France* (Mitchell Beazley, London, 1978). A magnificent book with superb photos. The only really good book about the top French restaurants.

Crewe, Quentin, *International Pocket Food Book* (Mitchell Beazley, London, 1980). An excellent reference book, by a top authority, and small enough for a vest pocket.

David, Elizabeth, *French Provincial Cooking* (Michael Joseph, London, 1960, with various paperback editions by Penguin). One of many such charming books by the one who did so much to transform England's cooking skills. Her *English Bread and Yeast Cookery* is also splendid.

Davidson, Alan, *Mediterranean Seafood* (Penguin, London, 1981) and *North Atlantic Seafood* (Penguin, London, 1979). Two scholarly works by one of our most entertaining and distinguished food writers. Essential reading and reference.

Deighton, Len, *Basic French Cooking* (Century Hutchinson, London, 1990).

Diat, Louis, *Gourmet's Basic French Cookbook: Techniques of French Cuisine* (Gourmet, New York, 1961). Louis Diat was the man César Ritz sent to be *chef de cuisines* at the Ritz Carlton in New York. This excellent book was compiled from his notes and papers.

Edelmann, Anton, *The Savoy Food and Drink Book* (Pyramid, London, 1988). Introduction by Kingsley Amis. Anton Edelmann occupies the top gastronomic job in England, chef at the *Savoy Hotel,* which keeps alive Escoffier's skillful mix of the best of French and British cooking. He does it with skill and unsurpassed dedication.

Eekhof-Stork, Nancy, English language edition edited by Adrian Bailey, *The World Atlas of Cheese* (Paddington Press, London, 1976). An illustrated guide in the style of Hugh Johnson's wine atlas. Highly recommended for reference or general reading.

Escoffier, Auguste, *A Guide to Modern Cookery* (Heinemann, London, 1907 and subsequent editions). An interesting work, which was the result of Escoffier's collaboration with two other chefs. One of the most useful of Escoffier's works: matter of fact and succinct. But of course it is intended for the professional chef.

Fisher, M. F. K., *The Cooking of Provincial France* (Time-Life Books, New York, 1968). A lavishly illustrated volume with many recipes. This is the best-known volume of the *Foods of the World* series.

Fitzgibbon, Theodora, *The Food of the Western World* (Hutchinson, London, 1976). A fine encyclopedia. Five hundred closely printed pages.

Girardet, Fredy, *La Cuisine Spontanée* (Laffont, Paris, 1982). A recipe book from a man widely regarded as the world's greatest chef.

Gray, Patience, *Honey from a Weed* (Harper & Row, New York, 1986). A wonderful antidote for anyone beginning to believe that life in some primitive Mediterranean village might be paradise. Patience Gray lived in many such places—some without electricity or running water, let alone shops—and writes of it in this "passionate autobiographical cookbook." A unique, fascinating and scholarly work.

Gray, Patience, and Primrose Boyd, *Plats du Jour* (Penguin, London, 1957). A first-class book of recipes covering dishes from France, Italy and Spain. Delightful illustrations.

Grigson, Jane, *The Art of Charcuterie* (Alfred Knopf, New York, 1968). This specialist book from the always reliable and remarkable Mrs. Grigson became a classic soon after publication and is still unsurpassed as far as I know. Heartily recommended for anyone prepared to roll up his sleeves and get down to some serious work. Or just to pretend.

Grigson, Jane, *Jane Grigson's Fruit Book* (Michael Joseph, London, 1982).

Grigson, Jane, *Jane Grigson's Vegetable Book* (Michael Joseph, London, 1982). A remarkable encyclopedia of recipes plus many helpful comments by a practical cook.

Hampstead, Marilyn, *The Basil Book* (Long Shadow Books [dist. Pocket Books, New York], 1984). The author runs an herb farm and inaugurated an annual Basil Festival at which prizes are given for the best *pesto*! The author says there are 150 species of basil, and recommends Genovese for tomatoes and salads but says *piccolo verde* is the one for *pesto*. Yes, mine is growing well.

Heath, Ambrose, *Madame Prunier's Fish Cookery Book* (Hutchinson, London, 1938, re-printed 1947). More of a directory than a recipe book. Madame Prunier had excellent restaurants in London and Paris.

Heyraud, H., *Le Manuel du restaurateur* (Flammarion, Paris, 1970). A typical repertory of recipes for the professional chef or for any skilled cook.

Hume, Rosemary, and Muriel Downes, *The Penguin Dictionary of Cookery* (Penguin, London, 1966). A useful lexicon.

Jones, Evan, *A Food Lover's Companion* (Harper & Row, New York, 1979). An exemplary food anthology with pieces by everyone from Chekhov to Child. Evans also wrote *American Food,* the best book on the subject I've yet found.

Ladenis, Nico, *My Gastronomy* (Ebury Press, London, 1987). A forthright account of cooking and running a restaurant by a respected chef who is not afraid to criticize his customers.

Lallemand, Roger, *Guide du découpage en cuisine* (Consances Ancerville, France, 1976). A detailed description of kitchen knives by a chef, published by a knife manufacturer.

Lang, Jennifer Harvey, *Tastings* (Crown Publishers, New York, 1986). A serious book that describes "pantry basics"—coffee, canned tomatoes, olive oil, ice cream, pasta and so on—in detail, then rates them by means of blind tastings. Anyone even remotely interested in what's in the cans and packets will find it very interesting.

Levy, Paul, *Out to Lunch* (Harper & Row, 1988). A fascinating collection of pieces by Britain's most influential food writer literally ranges the wide world of food.

McGee, Dr. Harold, *On Food and Cooking: the Science and Lore of the Kitchen* (Scribner's, 1984). The science and to some extent the history of food and cooking. Well-written, lucid and entertaining. Don't be put off by the rather dull illustrations and diagrams. This is a wonderful work and I notice it on the shelves of most top chefs I visit.

Maurois, Gerald, *Cooking with a French Touch* (Dolphin, New York, 1950). An unpromis-ing title, but the book (not all recipes) is instructive and entertaining.

Maximin, Jacques, *Couleurs, parfums et saveurs de ma cuisine* (Laffont, Paris, 1984). A recipe book from a top chef.

Montagné, Prosper, *Larousse Gastronomique* (English translation, Hamlyn, London, 1961). Staggering encyclopedia of French cooking that was compiled by one man and first published, with a preface by Escoffier, in 1938. The first English translation kept a team of four translators and two editors busy for over three years. In 1984 a new edition was supervised by Robert Courtine and in 1988 it appeared in English. This new volume is completely revised and very well designed with excellent illustrations, many of them in color. I heartily recommend it for anyone who wants the best reference book to French food.

Mosimann, Anton, *Cuisine à la carte* (Northwood Books, London, 1981). Well arranged, clearly expressed recipes are accompanied by excellent photos. French cooking from a world-famous chef with an emphasis upon creative and unusual combinations rather than traditional dishes. This remarkable chef went on to produce *Cuisine naturelle* (Macmillan, London, 1985), in which health was a theme for the recipes, and *Anton Mosimann's Fish Cuisine* (Macmillan, London, 1988), a date which marked the opening of his fabulous private restaurant—*Mosimann's.*

Olney, Richard, *Simple French Food* (Penguin, London, 1983). There are not many serious cookbooks available. Olney not only knows cooking but he knows about France. It's a rare combination to find in culinary writers.

Page, E. B., and P. W. Kingsford, *The Master Chefs: a History of Haute Cuisine* (Edward Arnold, London, 1971).

Pellaprat, H. P., *Modern Culinary Art* (Jacques Kramer, Paris, 1950). This translation of *L'Art culinaire moderne* has a special place on my shelf because it was the first serious cookbook I acquired. I believe Pellaprat remains the most respected authority for amateur and professional cooks in France. Despite prolific writing Pellaprat is always a practical chef.

Pépin, Jacques, *La Technique* (Knopf, New York, 1978). Subtitled *An Illustrated Guide to the Fundamental Techniques of Cooking,* this large book contains 1,500 photos to illustrate step by step 150 basic cooking procedures and recipes. A unique and wonderful book by means of which my 11-year-old son produced unfailing culinary coups and which my wife says never goes wrong.

Pépin, Jacques, *La Méthode* (Knopf, New York, 1983). A companion volume to the above *La Technique,* it is an essential instructional book for amateur and professional produced by a master chef with great experience in teaching. Pépin sticks to the basics of traditional French cooking.

Pépin, Jacques, *Everyday Cooking with Jacques Pépin* (Harper & Row, 1982). In other hands this book of step-by-step color photos might have been slight. But this is Pépin and it is first class and fun.

Pépin, Jacques, *The Art of Cooking,* Volumes One and Two (Alfred Knopf, New York, 1987 and 1988). Pépin, personal chef to three of France's heads of state, has now emerged as the most serious instructor (and arguably the most serious authority) on French cooking writing in English. This amazing, and delightfully personal, work reflects well upon its dedicated author and upon its enterprising American publisher. Suited to both professional chef and beginner, it includes about 3,000 step-by-step color photos. Every one of these pictures was taken in the kitchen of Pépin's home. This is the most complete and important work on cooking—mostly French but not exclusively so—available in the English language. It is difficult to imagine anyone doing it better. Buy, beg, borrow or steal it.

Phillips, Roger, *Mushrooms—and other fungi of Great Britian & Europe* (Pan Books, London, 1981). An inexpensive large format, limp cover, all-color guide to 914 species found over a five-year search in the course of which a new species was discovered. All concerned should be rightly proud of this book that bears the description—"The most comprehensively illustrated book on the subject this century." A wonderful work.

Point, Fernand, *Ma Gastronomie* (Flammarion, Paris, 1969; English translation, Lyceum Books, Wilton, Connecticut, 1974). One of the most important restaurateurs of this century offers memoirs, menus and recipes. The English translation is "adapted" to such an extent that it is virtually a different book from the original.

Pomaine, Edouard, *Cooking with Pomaine* (Farrar, Straus, 1976). A translation of the lively writing of the famous Professor Pomaine.

Revel, Jean François, *Culture and Cuisine* (Doubleday, Garden City, New York, 1982). Subtitled *A Journey through the History of Food,* this translation of *Un Festin en paroles* provides a scholarly history of cooking from the ancient Greeks to Carême.

Root, Waverley, *Food* (Simon & Schuster, New York, 1980). An encyclopedia with wonderful illustrations, some in color, by a gourmet and scholar. It is a book for readers interested in the history of food and strange and surprising exotica rather than for chefs or general readers interested in cooking dinner.

Root, Waverley, *The Food of France* (Knopf, New York, 1958; updated for paperback, Vintage Books, 1977). A classic compilation that takes France region by region to describe history and cuisine from the traveler's point of view rather than from the chef's, but there is an index of dishes.

Roux, Albert and Michel, with a chapter on wine by Michael Broadbent, illustrations by Paul Hogarth and photos by Anthony Blake, translated by K. Whiteman, *New Classic Cuisine* (Macdonald, London, 1983). What an astounding array of talent: delightful drawings by one of our very finest illustrators and photos (color and step-by-step) by the superb Anthony Blake. The text was written (in French) by the Roux brothers, who brought uncompromising standards to their English restaurants and gained Michelin's ultimate accolade. The text is workmanlike, lucid and sincere. Excellent design; a fine book in every way.

Roux, Albert and Michel, photos by Anthony Blake,. *The Roux Brothers on Pâtisserie* (Macdonald, London, 1986). Here the Roux brothers deal with a specialized subject in great detail. They go from croissants (prepare the dough 12 hours in advance) to Christmas pudding! But the design is chaotic! No matter, the Roux brothers know what they're talking about and explain it well.

Savarin, *Real French Cooking* (Faber & Faber, London, 1956). English translation of a chatty and informative discourse by a French journalist, who wrote *La Vraie Cuisine Française* using this pen name. In his dedication he rhymed "four" with "amour." The translators splendidly rendered it "kitchen stove" and "love."

Simon, André, and Robin Howe, *A Dictionary of Gastronomy* (Nelson, London, 1970).

Stevenson, Daniel R., *Professional Cookery: the Process Approach* (Hutchinson, London, 1985). For anyone who just can't stand the sight of another recipe book with pictures of colored plates in it, this down-to-earth book by a lecturer at Oxford Polytechnic provides serious instruction.

Stobart, Tom, *The Cook's Encyclopedia—Ingredients and Processes* (Batsford, London, 1980). Well worth hunting for, this erudite, idiosyncratic, if not to say eccentric notebook about food contains some illuminating facts, many of them due to Stobart's simple way of explaining chemistry. But I hope no one will be frightened off by the word chemistry, for this is an amusing and very readable bedside book with asides and anecdotes about the author's colorful adventures.

Stobart, Tom, *Herbs, Spices and Flavourings* (International Wine and Food Society, London, 1970). Mostly herbs with fine drawings, some in color. Stobart's erudition and charm come through. He gives foreign names, as well as Latin ones. Stobart is wonderful. There is a Penguin reprint without the color pictures.

Troisgros, Jean and Pierre, *Cuisiniers à Roanne: les Recettes originales de Jean et Pierre Troisgros* (Laffont, Paris, 1977).

Troisgros, Jean and Pierre, *The Nouvelle Cuisine,* edited and adapted by C. Conran (Macmillan, London, 1980). The Troisgros brothers' restaurant at Roanne has long been unique for the high quality of the cooking, the ingredients and the service. Jean is alas dead, but Pierre is still working and whatever he writes or says should be of interest to anyone who's ever brandished a sauté pan. So this translation and adaptation by the erudite and hard-working Mrs. Conran is important and valuable. For the original version (significantly not called *Nouvelle Cuisine*), *Cuisiniers à Roanne,* see above. It is easy to read even for the non–French speaker.

Troisgros, Jean and Pierre, *The Nouvelle Cuisine of Jean and Pierre Troisgros* (William Morrow, New York, 1978). An American publication that predated the English one.

Troisgros, Pierre and Michel, *Les Petits Plats de Pierre et Michel Troisgros* (Laffont, Paris, 1985). Pierre combines with his much-traveled chef son.

Tsuji, Shizuo, *Japanese Cooking: a Simple Art* (Kodansha International, dist. in America by Harper & Row, New York, 1980). Clear, concise book about Japanese cooking that shows it's not so simple. This is an outstanding work. To find out why it's listed here see **Tsuji** in the main text.

Vergé, Roger, edited and adapted by C. Conran, *Cuisine of the Sun* (Macmillan, London, 1979).

Vergé, Roger, *Ma Cuisine du Soleil* (Laffont, Paris, 1978).

Viard, Henry, *The Gourmet's Tour de France. 27 Great French Restaurants and their Favorite Recipes* (Little, Brown, Boston, 1984).

Welanetz, Diana and Paul von, *The von Welanetz Guide to Ethnic Ingredients* (J. P. Tarcher, Los Angeles, 1982). A unique book—over 700 pages—and an essential reference for anyone with a serious interest in unusual foods and ingredients.

Wells, Patricia, *The Food Lover's Guide to Paris* (Workman Publishing, New York, 1984), *The Food Lover's Guide to France* (Workman Publishing, New York, 1987). Two superb books about restaurants, markets and even cooking schools. They don't compete with Michelin and Gault Millau. I wish they did; I find Ms. Wells a far more interesting and enterprising companion than the established guides could ever be.

Werner, François, *Grandes Cuisines Rhône-Alpes* (Glenat, Grenoble, 1985). A book about the chefs of this region: Bise, Blanc, Bocuse, Chapel, Pic, Point and Troisgros.

Willan, Anne, *French Regional Cooking* (Hutchinson, London, 1981). A particularly interesting and attractive book on a difficult subject. Many pictures and recipes too.

Willan, Anne, *Great Cooks and Their Recipes: from Taillevent to Escoffier* (Elm Tree Books, London, 1977). A very well researched and lucidly written history with recipes.

Youell, Tessa, and George Kimball, *The Pocket Guide to French Food and Wine* (Xanadu, London, 1985). This is not a guide to hotels or restaurants. It's a slim, narrow, low-priced volume intended to be carried in the pockets and handbags of visitors to France who want to translate restaurant menus. As well as brief but excellent general advice about tackling France's varied types of eating places, there are guides (with small maps) to the regions and local wines, dishes and cheeses. The largest section is a glossary of about 3,000 menu terms (complete with pronunciation guide) that is, despite the brevity of each entry, knowledgeable and comprehensive.

Guides

Guide Gourmand de la France, Gault, Henri and Christian Millau, (Hachette, Paris, published annually).

Le Guide Michelin (published annually). A compact volume of well over a thousand pages in which are listed restaurants and hotels all over France. Symbols make it unnecessary to read French. Michelin invented a system of grading restaurants for their cooking (although confusingly they have rigid rules about what sort of establishment can get the top rating of three stars). This system of Michelin stars is the most commonly used one nowadays.

Periodicals

Petite Propos Culinaires, Ma Maison et la table, Gault and Millau Magazine, Wine and Food, Gourmet, Cuisine et vins de France, Bon Appétit, Cuisine, Food and Wine, A la carte, Taste, etc., etc.

Books with Several Authors

L'Art Culinaire Français (Flammarion, Paris, 1957). Subtitled *Les Recettes de cuisine pâtisserie, conserves, des mâitres contemporains les plus réputes,* this is a truly remarkable recipe book. With a minimum of editing, so that the recipes retain the style of the original, this massive tome provides the style and voice as well as the classic recipes of France's great chefs. Most importantly it predates *nouvelle cuisine.* This is the real thing. Use it and cook from it. You certainly won't get anything like this in even the finest of French restaurants. It is available in English translation.

The Cook's Catalogue (Avon Books, New York, 1975). A massive, 600-page directory of kitchen equipment with reviews and even recipes.

Cuisine du Terroir (Corgi Books, London, 1988). The association of France's master chefs (Maîtres Cuisiniers de France) pooled their experience and research to produce *Les Recettes du Terroir* in 1984. It was intended as a way to preserve and promote the tradition of regional cooking. The English translation omits only a few esoteric recipes, but the text is anglicized in that way that publishers demand; still the Corgi paperback edition is a bargain for such an amazing array of scholarship and talent.

The Good Cook: Techniques and Recipes (Time-Life Books). A series of 27 books including such titles as *Bread, Fruit, Lamb* and *Beverages,* each providing step-by-step instruction plus an anthology of recipes taken from many lands. Although Richard Olney is only credited as Chief Consultant, I hear that he has played a major part in compiling this amazing series. Recommended.

Masterpieces of French Cuisine (Macdonald, London, 1970). A translation of *Joies de la gastronomie: la cuisine aux étoiles.* Recipes and descriptions of notable French restaurants.

Six Grands Cuisiniers de Bourgogne (Editions Lattes, Paris, 1982). Up-and-coming French chefs give you their recipes.

The Taste of France (Webb & Bower, Exeter, England). This superb volume was based upon a series of articles in *The Sunday Times* color magazine and used the fine photos of Robert Freson. Contributors were all well-known experts and each was assigned to a region of France. A lovely book.

Notes

1 According to my conversations at the restaurant and confirmed by the Baumanière recipe in Louisette Bertholle, *Secrets of the Great French Restaurants* (Weidenfeld & Nelson, London, 1973).

2 Eugenie Fraser, *The House by the Dvina—a Russian Childhood* (Corgi Books, London, 1986).

3 Also present for this June lunch were Kingsley Amis, Ted Allbeury, Lionel Davidson, John le Carré, Frederick Forsyth, Gavin Lyall, Julian Symons, Miles Tripp, Harry Keating and Anthony Price. The full meal (as on the Savoy Hotel menu) was *la terrine de saumon à l'oseille, la salade meli-melo, le baron d'agneau rôti nouvelle saison* with *les légumes sur le plat* and *les pommes dauphinoise*. The dessert was *la tulipe de sorbet aux framboises* and after that came *les friandises, la bombe pralinée* and *le café Savoy*.

4 Fernand Point, *Ma Gastronomie* (Flammarion, Paris, 1969).

5 Quoted by Rudi Chelminski, "The Secrets of France's Super Chef, Paul Bocuse," *People*, date unknown.

6 Harry Waugh, "The Bordeaux Club," *Wine and Food* (Summer 1966).

7 According to Jacques Pépin, *La Méthode* (Knopf, New York, 1983).

8 Bob Campbell, the caviar and *foie gras* supplier of R. E. Campbell Ltd., Maidenhead, Berkshire.

9 Herr Wiemann, Hotel Gasthof, Ringstrasse 4, 8918 Riederau am Ammersee, Oberbayern. This chef is a notable exponent of south German cooking. I enjoyed it for many months.

10 Quoted by Chelminski, "The Secrets of France's Super Chef."

11 From Curnonsky's Preface to *Real French Cooking* by Savarin (*see* Bibliography, page 225).

12 Boudin, 6 rue de Buci, Paris 6ième.

13 Interview in *A la Carte* (February 1987).

14 "Exigez le véritable Cheddar Français," *Wine and Food,* no. 122 (Summer 1964).

15 René Fulconis, Le Vivier de Mougins, 20 Chemin de la Traversière, Quartier Vaumarre, 06250 Mougins, France.

16 Nico Ladenis, *My Gastronomy* (Ebury Press, London, 1987).

17 G. A. Escoffier, *A Guide to Modern Cookery* (Heinemann, London, 1907, and subsequent editions).

18 Jean and Pierre Troisgros, *The Nouvelle Cuisine of Jean and Pierre Troisgros* (W. Morrow, New York, 1978).

19 *Time* (9 February 1976).

20 Jacques Pépin, *La Technique* (Knopf, New York, 1978).

21 According to Anne Willan, Directrice of La Varenne Cookery School, Paris.

22 Fernand Point, *Ma Gastronomie* (Flammarion, Paris, 1969). Also mentioned in Quentin Crewe and Anthony Blake, *Great Chefs of France* (Mitchell Beazley, London, 1978).

23 James Bentley, *Life and Food in the Dordogne* (Weidenfeld & Nicholson, London, 1986).

24 Anne Willan, *French Regional Cooking* (Hutchinson, London, 1981).

25 Quoted by Patience Gray and Primrose Boyd in their excellent book, *Plats du Jour* (Penguin, London, 1957). (Now, like so many other books I've used, no longer in print.)

26 H. McGee in that essential work, *On Food and Cooking* (Scribner's, 1984).

27 Who had in fact got it from another famous woman chef *(cuisinière),* Mère Fillioux.

28 Elizabeth David, *French Provincial Cooking* (Michael Joseph, London, 1960).

29 Provided through the courtesy of that notable expert, Ms. Lyn Hall of La Petite Cuisine.

30 H. Heyraud, *Le Manuel du restaurateur* (Flammarion, Paris, 1970). This contains 2,500 brief recipes. There are many other such reference books, including some in English.

31 The repertoire says that glazed *ris de veau* (sweetbreads) is placed on *croûtons,* decorated with *soubise* (an onion purée) and with slices of truffle. When items such as *ris de veau* are on the menu they are prepared in advance. The glazed ones will have been blanched and then put into iced water. They will have been peeled and then put under a weight to cool. Then they are colored by frying in butter with a *mirepoix* and prepared with a wine and meat glaze. In case the chef has forgotten all this too, the repertoire will list it.

32 This is a recipe from the Rôtisserie de la Table du Roy, Paris 9ième, according to Louisette Bertholle, *Secrets of the Great French Restaurants.*

33 Michael Korda told this story about his uncle in that wonderful book *Charmed Lives* (Allen Lane, Harmondsworth, 1980).

34 *Business Weekly* (13 July 1987).

35 Quentin Crewe, *International Food Pocket Book* (Mitchell Beazley, London, 1980).

36 Richard Olney, *Simple French Food* (Penguin, London, 1983).

37 Vernon Jarratt, "The One Man Michelin," *Wine and Food* (Autumn 1964).

38 Jean Troisgros, quoted by Quentin Crewe and Anthony Blake, *Great Chefs of France.*

39 *Time* (February 1976).

Index